CREATING ENTREPRENEURIAL SPACE

CONTEMPORARY ISSUES IN ENTREPRENEURSHIP RESEARCH

Series Editor, Volumes 1–6: Gerard McElwee

CONTEMPORARY ISSUES IN ENTREPRENEURSHIP
RESEARCH, VOLUME 9B

CREATING ENTREPRENEURIAL SPACE: TALKING THROUGH MULTI-VOICES, REFLECTIONS ON EMERGING DEBATES

EDITED BY

DAVID HIGGINS
University of Liverpool, UK

PAUL JONES
University of Coventry, UK

PAURIC MCGOWAN
Ulster University, UK

United Kingdom – North America – Japan
India – Malaysia – China

Emerald Publishing Limited
Howard House, Wagon Lane, Bingley BD16 1WA, UK

First edition 2019

Reprints and permissions service
Contact: permissions@emeraldinsight.com

British Library Cataloguing in Publication Data
A catalogue record for this book is available from the British Library

ISBN: 978-1-78769-578-8 (Print)
ISBN: 978-1-78769-577-1 (Online)
ISBN: 978-1-78769-579-5 (Epub)

ISSN: 2040-7246 (Series)

Printed and bound by CPI Group (UK) Ltd, Croydon, CR0 4YY

ISOQAR certified
Management System,
awarded to Emerald
for adherence to
Environmental
standard
ISO 14001:2004.

Certificate Number 1985
ISO 14001

INVESTOR IN PEOPLE

CONTENTS

LIST OF CONTRIBUTORS

Ahmed Abdullah	University of South Wales, UK
Gareth Huw Davies	Swansea University, UK
David Deakins	Lancaster University, UK
Marian Evans	DeMontfort University, UK
Hanne Haave	Inland Norway University of Applied Sciences, Norway
Julie Haddock-Millar	Middlesex University, UK
Lucy Hatt	Northumbria University, UK
Inge Hermanrud	Inland Norway University of Applied Sciences, Norway
David Higgins	University of Liverpool, UK
Åse Storhaug Hole	Inland Norway University of Applied Sciences, Norway
Oswald Jones	University of Liverpool, UK
Paul Jones	Coventry University, UK
Neil Kaye	Middlesex University, UK
Daniela Lundesgaard	Inland Norway University of Applied Sciences, Norway
Oliver Mallett	University of Stirling, UK
Xiang Ying Mei	Inland Norway University of Applied Sciences, Norway
Pauric McGowan	University of Ulster, UK
Kamran Namdar	Mälardalen University, Sweden
Martin N. Ndlela	Inland Norway University of Applied Sciences, Norway
Robyn Owen	Middlesex University, UK
David Rae	DeMontfort University, UK
Sian Roderick	Swansea University, UK
Chandana Sanyal	Middlesex University, UK
Leandro Sepulveda	Middlesex University, UK

Victoria Konovalenko Slettli	Inland Norway University of Applied Sciences, Norway
Kjell Staffas	Aalborg University, Denmark
Stephen Syrett	Middlesex University, UK
Brychan Thomas	University of South Wales, UK
Roderick Thomas	Swansea University, UK
Gareth R. T. White	University of South Wales, UK
Michael D. Williams	Swansea University, UK

SERIES EDITOR'S PREFACE

The Institute of Small Business and Entrepreneurship (ISBE) Emerald Book Series aims to provide a platform for leading edge research that reflects on contemporary themes of interest to the entrepreneurship discipline. The volumes of this series are proposed and edited by established scholars drawn from the membership of the ISBE community. All contributions are double blind peer reviewed by subject experts from the discipline.

The ninth volume (A & B) in the series, *Creating Entrepreneurial Space: Talking through Multi-voices, Reflections on Emerging Debates* edited by David Higgins, Paul Jones and Pauric McGowan, has collected sufficient material to present two volumes. Particular thanks to David Higgins for leading the guest editing process from project initiation to completion. These collections were developed in recognition of the need for the entrepreneurship literature to engage more critically with the lived experiences of practising entrepreneurs through alternative approaches and methods, seeking to account for and highlighting the social, political and moral aspects of entrepreneurial practice (Tedmanson, Verduyn, Essers, & Gartner, 2012). Thus, this volume is an attempt to supplement and enhance this evidence base with studies drawn from several different contexts of entrepreneurial practice and behaviour.

Some words of thanks to conclude this introduction. To the guest editors, authors and reviewers, for all their hard work and diligence in taking this volume to completion. To Katy Mathers and Pete Baker and the Emerald production team, for their efforts in taking the volume through the production processes by the required deadlines. To ISBE, in supporting the development of the volume and its promotion. In line with the objectives of the series, this volume contributes a new peer-reviewed body of evidence, which provides fresh insights and perspectives and informs and further engages the entrepreneurship discipline.

Paul Jones
(*Editor – ISBE Emerald Book Series*)

REFERENCE

Tedmanson, D., Verduyn, K., Essers, C., & Gartner, W. (2012). Critical perspectives in entrepreneurship research. *Organization*, *19*(5), 531–541.

CHAPTER 1

PUTTING 'THOUGHT' INTO THE THEORY/PRACTICE DEBATE

David Higgins, Paul Jones and Pauric McGowan

The purpose of the two volumes of this book was to offer a unique combination of studies that illustrate critical perspectives of current entrepreneurship research (Higgins, Jones, & McGowan, 2018). We sought to offer new theoretical perspectives and approaches as a means of illustrating the inherently social embedded and contextualised nature of entrepreneurial practice. As a result, we seek to develop a more critical and constructive position towards current theories, methods, assumptions and beliefs, which seek to question the prevailing assumptions currently dominating entrepreneurial researching and practice. This volume covers a broad spectrum, in terms of topics and approaches, on diversity and critique in their perspectives towards entrepreneurial practice and scholarship. The second volume includes nine invited chapters, which are introduced next.

In Abdullah, White and Thomas's chapter we are introduced to the use of an extended stage model for the evaluation and adoption of e-business in the small business sector in the Middle East. Empirical studies of e-business adoption are rare in a developing country context and the chapter provides novel insights into this region, by evaluating the use of the extended stage model to explore adoption among Yemeni Institute for Small Business and Entrepreneurship (SMEs). Current technology adoption models imply that organisations adopt technologies in a linear fashion, gradually increasing complexity and capability. This chapter suggests that there are multiple points at which SMEs may 'enter' the technology-adoption ladder.

Hatt's chapter presents a study on the concepts critical to thinking as an entrepreneur to inform entrepreneurship curriculum development. There is a lack of entrepreneurship education research that integrates the external stakeholder perspective. Using a Delphi-style method with 12 entrepreneurs, 5 candidate entrepreneurship

Creating Entrepreneurial Space: Talking Through Multi-voices, Reflections on Emerging Debates
Contemporary Issues in Entrepreneurship Research, Volume 9B, 1–7
Copyright © 2019 by Emerald Publishing Limited
All rights of reproduction in any form reserved
ISSN: 2040-7246/doi:10.1108/S2040-72462019000009B001

threshold concepts were identified. Threshold concepts offer a potentially transformative effect on the learner, allowing the learner to make sense of previously isolated pockets of knowledge. This chapter contributes to the call for more research
grounded discussion on the quality and effectiveness of entrepreneurship education
initiatives. Designing curricula around the threshold concepts in entrepreneurship
will enable educators offer relevant support in areas where students are likely to
become 'stuck' and will facilitate constructive alignment with assessment.

The chapter by Evans explores the decision-making processes past the start-up
stage that small businesses employ to grow. The study examines how entrepreneurs
evaluate and make decisions on growth opportunities in their business environment; it employs a cognitive style as a theoretical lens to evaluate differences in
information processing. The chapter determines how intuitive and analytical cognitive styles are used by entrepreneurs and the contribution these make to decision-making. The chapter findings demonstrate that the two styles are versatile as
entrepreneurs adjust and adapt their style over time, in keeping with the situational
factors of their business environment. The study also found differences between
novice and mature entrepreneurs and that experienced entrepreneurs exhibited
greater levels of cognitive versatility, which was linked to prior experience.

The chapter by Ndlela, Storhaug Hole, Slettli, Haave, Mei, Lundesgaard,
Hermanrud, Staffas and Namdar explores the process of facilitation of entrepreneurial learning. The literature on entrepreneurial learning and education
emphasises the importance of facilitation, although it is yet to be addressed in-
depth. This chapter contributes to the further understanding of the role facilitators play in the entrepreneurial and transformative learning processes. Drawing
on the social constructionist approach to learning, the chapter discusses how
facilitators and learners (entrepreneurs) become co-creators of knowledge and
learning experiences. The findings offer an example of scholarship that demonstrates a commitment to the exploration of the research field, which is accessible
to readers in terms of their applied focus through capturing the experiences of
learners/readers as they enact in practice.

The chapter by Mallett examines the interactions of formal and informal
forms of small business support, characterised as interactions within an 'enterprise industry'. An analysis of the interactions revealed in the existing literature
for different forms of business support develops a new conceptual framework for
understanding those varied forms of external influence targeted at small businesses that constitute and extend a 'patchwork quilt' of provision. This chapter
focusses on how different forms of support and advice interact, the centrality of
state influence and how such interactions can be considered as a part of a firm's
regulatory context. This conceptualisation allows the consideration of both business support and state regulations to move beyond conceptions of positive or
negative impacts on factors such as firm growth. Instead, it offers a novel conceptual lens for considering how different forms of external influence can shape
practices and attitudes of small businesses and their owner-managers.

The chapter by Owen, Haddock-Millar, Sepulveda, Sanyal, Syrett, Kaye and
Deakins examines the role of volunteer business mentoring (VBM) in relation to
potentially improving financing and financial management in youth enterprises in

deprived under-served neighbourhoods. The chapter explores the following questions. To what extent is youth VBM associated with access to external finance? Where access to external finance takes place, does VBM improve business outcomes? Do VBMs make a difference to the performance of businesses receiving financial assistance? In the post-global financial crisis era of high youth unemployment, rising youth entrepreneurship and constrained business finance VBM offers the potential of improved youth business signalling and credibility, reducing information asymmetries and associated agency failures. Findings suggest that VBM is a positive opportunity, offering low-cost support and improvement to business financing and subsequent performance. VBM allied to microfinance offers a blueprint for future youth enterprise start-up policy.

The chapter by Davies, Roderick, Williams and Thomas provides a case study approach to evaluate the Technium initiative, started in Wales, to encourage business start-up and growth in the knowledge economy sector considering evidence from two decades. This case study helps address the evidence deficit by revisiting the initial Technium Swansea initiative and its subsequent development. A vibrant policy and practice debate subsequently emerged, together with strident media comment. The case study provides novel insights into what can realistically be expected of such initiatives in the short, medium and long terms, with realistic time-horizons for 'success' and the role of learning for knowledge-based development in similar initiatives and regions.

Rae's chapter explores three dimensions of the 'Open Space' of freely available resources for Entrepreneurship. Here, 'Open Entrepreneurship' is discussed as a unifying approach for value creation through a conceptual model combining 'Open' tools and resources. Open resources for digital and data-led entrepreneurship offer conditions for new, pervasive and distributed forms of value-creating entrepreneurial activity. Namely, what is 'Open' in the context of entrepreneurship? Secondly, why is Open Entrepreneurship important for conceptualisation, education and practice? Finally, can Open Entrepreneurship offer significant new opportunities for innovation, value creation and learning, and how can these be realised? These can create learning environments with rich access to data and resources, innovative connections and opportunities for co-creating value in multiple forms. This learning-centred approach builds on the concept of entrepreneurship as an educational philosophy of value creation for others.

In the final chapter, Jones provides an ethnographic account of a team involved in preparing a proposal and, subsequently, undertaking a small firm research project. Teamwork has become increasingly prevalent both in undertaking research projects and in preparing manuscripts for publication. There is limited literature considering this process in the Entrepreneurship discipline. Typically, existing studies discern between problems associated with task-based conflict and relationship-based conflict. This chapter profiles a major Economic and Social Research Council project initiative that funded 13 distinct projects. During a nine-month period of developing the research proposal, the research team worked extremely effectively with periods of intense knowledge sharing, which enabled the team to develop a successful bid. However, a major dispute between team members, during the early stages of the fieldwork, led to a period of both task-based and relationship-based conflict, which threatened to undermine the project. This chapter assists those who may find themselves operating in dysfunctional teams; it makes sense of the underlying tensions associated with 'academic knowledge creation'.

SOME THOUGHTS ...

The field of entrepreneurship is growing but the fundamental question of what it means to be an entrepreneur, what they do and how they engage in practice is becoming more obscured and fragmented, resulting in different conceptual perspectives (Higgins, Trehan, & McGowan, 2015; Ucbasaran, Westhead, & Wright, 2001; Watson, 2013). Gartner (2001) suggests that each discipline in the field has its own way of viewing what entrepreneurship is; but equally, it is difficult to fully appreciate the phenomenon of the entrepreneur by simply looking at its effect, we need to understand what it means to 'be' (Hjorth, 2004). The beauty, simplicity and yet complexity of what it means to be an entrepreneur cannot be decontextualised into constituent parts; it must be appreciated as an emergent dynamic whole. This is not to say that the knowledge we have gained about entrepreneurship is redundant rather what is being suggested is that we use this knowledge as an opportunity to seek alternative ways of exploring entrepreneurship. We need to be critical of the strengths and weaknesses of the current theories we have formulated. This involves taking time to understand and appreciate what we know (Anderson, 2000; Diochon & Anderson, 2011; Korsgaard & Anderson, 2011). Currently, many entrepreneurship scholars retain a narrow perspective of what entrepreneurship is and comprises of; if this view persists, as a field, we run the risk of systematically limiting our ability of seeing, alternative purposeful perspectives, hindering our ability to enquire and develop new ways, which may offer further insights and values.

This, of course implies, the question (an all too often ignored question): what value and insight would an alternative mode of inquiry give the field and to whom? To a degree, the contents of this book could be viewed as offering novel insight and interesting points of discussion, but, to others, it may sound obvious. Gartner (2001) suggested that words, such as entrepreneur or entrepreneurship, have now developed a wide variety of overlapping and contradictory meanings; a suggestion offered at the time was to encourage scholars to be more explicit about how and why they define entrepreneurship. Entrepreneurship is not simply a thing that we look upon but rather a social enactment, a living experience embodied in social action, shaped and mediated by context, a means of becoming, co-constructed in connection with others, as a practical measure of how it is and what they do (Anderson, Dodd, & Jack, 2012; Anderson, Park, & Jack, 2007).

Higgins et al. (2015) has argued for alternative approaches to entrepreneurial inquiry, which illustrates the contextualised nature of social practice. Placing human activity at the centre of how we understand and make sense of what it means to practice is critical. It is often recognised that entrepreneurial practice is a crafted form of art, which requires an appreciative and sensitive engagement with a range of sociocultural phenomena in the entrepreneurial setting (Blackburn & Kovalainen, 2009; Hjorth, Jones, & Gartner, 2008). Before any kind of research or theorising can occur, clarification in terms of what is going to be regarded as real in the social world and how we might evaluate and make sense of that knowledge becomes critical. The entrepreneur continually faces complex situations, as they engage in their everyday practice, dealing with new situations and seeking ways to overcome perceived barriers and maximise apparent opportunities. In this sense, the development of how we view and make sense of social action can be to assume that entrepreneurial action is emergent in nature. Such emergent behaviour is not unbounded; it is situated in a social context which has outcomes that are determined and mediated by social, historical and cultural elements. This is consistent with the perspective of Steyaert (2007) and Johannisson (2011), who view the practice of 'entrepreneuring' with that of everyday life.

The problematic nature of how we view and approach entrepreneurial research is matched by the lack of agreement on the most appropriate conceptual and theoretical foundations within the field. Watson (2013) argues that entrepreneurship and scholarly activity need to break away from the more traditional perspectives of economies, psychology or positivist perspectives, and instead towards more sociological perspectives and theories, which could provide more appreciative and explanatory powers/means. The importance of developing a scholarly voice, which seeks to foster innovative and accessible scholarly writing, is of crucial importance to any research field. In this context, the role of our own attentiveness, what it means to be reflexively aware, in our practice, as custodians of knowledge, becomes extremely important – how we perceive our roles as lecturers, researchers, writers and editors, how we enact our relationships with our audiences and wider communities in a meaningful way. A thoughtful inquiry requires the questioning of the relationship between ourselves, our community and the theories/concepts we work with. As we learn through action, the need to become reflexively aware in terms of how we construct our knowing becomes critical.

Through the influence of the field, we have come to understand the social world by creating meaning through our research practice. The social world cannot exist independently from us; rather, it is our actions, which shape, mediate, maintain, and are represented in and through our ongoing daily interactions. Our ability to explore and pose questions to these often-overlooked relationships and the manner in which we seek to make sense of our social world is key. The need to move beyond simple what, how and why questions, to questions which provoke and challenge such as where, when and who as a method of unlearning and advancing the discipline. At the basest level, these questions involve thoughtfully considering the relevance and application of existing knowledge, by offering novel insight and future debate. Connecting these question sets offers the possibility of drawing connections towards research material, which reveals the relational orientations of enacted learning. Such a practice opens up the possibility to introduce different perspectives to now we view and practice in the subject area of action learning.

The importance of creating a voice, which asks questions that seek to challenge and push boundaries, is an important core value of our scholarship. When we consider the meaning of dialogue, and begin to recognise the importance of our voice as a means of dialogue, we look towards the view that none of the things we do as humans happens in a vacuum, speaking, writing, reading, thinking or listening. In this sense, positioning ourselves as active participants in the process of shaping our actions means thinking reflexively about our relationship with self and the field. This could mean the following:

• the questioning of our assumptions, who we are and what is it that we want to achieve;
• the questioning of what really makes sense, of how we live and experience, our own and others voices and conversations; and
• understanding our relationship with our social world and recognising its dynamic and emergent nature.

Although I refer to the term 'self', I am conscious that I am implying an individualistic stance; rather, I am recognising self, in a reflexive context which incorporates the understanding that we are in relation to others and thus need to consider the nature of those relationships as a collective mediated voice. The ability of any scholarly publication, to develop material, which engages with practical experience and action must be a key priority in the advancement of future practice and scholarship. One of the most important contributing factors for the advancement of our scholarly knowledge and field is the questions we ask and, in particular, the manner in which we pose questions. Our capacity to ask meaningful and insightful questions is critically more important than finding a right answer. In this sense, the creation of academic/practice-oriented material, which offers to the reader the opportunity to build upon our capabilities to become more informed and knowledgeable is one of the most impactful attributes any book can offer, to both contributor and readers. As such, the need for academic publications to engage with and appeal to different communities as a means of encouraging writers and readers to ask explorative questions is a challenge but one, which is of increased importance. If, as a scholarly community, we are serious about developing and constructing our practice, we must be mindful not to be afraid to question our assumptions and beliefs, in doing so reframing and extending the manner in which we seek meaning, through the questions we ask and how we ask those questions.

REFERENCES

Anderson, A. R. (2000). Paradox in the periphery: An entrepreneurial reconstruction? *Entrepreneurship and Regional Development, 12*(2), 91–109.
Anderson, A. R., Dodd, S. D., & Jack, S. L. (2012). Entrepreneurship as connecting: Some implications for theorising and practice. *Management Decision, 50*(5), 958–971. http://dx.doi.org/10.1108/00251741211227708
Anderson, A. R., Park, J., & Jack, S. L. (2007). Entrepreneurial social capital: Conceptualizing social capital in new high-tech firms. *International Small Business Journal, 25*(3), 243–267.
Blackburn, R., & Kovalainen, A. (2009). Researching small firms and entrepreneurship: Past, present and future. *International Journal of Management Reviews, 11*(2), 127–148.

Diochon, M., & Anderson, A. R. (2011). Ambivalence and ambiguity in social enterprise; Narratives about values in reconciling purpose and practices. *International Entrepreneurship and Management Journal, 7*(1), 93–109.

Gartner, W. B. (2001). Is there an elephant in entrepreneurship? Blind assumptions in theory development. *Entrepreneurship Theory and Practice, 25*(4), 27–39.

Higgins, D., Jones, P., & McGowan, P. (2018). *Creating entrepreneurial space: Talking through multivoices, reflections on emerging debates.* Contemporary Issues in Entrepreneurship Research (Vol. 9A). Bingley: Emerald Publishing.

Higgins, D., Trehan, K., & McGowan, P. (2015). Developing perspectives and challenging the 'status quo'. *International Journal of Entrepreneurial Behavior & Research, 21*(3). https://doi.org/10.1108/IJEBR-03-2015-0061

Hjorth, D. (2004). Creating space for play/invention – Concepts of space and organizational entrepreneurship. *Entrepreneurship & Regional Development, 16*(5), 413–432.

Hjorth, D., Jones, C., & Gartner, W. (2008). Introduction to 'recreating/recontextualising' entrepreneurship. *Scandinavian Journal of Management, 24*(2), 81–84.

Johannisson, B. (2011). Towards a practice theory of entrepreneuring. *Small Business Economics, 36*(2), 135–150.

Korsgaard, S., & Anderson, A. R. (2011). Enacting entrepreneurship as social value creation. *International Small Business Journal, 29*(2), 135–151.

Steyaert, C. (2007). 'Entrepreneuring' as a conceptual attractor? A review of process theories in 20 years of entrepreneurship studies. *Entrepreneurship and Regional Development, 19*(6), 453–477.

Ucbasaran, D., Westhead, P., & Wright, M. (2001). The focus of entrepreneurial research: Contextual and process issues. *Entrepreneurship Theory and Practice, 25*(4), 57–80.

Watson, T. (2013). Entrepreneurship in action: Bringing together the individual, organizational and institutional dimensions of entrepreneurial action. *Entrepreneurship and Regional Development, 25*(5–6), 1–19.

CHAPTER 2

AN EXTENDED STAGE MODEL FOR ASSESSING YEMENI SMES' E-BUSINESS ADOPTION

Ahmed Abdullah, Gareth R. T. White and Brychan Thomas

ABSTRACT

This chapter discusses the use of an extended stage model for the evaluation of the adoption of e-business in small and medium-sized enterprises (SMEs). Empirical studies of e-business adoption are rare in Middle Eastern and developing countries and the chapter provides valuable insight into this region, by presenting an account of the use of the extended stage model to explore the level of e-business adoption among Yemeni SMEs.

In making this examination, the challenges and opportunities that accompany e-business adoption are revealed. The internal drivers and barriers, such as finance and skills, are recognised along with the external factors that include infrastructure and legislation. It also provides valuable insight into the macro-level sociopolitical determinants of e-business adoption that have not previously been appreciated; the study was undertaken during the Yemen Civil War in 2016.

Current adoption models imply that organisations adopt technologies in a linear fashion, gradually increasing complexity and capability. This study makes an important contribution by recognising that there are multiple points at which SMEs may 'enter' the technology-adoption ladder.

Keywords: SMEs; Yemen; e-business; adoption; drivers; barriers

Creating Entrepreneurial Space: Talking Through Multi-voices, Reflections on Emerging Debates
Contemporary Issues in Entrepreneurship Research, Volume 9B, 9–26
Copyright © 2019 by Emerald Publishing Limited
All rights of reproduction in any form reserved
ISSN: 2040-7246/doi:10.1108/S2040-72462019000009B002

INTRODUCTION

In both developed and developing countries, small and medium-sized enterprises (SMEs) are becoming more important to national economies due to their strategic significance in developing different industrial sectors (Afolayan, Plant, White, & Jones, 2015; Maad & Liedholm, 2008). SMEs play a major role in an economy by significantly contributing to gross domestic product, creating more job opportunities and through developing skilled labour. The integration of information and communication technology (ICT) can have a significant impact within organisations and their employees by improving productivity and subsequently lowering unit costs (Andam, Programme, & Force, 2003; Jones, Packham, Pickernell, Thomas, & White, 2013). Furthermore, it is considered to be one of the most important strategic capabilities that can effectively help SMEs to enhance their business performance (Sin Tan, Choy Chong, Lin, & Cyril Eze, 2009). ICT can provide SMEs with several competitive advantages, such as integrating supply chain partners, organisational functions and offering critical information at the right time (Chaffey & White, 2011; Sharma & Sheth, 2010; White, Afolayan, & Plant, 2014). However, there are barriers for SMEs adopting e-business, such as the lack of skilled labour (Bolongkikit, 2006; Hamed, Ball, Berger, & Cleary, 2008; Kaynak, Tatoglu, & Kula, 2005; Middleton, 2011; OECD, 2012), cost (Hamed et al., 2008; Middleton, 2011; Ntoko, 2008; Pahladsingh, 2006; Parazoglou, 2006; Parida, Johansson, Ylinenpää, & Baunerhjelm, 2010; Zolait, Abdul Razak, & Ahmad, 2010) and size (Hamed et al., 2008; Middleton, 2011; Parazoglou, 2006). ICT has become a vital component of economic development, business strategy and operations (Al-Marti, 2008).

There are a number of different interpretations of the terms e-commerce and e-business. For example, Chaffey (2011, p. 12) argues that e-commerce is a subset of e-business, whereas IBM defined e-business in 1997 as 'the transformation of key business processes through the use of internet technologies' (Chaffey, 2011, p. 12). Parazoglou (2006) and Turban (2010) argue that e-business is more than buying and selling products and services; it is about customer services, collaborating with business suppliers and partners, as well as making transactions electronically inside the organisation. However, Fillis, Johannson, and Wagner (2004) identify e-businesses as companies that employ ICT in their business operations, but exclude sending and receiving text-based e-mail messages. Many researchers (Chaffey, 2011; Fillis, Johannson, & Wagner, 2004; Parazoglou, 2006; Turban, 2010) state that e-business and e-commerce are similar in terms of selling and buying products on the Internet and others define e-business and e-commerce as distinct. Most studies of stage model adoption, identify e-commerce as a subset of e-business (Davis & Benamati, 2003). This study adopts the definition of e-business as information technology that supports the range of business processes using electronically mediated information exchanges, both inside and outside the organisation, including e-commerce activity (Chaffey, 2011).

E-adoption models have been used by numerous researchers as a way of depicting the progressive adoption of increasingly sophisticated, and valuable, information technologies (Hoque, 2000; Jones, Beynon-Davies, & Muir, 2003;

Teo & Pian, 2004; Vosloo, 2003; Willcocks & Sauer, 2000). Many studies have explored e-commerce adoption but the majority of these have focussed on comparatively well-developed countries, such as Wales (Thomas & Simmons, 2010), South Africa (Cloete, Courtney, & Fintz, 2002), New Zealand (Al-Qirim, 2007), parts of Asia (Sharma & Sheth, 2004) and the United Kingdom (Simpson & Docherty, 2004). Comparatively few studies have concentrated on the adoption of e-business in developing economies (Li & Xie, 2012). This study addresses that gap by exploring e-business adoption in Yemeni SMEs.

E-BUSINESS IN YEMENI SMES

The definition of an SME varies between countries. To define a company as an SME, there is a need to identify the number of employees, annual turnover and balance sheet. In Europe, a medium-sized enterprise is defined as a firm having between 50 and 249 employees, and an annual turnover less or equal to 50 million Euros. A small-sized enterprise is a firm with employees between 10 and 49, and annual turnover less or equal to 10 million Euros (EC, 2005). Whereas, the Yemen Government defines SMEs as: medium-sized enterprises are firms with 10 to 50 employees and small-sized enterprises are firms with four to nine employees (Yemeni Ministry of Industry and Trade (YMIT), 2014).

The YMIT (2014) states that the number of SMEs in Yemen comprises around 27,796 companies in the manufacturing sector. The 0.51% of enterprises are large companies, 1.91% are medium-sized, 19.15% are small and 78.43% are micro-businesses. Most SMEs are located in Sana'a (18.06%), Taiz (13.93%) and 68.01% and are distributed among the rest of the cities in the country. Most SMEs are in the field of food products and beverages (43.75%), fabricated metal products (14.78%), non-metallic mineral products (11.02%), apparel products (10.80%) and various other activities, services and retail (19.65%).

There has been a comparatively large investment by the Yemeni government towards ICT in the desire to achieve greater productivity. Most government organisations use computers in their daily work life, to expedite work. In addition, to improve information systems and implement effective infrastructure, the Yemeni government has established IT departments in most of its ministries and governorates. The private sector in Yemen has an influence on ICT policy through their investment to improve ICT resources. For example, to improve information technology literacy, a number of institutes have established courses for students to learn how to use computers.

According to the international telecommunication union (ITU) (2012) report, the Yemen Ministry of Communications and Information Technology aims to provide, develop and expand the spread of telecommunications and postal services in the Republic to meet the needs of economic and social development and encourage investment in these areas in accordance with the constitution and state public policy, laws and regulations in force. The 3G network coverage is limited to some cities in Yemen using the technology called EV-DO Rev A. Yemen commercial broadband technology includes: Fixed (wired)-broadband technology (DSL) and three technology wireless-broadband technologies (CDMA EVDO, WiMAX and another Terrestrial Fixed Wireless Broadband Technology). The telecom sectors have increased since 2000 to four telecom operators, but the Yemen government is still the only internet provider in the country.

Yemen's telecom sector is representative of the growth opportunities that abound in such a developing market. Fixed-line subscriptions are increasing, with a penetration rate of less than 5% indicating significant room for growth. Given that over 60% of the population lives in rural areas a significant amount of fixed-line investment has been in the form of wireless local loops based on a variety of technologies. In addition, the telecom sector has invested in core and transmission network infrastructure to expand bandwidth and support the ability to offer new products and services (BuddeComm, 2012).

Al-Marti (2008) has argued that e-business concepts are comparatively unknown and untrusted among Yemen SMEs and its population. However, the Yemen e-business sector is witnessing rapid growth which has exceeded expectations and has recently become the dominant sector of shopping (Almotamar, 2014). The Warzan website and mail was established as the first Yemeni site to offer free online sales and attracts tens of thousands of monthly visitors, who are looking for a unique shopping experience and convenient delivery service (Almotamar, 2014). According to Almotamar (2014), there is now increasing reliance on e-commerce and goods that enter Yemen through this medium are to the tune of millions of dollars annually.

E-BUSINESS ACTIVITIES: BENEFITS AND BARRIERS

In the current global economy e-business has increased and become an important component of business strategy and economic development (Kumar & Kumar, 2014). Indeed, one of the most important strategies that can effectively assist SMEs to enhance their business performance is the utilisation of ICT (Sin Tan et al., 2009). ICT can provide SMEs with several competitive advantages, such as integrating supply chain partners, organisational functions and offering time critical information (Sharma & Sheth, 2010). The adoption of ICT and e-business can offer SMEs a wide range of benefits for their business process (OECD, 2004). For example, adopting ICT and its applications offers organisations more efficient resource management as well as making communication faster. E-business and the Internet can provide SMEs with significant benefits, such as reducing transaction costs and increasing the speed and reliability of the transaction (OECD, 2004).

However, the characteristics of SMEs, such as structure, resource constraints and size, generate several challenges and difficulties in relation to the adoption of ICT. According to MacGregor and Vrazalic (2005), despite the rapid growth of ICT within SMEs, the level of ICT adoption by small and medium enterprises remains comparatively low. The lack of financial resources required for ICT development and maintenance is one of the main reasons preventing SMEs from adopting ICT (Parida et al., 2010). Indeed, as stated by Ghobakhloo, Hong, Sabouri and Zulkifli (2012), SMEs have less tolerance in accepting cost and risk associated with adopting new technologies. Furthermore, the lack of ICT literacy among owners and employees is another barrier that inhibits effective ICT deployment within SMEs (Mehrtens, Cragg, & Mills, 2001).

Prior research has shown that e-business offers solutions for businesses to meet the challenges of a changing environment, even though studies related to SMEs in developing countries reveal a delay or failure of SMEs in adopting e-business. Numerous studies have reported many barriers for e-business adoption in SMEs such as (Kaynak et al., 2005), who state that it is difficult to find and retrain employees with the required skills and knowledge. Bolongkikit (2006) reports that there is a need for a high degree of human collaboration in SME markets but Hamed et al. (2008) state that it is difficult for many SMEs to obtain the levels of e-business skills to benefit from ICT investment in e-business. Parazoglou (2006) argues that the main challenge that may impact on the adoption of e-business is company size along with uncertainty of the financial benefits, lack of a clear e-business strategy, technological concerns, security concerns, privacy and legal issues, suspicion regarding new partnership loyalties, and the high cost of computing technology. Pahladsingh (2006) also finds that ICT infrastructure, internet connection speed and cost, the cost of hardware and software services, government policies, credit card interest, regulation, security, country's culture, language and e-business ethics are barriers to the adoption of e-business. The OECD (2012) reports that even though 94% of SMEs in OECD countries have a high-speed internet connection, only 35% are using online purchasing and 18% are selling products and services online. Li and Xie (2012) mention other barriers that prevent SMEs from adopting e-commerce and these include institutional environment, legal system, proactive government policy, ICT infrastructure, tax policy for online transactions, national e-commerce strategy, government e-commerce use and e-commerce training.

The nature of the country may also have an impact upon ICT and e-business adoption. For instance, Al-Madhagy (2013) argues that the main barriers that lead prevent a country from benefitting from communication and information systems are a difficult topography, scattered population group with low density and a low level of distribution networks in cities and rural areas. However, Middleton (2011) highlights the barriers to e-business adoption that comprise cost, technology, SMEs' education and skills sets, lack of skilled labour and access to trusted advisors and consultants, red tape and bureaucracy, lack of time and resistance to growth. Although there are differences between developing countries, they have similar barriers for the adoption of e-commerce, such as lack of infrastructure, financial problems (Jones, Beynon-Davies et al., 2003) along with lack of awareness, the absence of trust, weak income, poor economy, purchases made online, online payment services, regulation, cost, technology and suitable infrastructure (Hamed et al., 2008; Ntoko, 2008; Zolait et al., 2010). In accord with the context of this study, PayPal (2013) reports that online fraud and security are a concern to all e-commerce shoppers in the Middle East, whereas Berthon, Pitt, Berthon, Campbell and Thwaites (2008) find that corruption has a strong effect on e-business adoption and development in the Yemen, and Al-Marti (2008) notes that the country has weak internet infrastructure.

THE DEVELOPMENT OF STAGE ADOPTION MODELS

The first information technology–adoption stage model was developed by Richard L. Nolan in 1973 and initially comprised four stages: initiation, contagion, control and integration (Nolan, 1973). Later, as information technology availability and usage increased, this adoption model was extended to incorporate further adoption levels: initiation, contagion, control, integration, data administration and maturity (Nolan, 1973). Since then, a multitude of studies have described the stages of e-business adoption (Daniel, Wilson, & Myers, 2002; Martin & Matlay, 2001; Poon & Swatman, 1999; Taylor & Murphy, 2004; Zhang, Cheng, & Boutaba, 2010), most of which have consisted of four to six stages (see Table 1).

The e-adoption model used by a number of researchers is typically a 'step-by-step' indicator, which starts with an email communication followed by basic website, ecommerce, e-business until the point of the transformed organisation (Hoque, 2000; Jones et al., 2000; Jones, Beynon-Davies et al., 2003; Teo & Pian, 2004; Vosloo, 2003; Willcocks & Sauer, 2000). Martin and Matlay (2001) depict the Department of Trade and Industry adoption ladder. The model was intended to be a useful way for SMEs to review their relative level of e-business adoption; however, it faced criticism because it was perceived to be too simplistic and its linear progression could not capture the complex nature of small firm activities (Parker & Castleman, 2009).

Table 1.   E-Business Adoption Models.

Model	Description	Authors
Stages of computer budget growth	Stage 1: Initiation (computer acquisition). Stage 2: Contagion (intense system development). Stage 3: Control (proliferation of controls). Stage 4: Integration (user/service orientation).	Nolan (1973)
Six stages of growth	Stage 1: Initiation (computer acquisition). Stage 2: Contagion (intense system development). Stage 3: Control (proliferation of controls). Stage 4: Integration (user/service orientation). Stage 5: Data administration. Stage 6: Maturity.	Nolan (1979)
A five-stage model referring to the development of sell-side e-commerce	Stage 1: Image and product information. Stage 2: Information collection. Stage 3: Customer support and service. Stage 4: Internal support and service. Stage 5: Transactions.	Quelch and Klein (1996)
Web technology adoption levels	Level 1: Information access. Level 2: Work collaboration. Level 3: Core business transactions.	Nambisan and Wang (1999)
Australian national audit office-office for government online (ANAO-OGO) model of service delivery by the Internet	Stage 1: Website presence. Stage 2: Database queries online. Stage 3: Agency interaction. Stage 4: Agencies receiving authenticated information share data with other agencies with prior approval of individual clients.	Office, Nicoll, and Turner (1999)
Intranet technology use modes	Stage 1: Publishing. Stage 2: Transacting. Stage 3: Interacting. Stage 4: Searching. Stage 5: Recording.	Damsgaard and Scheepers (1999)

Table 1. (*Continued*)

Model	Description	Authors
Moving to e-business	Stage 1: Web presence.	Willcocks and
	Stage 2: Access information and transact business.	Sauer (2000)
	Stage 3: Further integration of skills, processes and technologies.	
	Stage 4: Capability, leveraging experience and know-how to maximise value.	
Four stages of development (technology levels)	Stage 1: Website containing 'packaged' information about the agency and its services.	Statskontoret (2000)
	Stage 2: Website containing 'interactive' information about the agency and its services.	
	Stage 3: Website and communicative functions that allow the visitor to submit and retrieve personal information.	
	Stage 4: Website and network functions for joined-up services involving several agencies and institutions.	
Three levels of e-business	Phase 1: Experimentation.	Hackbath and Kehinger (2000)
	Phase 2: Integration.	
	Phase 3: Transformation.	
e-Adoption ladder	Stage 0: No internet connection.	Martin and Matlay (2001)
	Stage 1: E-mail.	
	Stage 2: Website.	
	Stage 3: E-commerce.	
	Stage 4: E-business.	
	Stage 5: Transformed organisation.	
Dimensions and stages of e-government development	Stage 1: Cataloguing.	Layne and Lee (2001)
	Stage 2: Transaction.	
	Stage 3: Vertical integration.	
	Stage 4: Horizontal integration.	
Stages of e-government	Stage 1: Information.	Hiller and Bélanger (2001)
	Stage 2: Two-way communication.	
	Stage 3: Transaction.	
	Stage 4: Integration.	
	Stage 5: Political participatio	
Level of Internet adoption	Level 0: E-mail adoption.	Teo and Pian (2003)
	Level 1: Internet presence.	
	Level 2: Prospecting.	
	Level 3: Business integration.	
	Level 4: Business transformation.	
A stage model for e-commerce development	Stage 1: Presence.	Rao, Metts, and Monge (2003)
	Stage 2: Portals.	
	Stage 3: Transactions Integration.	
	Stage 4: Enterprises Integration.	
Buy-side e-commerce stages	Level 1: No use of the web.	Chaffey (2003)
	Level 2: Review and selection from competing suppliers using intermediary Websites, B2B exchanges and supplier websites. Orders placed by conventional means.	
	Level 3: Orders placed electronically through electronic data interchange (EDI), via intermediary sites.	
	Level 4: Orders placed electronically with integration of company's procurement Systems.	
	Level 5: Orders placed electronically.	

Table 1.   (*Continued*)

Model	Description	Authors
Sell-side e-commerce stage model	Level 0: No website or presence on web.	Chaffey (2003)
	Level 1: Basic web presence.	
	Level 2: Simple static informational website.	
	Level 3: Simple interactive site.	
	Level 4: Interactive site supporting transactions with users.	
	Level 5: Fully interactive site supporting the whole buying process.	
Ladder of connectivity	Six stages	Murphy and Symonds (2004)
	Stage 0: (not started).	
	Stage 6: (advanced e-commerce).	
Six-stages of e-business adoption	Stage 0: Not connected to the Internet.	Molla and Licker (2005)
	Stage 1: Connected to the Internet with e-mail.	
	Stage 2: Static web.	
	Stage 3: Interactive web presence.	
	Stage 4: Transactive web.	
	Stage 5: Integrated web.	
The e-commerce stairway	Six stages	Brychan, Christopher, Gary, and Geoff (2009)
	Stage 0: (not started).	
	Stage 6: (advanced e-commerce).	
E-commerce adoption ladder	Five steps	Thomas, Williams, Thompson, and Packham (2013)
	Step 0: (not started).	
	Step 5: (transformed organisation).	
Organisation level of e-commerce adoption	Five stages	Al-Somali and Clegg (2013)
	Stage 0: (no online capability).	
	Stage 5: (integrated web).	
Stages of the e-commerce adoption ladder	Six stages	Beynon-Davies (2010)
	Stage 0: (have not started yet).	
	Stage 6: (use advanced e-commerce).	
New stage model of electronic business adoption	Eight stages	Abdullah, White, and Thomas (2016); Abdullah, Thomas, and Metcalfe (2016); Abdullah, Thomas, Lyndon, and Plant (2018)
	Stage 0: No internet access.	
	Stage 1: Email.	
	Stage 2: Social media.	
	Stage 3: Website.	
	Stage 4: e-Commerce.	
	Stage 5: Mobile Apps.	
	Stage 6: Cloud service.	
	Stage 7: e-Business.	
	Stage 8: Transformed organisation.	

This study utilises an extended stage model of electronic business adoption (Abdullah et al., 2018). Building upon previous adoption stage models, it recognises the recent developments in information technology that businesses have harnessed, social media, for example, has become a significant influence upon the way businesses and consumers interact (Chaffey & White, 2011). The extended stage model utilised here incorporates 'social media', mobile applications' and 'cloud technologies'.

The term 'social media' is troublesome to define, being a general term for virtual communications and a term that encompasses a range of technologies. Consequently, numerous typologies of social media platforms have been proposed (Grahl, 2015; Hyatt, 2013; Lake, 2009; Myers, 2015; Nations, 2015). Initially seen as a marketing vehicle, for increasing the virtual presence of a business, it has become a dyadic enabling mechanism between businesses and their customers (Clapperton, 2012). However, it has also been considered a catalyst for non-productive employee effort (Carter, 2012). Access to social media is relatively easy for both businesses and consumers and this has underpinned its rapid uptake. The extended stage model incorporates social media platforms and techniques at stage 2 (Fig. 1).

Chaffey (2007, p. 132) defines mobile commerce as 'electronic transactions and communications conducted using mobile devices such as laptops, PDAs and mobile phones, and typically with a wireless connection'. Mobile applications have become an additional platform for retailers to expand the market for distance selling, enabling consumers to make online transactions anytime and anywhere (Saidi, 2009). According to Shankar, Venkatesh, Hofacker, and Naik (2010), mobile applications are able to offer SMEs more than just a new platform for organisations to attract consumers: they are bidirectional and also offer consumers the opportunity to interact with the organisation and explore the information of products and services while shopping in- and out of- store. They are, therefore, vehicles for creating relationships between SMEs and customers, and improve retailers' engagement with the rising trend to engage in online shopping (OCED, 2013). The extended stage model incorporates mobile applications at stage 5 (Fig. 1).

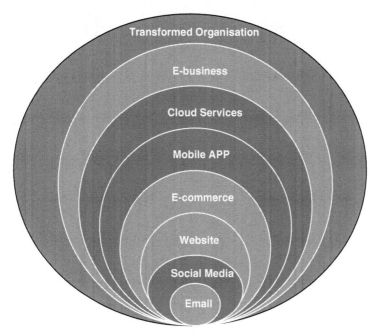

Fig. 1.   New Stage Model of Electronic Business Adoption (Abdullah et al., 2018).

The term 'cloud computing' covers a multitude of usages of information technologies that are developing rapidly and thereby preclude simple definition (MacVittie, 2008). In basic terms, cloud computing involves accessing rented web-based capacity or services. Data storage capacity can be quickly and cheaply sourced allowing for rapid expansion without the hindrance of the associated need to expand a company's own server room. Furthermore, during times of organisational restructuring or contraction, cloud-based storage can easily be cancelled, thus saving money. Similarly, data processing or software needs, termed Software as a Service can also be sourced via the cloud. Companies may operate a 'pay-per-use' system where they are charged only for the time that they use applications. The benefits of cloud technologies are widely reported and have underpinned their rapid adoption (Armbrust et al., 2010). However, these introduce many challenges that need to be addressed (ISACA, 2012). The extended stage model incorporates cloud services platforms and techniques at stage 6 (Fig. 1).

METHODOLOGY

This study has utilised mixed methods, following a sequential exploratory design (Creswell, 2013), involving a questionnaire survey technique to collect quantitative data, and semi-structured interviews to collect qualitative data. The study integrates different methods to facilitate a deep understanding of the adoption level of e-business in SMEs in Yemen.

The SMEs' contact details were sourced from the Ministry of Trade in Yemen. The SMEs' survey characteristics are: size: 1–50 employees based on Yemeni SMEs' definition (YMIT, 2014), location: the capital of Yemen (Sana'a). The CEOs/Managers/Owners of the SMEs were asked to complete a two-page questionnaire, which takes around 15 minutes to complete. Identities have been kept anonymous and responses confidential, with respondents free to withdraw at any time with no prior notice. The questionnaire was split into three parts. Part 1 described the nature and purpose of the research, including definitions of e-business, e-commerce, cloud services, social media and mobile apps, to enable the respondents to understand these concepts before answering the questions. Part 2 asked about e-business activities that the company has adopted. Part 3 was used to generate information about the company's background, such as the number of employees, the age of the company, type of company and the position of the participant.

Questionnaires were distributed to 768 SMEs in Yemen. The questionnaires were distributed by a hand and online using Qualtrics survey software, and based on stratified random sampling. To perform stratified sampling, the researcher grouped the target sample into four groups. Group A (represents Manufacturing), group B (represents Retail and Wholesale), group C (represents Services) and group D (represents Other sectors). Each group had a target of 192 questionnaires. 238 questionnaires were returned, giving a response rate of around 31%. Thirty-two incomplete questionnaires were removed. A total of five interviews were conducted with SME owners and managers to confirm the interpretation of the statistical analyses. The interviews were conducted through Skype, and recorded and thematically analysed.

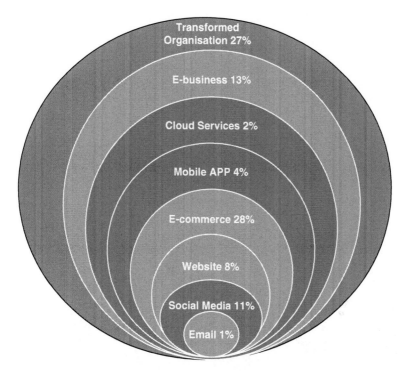

Fig. 2. E-Business Evolution Stage Model Results.

the technology. For example, as reported above, SMEs have adopted e-commerce activities and they sell and buy products online, but they receive payments either by bank transfer of cash which means SMEs have still not fully adopted e-commerce. In addition, the results outline that SMEs have adopted e-business activities, even though they are still using traditional ways more than these technologies. Although, many SMEs claim to have adopted a website and social media, usage is still quite limited.

E-business development in organisations is assumed to be a phased process in which firms are found to move from email, through to social media, a website, e-commerce, and mobile apps, to more advanced technology, such as e-business, and becoming transformed organisations that enable SMEs to carry out online selling and buying. Utilising electronic payments, for example, while being an e-transformed organisation allows transactions and communications to be conducted electronically and automated. This study confirms that e-business development in some organisations does progress from email towards more advanced technology and being a transformed organisation.

The study findings are significant due to identifying new entry points in the stage-adoption model (Fig. 3). Typically, stage-adoption models have assumed that technology adoption begins at the lowest level and progresses relatively linearly through to the higher levels. However, this study has found that contemporary

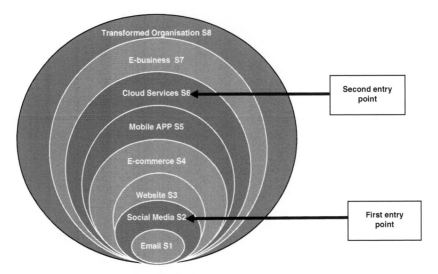

Fig. 3 Multiple Adoption Entry Points.

technologies, which have been included in the extended stage model that was used, permit entry to the adoption ladder at higher levels. These two entry points are stage 1 (email) and stage 6 (cloud services). Note, however, that entry to technology at stage 6 does not necessarily preclude the later adoption of technologies from stages 1–5. Where finance and capabilities have an influence, SMEs may retrospectively adopt 'lesser' technologies.

CONCLUSION

E-business is one of the opportunities for SMEs to improve their economic condition. Many businesses in developing countries are closely linked to a traditional pattern of commerce in their operations locally and abroad, which means the transition to e-commerce first requires understanding the importance and usefulness of trade over the Internet and adoption policies progress to develop strategies for the transition to e-commerce (Al-Marti, 2008). Studies of information technology adoption in developing countries are rare, and this is the first study to explore the adoption patterns of SMEs in the Yemen. Its findings are valuable for Yemeni SMEs, as well as the government and for developers of infrastructure.

The extended adoption model used in this study provides a useful framework for assessing the levels of adoption of contemporary information technologies. As such, it affords managers and researchers alike a more accurate means of examining the information technologies that are used in organisations. Efforts should be made to continually review and revise stage-adoption models as new information technologies are developed and become widely used. For instance, there may be a need to accommodate 'artificial intelligences' that are rapidly growing in capability and application.

In addition to continually refining stage-adoption models, future research should explore the vagaries of information technology adoption in other Middle Eastern countries. Examinations should also be made of the specific challenges and practices of micro-sized firms as these may be precursors to the development of SME enterprises. Similarly, the needs of large organisations are not fully understood in developing nations and their influence upon policy and infrastructure development may be valuable in supporting the technological development and overall growth of smaller organisations.

REFERENCES

Abdullah, A., Thomas, B., & Metcalfe, S. (2015). Measuring the e-business activities of SMEs in Yemen. *Asia Pacific Journal of Advanced Business and Social Studies*, 2(1), 1–8.

Abdullah A., Thomas B., & Metcalfe, S. (2016). Measuring the E-Business Activities of SMEs in Yemen. *Asia Pacific Journal of Advanced Business and Social Studies*, 2(1).

Abdullah, A., Thomas, B., Murphy, L., & Plant, E. (2018). An investigation of the benefits and barriers of e-business adoption activities in Yemeni SMEs. *Strategic Change*, 27(3), 195–208.

Abdullah, A., White, G. R. T., & Thomas, B. (2016). Conceptualising a new stage model of electronic business adoption in Yemeni SMEs. *The 39th annual conference of the institute for small business and entrepreneurship*, ISBE, Paris, France, October 26–27.

Afoloyan, A., Plant, E., White, G. R. T., Jones, W. P., & Beynon-Davies, P. (2015). Information technology usage in SMEs in a developing economy. *Strategic Change*, 24(5), 483–498.

Al-Marti A. (2008). *E-Commerce in Yemen to the Challenges and the Evolution of the Internet.* Available at: http://www.marebpress.net/news_details.php?sid=10488.

Al-Madhagy. (2013). *ICT Policy in Yemen.* Available at: https://www.academia.edu/5029849/ICT_Policy_in_ Yemen.

Almotamar news. (2014). *Repaid Growth in e-commerce in Yemen.* Available at: http://www.almotamar.net/ news/115930.htm.

Andam, Z. R., Programme, U. A. P. D. I., & Force, e.-A. T. (2003). *E-commerce and E-business: e-ASEAN Task Force.* (Retrieved October 22, 2010). www.apdip.net/publications/iespprimer.

Al-Qirim N. (2007). The adoption of eCommerce communications and applications technologies in small businesses in New Zealand. *Electronic Commerce Research and Applications,* 6(4), 462–473.

Armbrust, M., Fox, A., Griffith, R., Joseph, A. D., Katz, R., Konwinski, A., & Stoica, I. (2010). A view of cloud computing. *Communications of the ACM*, 53(4), 50–58.

Al-Somali, S. A., & Gholami, R. (2015). A stage-oriented model (SOM) for e-commerce adoption: a study of Saudi Arabian organizations. *Journal of Manufacturing Technology Management*, 26(1), 2–35.

Berthon, P., Pitt, L., Berthon, J.-P., Campbell, C., & Thwaites, D. (2008). e-Relationships for e-readiness: Culture and corruption in international e-B2B. *Industrial Marketing Management*, 37(1), 83–91. http://dx.doi.org/10.1016/j.indmarman.2007.06.014

Beynon-Davies, P. (2010). eBusiness as a driver for regional development. *Journal of Systems and Information Technology*, 12(1), 17–36. doi:10.1108/13287261011032634

Bolongkikit, J. (2006). An exploratory research of the usage level of e-commerce among SMEs in the west coast of Malaysia. *Journal of Internet Banking and Commerce.* 11(2).

Brychan, T., Christopher, M., Gary, P., & Geoff, S. (2009). The role of web sites and e-commerce in the development of global start-ups. In L. In (Ed.), *Electronic business: Concepts, methodologies, tools, and applications* (pp. 1002–1022). Hershey, PA: IGI Global.

BuddeComm. (2012). Yemen – Telecoms, mobile, broadband and forecasts. Retrieved from http://www.budde.com.au/Research/Yemen-Telecoms-Mobile-Broadband-and-Forecasts.html

Carter, S. (2012). Social media software provides no real benefit to the corporate culture. *Engineering & Technology*, 7(5), 31–31.

Chaffey, D. (2003). Business information systems. *Technology, Development and Management for the e-Business* (3rd ed). Harlow: Financial Times/Prentice Hall.

Chaffey, D. (2011). *E-business & e-commerce management: Strategy, implementation and practice.* Upper Saddle River, NJ: Pearson/Financial Times, Prentice Hall.

Chaffey, D., & White, G. R. T. (2011). *Business information management* (2nd ed.). London: Pearson Education.

Clapperton G. (2012). *This is Social Media: Tweet, blog, link and post your way to business success,* London: Amazon.

Cloete, E., Courtney, S., & Fintz, J. (2002). Small businesses' acceptance and adoption of e-commerce in the Western Cape Province of South Africa. *The Electronic Journal of Information Systems in Developing Countries, 10*(4), 1–13.

Creswell, J. W. (2013). *Research design: Qualitative, quantitative, and mixed methods approaches.* New York, NY: SAGE Publications.

Dali, N. R. S. B. M., Harun, M. Z. M. B., Khalid, F. B. M., & Hamid, H. B. A. (2003). Islamic business and e-commerce challenges and opportunities. Paper presented at the Uniten Score Conference, Mossaic Communications.

Damsgaard, J., & Scheepers, R. (1999). Power, influence and intranet implementation: A safari of South African organizations. *Information Technology & People, 12*(4), 333–358.

Daniel, E., Wilson, H., & Myers, A. (2002). Adoption of e-commerce by SMEs in the UK: Towards a stage model. *International Small Business Journal, 20*(3), 253–270.

Davis, W. S., & Benamati, J. (2003). *E-commerce basics: Technology foundations and e-business applications.* Boston, MA: Addison-Wesley.

EC. (2005). *The new SME definition, user guide and model declaration.* Retrieved from http://ec.europa.eu/enterprise/policies/sme/files/sme_definition/sme_user_guide_en.pdf

Fillis, I., Johannson, U., & Wagner, B. (2004). Factors impacting on e-business adoption and development in the smaller firm. *International Journal of Entrepreneurial Behaviour & Research, 10*(3), 178–191. doi:10.1108/13552550410536762.

Ghobakhloo, M., Hong, T. S., Sabouri, M. S., & Zulkifli, N. (2012). Strategies for successful information technology adoption in small and medium-sized enterprises. *Information, 3*(1), 36–67.

Grahl, T. (2015). The 6 types of social media. Retrieved from http://outthinkgroup.com/tips/the-6-types-of-social-media

Hackbarth, G., & Kettinger, W. J. (2000). Building an e-business strategy. *Information Systems Management, 17*(3), 78–93.

Hamed, A., Ball, D., Berger, H., & Cleary, P. (2008). The three-quarter moon: A new model for e-commerce adoption. *Communications of the IBIMA. 4*(11), 88–96.

Hiller, J. S., & Bélanger, F. (2001). Privacy strategies for electronic government. *E-government, 200,* 162–198.

Hoque, F. (2000). *E-enterprise: Business models, architecture, and components.* Cambridge: Cambridge University Press.

Hyatt, M. (2013). 10 types of social media updates – How many are you using? Retrieved from http://michaelhyatt.com/10-types-of-social-media-updates.html

ISACA. (2012). ISACA survey. Retrieved from http://www.isaca.org/About-ISACA/Press-room/News-Releases/2012/Pages/ISACA-Survey-90-Say-Online-Privacy-Is-Threatened-Yet-Risky-Behaviors-Persist.aspx

ITU. (2012). Connect Arab Summit 2012, connecting the unconnected by 2015: ICT adoption and prospects in the Arab Region. Retrieved from http://www.itu.int/dms_pub/itu-d/opb/ind/D-IND-AR-2012-PDF-E.pdf. Accessed on January 30, 2014.

Jones, C., Hecker, R., & Holland, P. (2003). Small firm Internet adoption: Opportunities forgone, a journey not begun. *Journal of Small Business and Enterprise Development, 10*(3), 287–297.

Jones, P., Beynon-Davies, P., & Muir, E. (2003). Ebusiness barriers to growth within the SME sector. *Journal of Systems and Information Technology, 7*(1/2), 1–25. doi:10.1108/13287260380000771

Jones, W. P., Packham, G., Pickernell, D., Thomas, B. C., & White, G. R. T. (2013). E-commerce trading activity and the SME sector: An FSB perspective. *Journal of Small Business and Enterprise Development, 20*(4), 866–888.

Jones, S., Wilikens, M., Morris, P., & Masera, M. (2000). Trust Requirements in E-Business. Communications of the ACM. *43*(12), 81–87.

Kaynak, E., Tatoglu, E., & Kula, V. (2005). An analysis of the factors affecting the adoption of electronic commerce by SMEs: Evidence from an emerging market. *International Marketing Review, 22*(6), 623–640.

Kumar, M. P., & Kumar, T. S. (2014). E-business: Pros and cons in customer relationship management. *International Journal of Management and International Business Studies, 4*(3), 349–356.

Lake, C. (2009). What is social media? Here are 34 definition. Retrieved from http://econsultancy.com/blog/3527-what-is-social-media-here-are-34-definitions

Layne, K., & Lee, J. (2001). Developing fully functional e-government: A four stage model. *Government Information Quarterly, 18*(2), 122–136.

Li P., & Xi W. (2012). A strategic framework for determining e-commerce adoption. *Journal of Technology Management in China, 7*(1), 22–35.

Maad, D. C., & Liedholm, C. (2008). The dynamics of micro and small enterprises in developing countries. *Journal of Finance, 26*(1), 61–74.

MacGregor, R. C., & Vrazalic, L. (2005). A basic model of electronic commerce adoption barriers. *Journal of Small Business and Enterprise Development, 12*(4), 510–527. doi:10.1108/14626000510628199

MacVittie, L. (2008). Defining cloud computing. Retrieved from http://www.computerweekly.com/opinion/Defining-cloud-computing

Martin, L. M., & Matlay, H. (2001a). *e-Benchmarking report*. London: Department of Trade and Industry.

Martin, L. M., & Matlay, H. (2001b). "Blanket" approaches to promoting ICT in small firms: Some lessons from the DTI ladder adoption model in the UK. *Internet Research, 11*(5), 399–410. doi:10.1108/EUM0000000006118

Mehrtens, J., Cragg, P. B., & Mills, A. M. (2001). A model of Internet adoption by SMEs. *Information & Management, 39*(3), 165–176. http://dx.doi.org/10.1016/S0378-7206(01)00086-6

Middleton, C. (2011). Understanding the costs and benefits associated with advanced e-business solutions in Canadian small and medium-sized enterprises. Report for Industry Canada.

Molla, A., & Licker, P. S. (2005). eCommerce adoption in developing countries: A model and instrument. *Information & Management, 42*(6), 877–899. http://dx.doi.org/10.1016/j.im.2004.09.002.

Murphy, L., & Symonds, W. (2004). *Measuring the e-business receptiveness of SMEs in rural mid wales*. ISBA Conference, University of Teeside.

Myers, A. (2015). 13 Types of social media platforms and counting. Retrieved from http://decidedlysocial.com/13-types-of-social-media-platforms-and-counting/

Nambisan, S., & Wang, Y.-M. (1999). Technical opinion: Roadblocks to web technology adoption? *Communications of the ACM, 42*(1), 98–101.

Nathan, R. J. (2009). Electronic commerce adoption in the Arab countries: An empirical study. *International Arab Journal of e-Technology, 1*(1), 29–37.

Nations, D. (2015). What is social media? Retrieved from http://webtrends.about.com/od/web20/a/social-media.htm

Nolan, R. L. (1973). Managing the computer resource: A stage hypothesis. *Communications of the ACM, 16*(7), 399–405.

Nolan, R. L. (1979). Managing the crises in data-processing. *Harvard Business Review, 57*(2), 115–126.

Ntoko, A. (2009). e-Business: A technology strategy for developing countries. *International Telecomunication Union*. Geneva, Switzerland: ITU.

OECD. (2004). *Information technology outlook*. Paris: OECD Publishing.

OECD. (2012). *Internet economy outlook*. Paris: OECD Publishing.

OECD. (2015). *Digital economy outlook*. Paris: OECD Publishing.

Pahladsingh, S. (2006). Barriers to effective e-business. Retrieved from http://www.emarketservices.com/clubs/ems/prod/eMarket,Services/20Barriers/to/effective/e-business.pdf. Accessed on April 6, 2014.

Parazoglou, M. P. (2006). *E-business organisational & technical foundations*. Hoboken, NJ: Wiley Limited.

Parida, V., Johansson, J., Ylinenpää, H., & Baunerhjelm, P. (2010). *Barriers to information and communication technology adoption in small firms*. Working paper, Swedish Entrepreneurship Forum.

Parker, C. M., & Castleman, T. (2009). Small firm e-business adoption: A critical analysis of theory. *Journal of Enterprise Information Management, 22*(1/2), 167–182.

Parliamentary Office of Science and Technology. (2006). Postnote: ICT in developing countries. Retrieved from http://www.parliament.uk/documents/post/postpn261.pdf

PayPal. (2013). *E-commerce in the Middle East*. Retrieved from www.paypal.com.

Poon, S., & Swatman, P. M. (1999). An exploratory study of small business Internet commerce issues. *Information & Management, 35*(1), 9–18.

Quelch, J. A., & Klein, L. R. (1996). Opinion: The Internet and international marketing. *Sloan Management Review, 37*(3), 60.

Rao, S. S., Metts, G., & Monge, C. A. M. (2003). Electronic commerce development in small and medium sized enterprises: A stage model and its implications. *Business Process Management Journal, 9*, 11–32.

Saidi, E. (2009). Mobile opportunities, mobile problems: Assessing mobile commerce implementation issues in Malawi. *Journal of Internet Banking and Commerce, 14*(1).

Simpson, M., & Docherty, A. J. (2004). E-commerce adoption support and advice for UK SMEs. *Journal of Small Business and Enterprise Development, 11*(3), 315–328. doi:10.1108/14626000410551573.

Sin Tan, K., Choy Chong, S., Lin, B., & Cyril Eze, U. (2009). Internet-based ICT adoption: Evidence from Malaysian SMEs. *Industrial Management & Data Systems, 109*(2), 224–244. doi:10.1108/02635570910930118

Sharma, A., & Sheth, J. N., (2010). A framework of technology mediation in consumer selling: Implications for firms and sales management, *Journal of Personal Selling and Sales Management, 30*(2), 121–129.

Shankar, V., Venkatesh, A., Hofacker, C., & Naik, P. (2010) Mobile marketing in the retailing environment: Current insights and future research avenues. *Journal of Interactive Marketing, 24*(2), 111–120.

Statskontoret, S. (2000). *The 24/7 agency: Criteria for 24/7 agencies in the networked public administration*. Swedish Agency for Administrative Development.

Taylor, M., & Murphy, A. (2004). SMEs and e-business. *Journal of Small Business and Enterprise Development, 11*(3), 280–289.

Teo, T. S., & Pian, Y. (2003). A contingency perspective on Internet adoption and competitive advantage. *European Journal of Information Systems, 12*(2), 78–92.

Teo, T. S., & Pian, Y. (2004). A model for web adoption. *Information & Management, 41*(4), 457–468.

Thomas, C. B., & Simmons, G. (Eds.). (2010). *E-commerce adoption and small business in the global marketplace: Tools for optimization*. Hershey, PA: IGI Global.

Thomas, C. B., Williams, R., Thompson, P., & Packham, G. (2013). Use of the internet and SME characteristics to expand scale and geographic scope of sales: The case of the United Kingdom. *International Journal of Technology Diffusion, 4*(3), 1–37. doi:10.4018/ijtd.2013070101.

Turban, E. (2010). *Electronic commerce 2010: A managerial perspective*. London: Pearson Education.

United Nations. (2009). Economic and social commission for Western Asia (ESCWA): National profile of the information society in Yemen. Retrieved from http://www.escwa.un.org/wsis/reports/docs/Yemen-07-E.pdf

Vosloo, G. J. (2003). *A conceptual framework of critical success factors for organisations to consider as they move towards full-scale B2B e-commerce*. Stellenbosch: Stellenbosch University.

White, G. R. T., Afolayan, A., & Plant, E. (2014). *Challenges to the adoption of e-commerce technology for supply chain management in a developing economy: A focus on Nigerian SMEs*. In E. Lacka, H. K. Chan, & N. Yip, (Eds.), *E-commerce platform acceptance: Suppliers, retailers and consumers*. London: Springer.

Willcocks, L., & Sauer, C. (2000). Moving to e-business: An introduction. In L. Willcocks, & C. Sauer (Eds.), *Moving to e-business: The ultimate practical guide to effective e-business* (pp. 1–19). London: Random House.

YMIT. (2014). *General report of the result of the comprehensive industrial survey 2010*. Retrieved from http://www.moit.gov.ye/moit/ar/print/2181

Zappalà, S., & Gray, C. (2006). *Impact of E-commerce on consumers and small firms*. London: Ashgate.

Zhang, Q., Cheng, L., & Boutaba, R. (2010). Cloud computing: State-of-the-art and research challenges. *Journal of Internet Services and Applications, 1*(1), 7–18. doi:10.1007/s13174-010-0007-6.

Zolait, A. H. S., Abdul Razak, I., & Ahmad, F. (2010). A study on the internet security and its implication for e-commerce in Yemen. *International Journal of Technology Diffusion, 1*(3), 34–47. doi:10.4018/jtd.2010070102

CHAPTER 3

WHAT DOES IT MEAN TO THINK AS AN ENTREPRENEUR? USING THE THRESHOLD CONCEPT FRAMEWORK TO INFORM ENTREPRENEURSHIP EDUCATION

Lucy Hatt

ABSTRACT

Entrepreneurs make a significant contribution to the health of any economy and higher education is regarded as pivotal in efforts to grow entrepreneurial talent. Entrepreneurship education has grown rapidly; yet, there is still controversy over the best way to educate and assess students. This chapter presents a study gathering a consensus of entrepreneur opinion on the concepts critical to thinking as an entrepreneur, in order to inform entrepreneurship curriculum development. There is a general lack of entrepreneurship education research that integrates the external stakeholder perspective in this way.

Using a Delphi-style method with twelve entrepreneurs, five candidate entrepreneurship threshold concepts are identified. Threshold concepts have a powerfully transformative effect on the learner, and important integrative qualities, allowing the learner to make the sense of previously isolated pockets of knowledge. A 'new world-view' or episteme can be constructed – a kind of disciplinary thinking, peculiar in this case, to entrepreneurs.

Creating Entrepreneurial Space: Talking Through Multi-voices, Reflections on Emerging Debates
Contemporary Issues in Entrepreneurship Research, Volume 9B, 27–44
ISSN: 2040-7246/doi:10.1108/S2040-72462019000009B003

This chapter contributes to the call for more research grounded discussion on the quality and effectiveness of entrepreneurship education initiatives. Designing curricula around the threshold concepts in entrepreneurship will enable educators to offer particular support in areas where students are likely to get 'stuck' and will facilitate constructive alignment with assessment.

Keywords: Threshold concepts; entrepreneurship education; Delphi; entrepreneur; pedagogy; threshold concept framework

INTRODUCTION

Entrepreneurship is generally regarded as an important factor in economic growth (UNCTAD, 2012), and higher education is regarded as an appropriate place for the development of entrepreneurship (QAA, 2012). However, there is a lack of consensus regarding how best to educate students for entrepreneurship in higher education (Pittaway & Cope, 2007) or indeed what educating students for entrepreneurship really means. Identifying concepts that are distinct to the field of entrepreneurship may open up new approaches to teaching it. Exploring the distinctive ways entrepreneurs think could reveal such concepts.

This chapter presents a study to gather a consensus of expert opinion on the concepts critical to thinking as an entrepreneur, as part of a doctoral research project using transactional curriculum inquiry (Cousin, 2008) to enhance entrepreneurship education. The concepts which are critical to thinking as an entrepreneur, and consequently to entrepreneurship, may be termed threshold concepts (Meyer & Land, 2003, 2005), and are characterised by their transformative, irreversible and integrative qualities.

Using a Delphi-style method, individual interviews with 12 expert entrepreneurs were conducted, transcribed, coded and analysed, and a list of candidate threshold concepts drawn up. Two further data sets were collected. In the first round of data collection following the interviews, the panel of interviewees were asked to rate the importance of the threshold concepts using an online survey, and suggest modifications. In the second round of data collection, the results of the first round were shared with the panel of interviewees and they were asked via email to indicate if each concept was critical or not to thinking as an entrepreneur.

By applying the threshold concept framework to entrepreneurship education, the author hopes to offer suggestions for the improvement of the effectiveness of programmes and modules claiming this specialisation. Using threshold concepts to distinguish ways of thinking as an entrepreneur will indicate ways in which entrepreneurship is distinctive. Further stages of this research will take the threshold concepts identified here and use them as a lens to examine existing entrepreneurship education programmes in the UK higher education. In addition, they will be used to research the perspective of students studying entrepreneurship in higher education, and ultimately findings will enable the recommendation of changes to curricula that are likely to have a positive impact on the effectiveness of entrepreneurship programmes, and the development of an understanding of entrepreneurship in graduates of these programmes.

Most higher education institutions now offer some sort entrepreneurship classes ranging from extracurricular activities to specialised optional and core modules, as well as entire degree programmes. A general lack of research-grounded discussion on the quality of entrepreneurship education initiatives has been highlighted however (Béchard & Grégoire, 2007), particularly in relation to what makes pedagogical innovations effective. Further stages of this study will use an analytical framework to understand a number of such educational initiatives in order to make recommendations regarding quality enhancement.

KEY LITERATURE

Threshold Concepts

Threshold concepts may be described as 'conceptual gateways' or 'portals' that lead to previously inaccessible ways of thinking about something – particularly in the context of academic disciplines (Meyer & Land, 2005). These conceptual gateways may be recognised by their *transformative, irreversible* and *integrative* characteristics. In transforming the learner, they change the learner's perceptions, subjectivities and worldview. There is a 'repositioning of the self' (Meyer & Land, 2005, p. 374); an ontological as well as a conceptual shift. This can often be uncomfortable and is sometimes resisted, so a threshold concept may also be characterised as troublesome. The transformational effects of threshold concepts are important both for ways of thinking, and for identity and discourse. Mastery of a threshold concept simultaneously changes an individual's idea of what they know and who they are (Cousin, 2009). Such changes are likely to be irreversible, and are also unlikely to be forgotten or unlearned. They are integrative in that they expose how other things can be related to each other. When individuals master the threshold concepts, they can see the relationships between other important concepts in the subject discipline. Examples of threshold concepts have included *precedent* in Law, *depreciation* in Accounting, *pain* in Physiology, *irony* in Literary Studies and *entropy* in Physics (Meyer & Land, 2005).

A threshold concept is also likely to be *bounded* in that 'any conceptual space will have terminal frontiers, bordering with thresholds into new conceptual areas' (Meyer & Land, 2006, p. 8). In recognising the threshold concepts in a subject area such as entrepreneurship, individuals recognise how it is qualitatively different to other subject areas and disciplines such as management or design (Donovan, 2017). A threshold concept can be a form of disciplinary property (Cousin, 2006) and offers a useful way of identifying and distinguishing a discipline, subject, profession or field of study. Land, Meyer, and Smith (2008) suggest they may define the boundaries of academic territories, and are being used to do this here. This study attempts to define a list of entrepreneurship threshold concepts that are bounded and separate and not simply a list of activities entrepreneurs engage in, that may or may not be distinctive of entrepreneurship.

Entrepreneurship

Theories of entrepreneurship are full of paradox and uncertainty and necessitate a level of improvisation (Schumpeter, 1934). According to Schumpeter (1934), the world of the entrepreneur is 'messy and paradoxical' (p. xii) and it is important to be prepared for 'complexity and uncertainty' (p. xii), and 'a continuous bombardment of new challenges and opportunities' (p. xii). To further add to the complexity, 'There are many entrepreneurships in terms of focus, definitions, scopes and paradigms' (Murphy, Liao, & Welsch, 2006, p. 5). However, if entrepreneurship is to be taught and curricula are to be developed which enable students to understand what it means to think like an entrepreneur, then it would be useful, to say the least, to identify a knowledge base for entrepreneurship.

From an economic perspective, entrepreneurship has been conceptualised in terms of financial risk, serving to compensate for discrepancies between supply and demand by buying something cheaply and selling it again at as high a price as possible (Schumpeter, 1934). The entrepreneur obtains and distributes resources at his or her own risk, thereby bringing the economy into equilibrium (McClelland, 1961). Gartner (1988) refers to Knight in the 1900s who stated the function of the entrepreneur was to carry the inherent uncertainty within the economy on his shoulders. Where different outcomes in the future exist and are known, the entrepreneur's role was to calculate probabilities and make decisions based on them. Where different outcomes in the future exist and are not known, the entrepreneur's role was to guess outcomes (based on a defined range of possible outcomes) with incremental certainty based on the accuracy of previous guesses, gradually building a picture of a likely future outcome. Where different outcomes in the future cannot be known, entrepreneurs receive profits as compensation or reward for taking risks.

Entrepreneurship can also be regarded purely as an investment alternative, and a mechanism for growing capital. A distinction can be made between people who supply funds and people who create profit (Carland, Carland, Hoy, & Boulton, 1988). Pittaway (2005) argued that the entrepreneur in fact bears no risk, instead, it is the venture capitalist who allocates the funds to the entrepreneur who bears the uncertainty and risk in the economy. Entrepreneurship therefore can be about the maximisation of return on investment. The creation of profit in entrepreneurial businesses may be distinguished from that of businesses in general because it can be argued as resulting from a strategy of aggressive expansion, and dissatisfaction with the status quo (Enterprising Oxford, 2010). An entrepreneur may be defined as anyone who practises entrepreneurship (in this way).

Schumpeter (1934) also argued that entrepreneurship is a proactive and creative activity, generating new opportunities and organisations in the economy by combining existing things, and arguably acting as the main source of development in the economy. Increasingly, concepts of entrepreneurship have become centred on innovation and the creation of value – where new venture creation is only one of many possible outputs. Entrepreneurship can be regarded as innovation (Schumpeter, 1934) and the act of value creation.

If an entrepreneur is someone who comes up with new ideas, recognises opportunities and translates these into added value for society by assuming the risk of starting a new business (Baron, 1998), then perhaps entrepreneurship can be regarded as anything that an entrepreneur does. However, many would argue that entrepreneurship is not only possible in the context of starting a new business.

A more holistic conceptualisation of entrepreneurship has also been extended to the human condition; 'We are entrepreneurs of the self' (Lazzarato, 2012, pp. 106–107). Entrepreneurship has thus been used to describe behaviours within corporate contexts (Nielsen, Klyver, Evald, & Bager, 2012) and therefore may not exclusively be about the creation of new and independent organisations. Entrepreneurship can be regarded as being about more than just starting an independent organisation, but a complex phenomenon that occurs in many different contexts, varying in terms of scope, process and output (Nielsen et al., 2012). Entrepreneurship therefore becomes possible for employees, and is thus transformed into the concept of 'intrapreneurship' (Pinchot, 1987). However, others would argue against this conceptualisation as it neglects the extent of personal financial risk normally involved in new venture creation.

Risk has often traditionally been associated with courage, masculinity and lone, heroic acts. Entrepreneurship has often been conceptualised as a form of heroism, and entrepreneurs are frequently portrayed in the media as 'today's heroes' (Nielsen et al., 2012, p. 3). Rags-to-riches stories in which our resourceful entrepreneur creates a new venture and becomes rich and famous are common and widespread.

Entrepreneurship has also been conceptualised as a type of vocation or calling, similar to that of an artist, musician or explorer,

> Entrepreneurship, particularly if you're a founder, is a calling, not a job. That's the biggest piece of advice I could give any entrepreneur. The problem today is that it's cool and trendy, so you think you should do it. Entrepreneurship is for crazy people, much like an artist. You don't get assigned to be a sculptor, a painter or a writer. It's something that you can't get rid of. It's inside of you, dying to get out. (Blank, 2014)

This would also suggest that entrepreneurs are born, not made, which is problematic for entrepreneurship educators.

Entrepreneurship has been conceptualised in terms of specific personality traits such as creativity, opportunism and persuasiveness combined with an unusually low level of aversion to uncertainty. These traits may be inherent, developed or a combination of the two. Repeated research attempts have attempted to distinguish those who engage in entrepreneurship through having a particular psychological mentality (Autio, 2007). The 'need to achieve' (Atkinson, 1957) amongst the actors in a given society could explain why some people concentrate on economic activity and are successful and others are not, and also why societies starting from similar points achieve different economic outcomes. A high level of self-efficacy is also frequently cited as a defining characteristic of entrepreneurs (Hechevarria, Ingram, Justo, & Terjesen, 2012).

However, the literature exploring the personality traits of successful entrepreneurs has been challenged on three main fronts. Firstly, the interdependency of traits and the influence of environmental factors have been largely ignored and are challenging or impossible to quantify. Secondly, such a wide range of traits have been generated as to render the concept of the characterisation of 'a successful entrepreneur' meaningless, and finally, the identification of 'the entrepreneurial personality' has not yet been empirically possible (Kolb, 1984).

Considering an entrepreneur as anyone practising entrepreneurship, and anyone practising entrepreneurship as an entrepreneur, the problem of definition and distinction of an entrepreneur and entrepreneurship is not progressed. This is the basis of the longstanding 'structure–agency' debate. Privileging structure (the entrepreneurial context or ecosystem) over agency (the individual entrepreneur) reifies some features of the social world, which are then assumed to structure other features, negating agency and creativity in humans, which, in turn, are assumed to be predictable and robotic processors of information (Garud, Hardy, & Maguire, 2007). Privileging agency (the individual entrepreneur), however, promotes heroic models of actors and can be criticised for being historically inaccurate, decontextualised and so broad as to be meaningless. By emphasising intentionality, little attention is afforded to the unintended consequences of action, which can be a critical contributor to innovative breakthroughs.

Whichever conceptualisation or combination of conceptualisations one chooses for entrepreneurship, the fact remains that none of them tell the whole story, so far. None is sufficient on its own; many people with supposedly entrepreneurial traits have not set up new ventures, and many self-employed people or small business founders do not display an entrepreneurial approach.

It is argued that the missing dimension might be the entrepreneurial context, the environmental factors or ecosystem within which the person embodying an entrepreneurial predisposition finds himself or herself. It could be the interplay between the processes of new venture creation, the individual and the context of external factors such as financial support (Prahalad, 2005) that might enable the prediction of entrepreneurial activity and hence offer the key to economic development and success.

Entrepreneurship has been explained by considering the nexus of enterprising individuals and valuable opportunities (Shane, 2000) and other researchers have attempted to address these issues by offering theoretical perspectives that combine structure and agency in some form of mutually constitutive duality. Bourdieu (1990), for example, overcomes what he sees as the false antimony between agency and structure, replacing this with a focus on practice. According to these researchers, structure is both the medium and outcome of social practices; instead of being in opposition, structure and agency presuppose each other and are mutually constitutive (Sewell, 1992). Entrepreneurship threshold concepts, when defined as ways of thinking and practising, may exist within, and help to explain, the individual – opportunity nexus.

This chapter builds on work by Cope (2005), Rae and Carswell (2001), Politis (2005) and others who look at understanding entrepreneurship from a learning perspective. Cope (2005) sets out five broad areas of content – the 'what' entrepreneurs need to learn about; oneself; the business; the environment and entrepreneurial networks; small business management; and the nature and management of relationships. Entrepreneurs learn most from experience and discovery (Deakins & Freel, 1998; Gibb, 1987; Politis, 2005); particularly, critical experiences, routine and regular activity and reflection. This last activity can give rise to generative learning (Senge, 1990) where learning from past experiences can be brought forward and applied to different experiences in the future. It is also interesting to note the importance of the social aspect of learning for the entrepreneur and the role of vicarious learning (Cope, 2005).

Focussing on the distinctive ways in which entrepreneurs think and practise is particularly appealing in an educational context notwithstanding the many challenges this approach presents to the educator. Not least of these is the task of identifying the threshold concepts of entrepreneurship (the focus of the research presented here) and the means whereby they might be assessed, which is indicated as an area for future research. Hence, this study attempts to answer the question, 'What does it mean to think as an entrepreneur?' Exploring the distinctive ways entrepreneurs think will enable the identification of entrepreneurship threshold concepts, and contribute towards the understanding of how entrepreneurs develop entrepreneurial knowledge that indirectly enables them to recognise and act on entrepreneurial opportunities and organise and manage new ventures. This in turn will open up new approaches to learning and teaching entrepreneurship.

METHODOLOGY

The Delphi Method

It is argued that a shared understanding of threshold concepts is critical and therefore a level of consensus is invaluable to their identification in any field or discipline (Barradell, 2013). The Delphi method was chosen here as it achieves a shared consensus amongst experts, and is regarded as an appropriate method for collecting data where knowledge is incomplete (Amos & Pearse, 2008).

It is appropriate if the problem at hand does not lend itself to precise analytical techniques but can benefit from subjective judgements on a collective basis and more individuals are needed than can effectively or realistically (from a logistical perspective) interact in a face to face exchange. The main advantage of the technique is that it allows the heterogeneity of the participants to be preserved assuring greater validity of results, as the group is not open to domination by quantity or by strength of personality from any particular individual or group of individuals (Linstone & Turoff, 1975).

The term 'Delphi' has been extended over the years to cover a wide variety of types of group interaction (Linstone & Turoff, 1975). Most can be characterised as follows:

- The exercise involves a group.
- The goal of the exercise is information (i.e. the exercise is an inquiry).
- The information being sought is uncertain the minds of the group.
- Some pre-formulated systematic procedures are followed in obtaining group output.

A way of gathering expert opinion, it may be considered a remote group inter-view or focus group where the participants are aware of the perspectives of each other but are not aware of which participant has which perspective. The inten-tion is that participants are influenced by each other's perspectives according to the content and not the author. Opinion is gathered over several rounds inter-spersed with a controlled feedback until the results become stable or consensus is achieved (Amos & Pearse, 2008). The researcher alternates between discovering and interpreting the data with the aim of approaching a consensus of opinion which is more informed and sophisticated than any of the preceding construc-tions including that of the researcher (Guba & Lincoln, 1994).

A number of studies concerned with entrepreneurship have used the Delphi method to collect research data (Amos & Pearse, 2008; Gartner, 1990; Morris, Webb, Fu, & Singhal, 2013; Robles & Zárraga-Rodríguez, 2015). As the goal of this exercise is not information as such, but threshold concepts, and the partici-pants' responses have been treated as self-reports, the method used here may be described as a Delphi-inspired survey process to obtain expert consensus.

DESCRIPTION OF THE STUDY

Any research paradigm, as a set of basic beliefs, represents a human construction that has been devised as the most informed and sophisticated view the researcher is capable of. As a human invention, it will be subject to human error so cannot be presented as incontrovertibly 'right', but must rely on persuasiveness and utility rather than proof (Guba & Lincoln, 1994). This research adopts a constructivist paradigm where many realities are constructed from social and experiential bases which are local and specific in nature. Constructions are therefore only more or less informed and/or sophisticated rather than more or less 'true' in any kind of absolute sense (Guba & Lincoln, 1994). Therefore, the aim of this inquiry, adapted from Guba and Lincoln (1994, p. 112), is to understand and reconstruct concepts that might be critical to thinking as an entrepreneur regarding reality as relative and socially constructed.

A three-stage Delphi-inspired process was used to identify and obtain expert consensus on entrepreneurship threshold concepts. The first stage consisted of semi-structured interviews conducted with expert entrepreneurs. The aim of the interviews was to answer the overarching research question, 'What does it mean to think as an entrepreneur?' Twenty-three individuals were approached to par-ticipate in the interview stage. Seventeen agreed to participate and interviews of around 40 minutes were conducted and transcribed (nine were conducted face-to-face and eight over the telephone).

A purposive sample of entrepreneur interviewees was identified from the mem-bership records of the Entrepreneurs' Forum. The Entrepreneurs' Forum (2017) is a members' organisation in the North East of England dedicated to helping their members develop, create new opportunities and grow their businesses. All members are owner/managers of businesses who work full-time on their busi-ness, which must have an annual turnover in excess of £250,000. Further participants were introduced by individuals in the initial participant set, in a snowball fashion. Two additional participants were known personally by the author and served to pilot the research communication and interview questions. For additional context, four other individuals were also interviewed, including an expert in venture capital, founders of smaller businesses and an expert in entrepreneurship education.

One of the criticisms of the Delphi technique is the lack of universal guidelines and the fact that there are no established rules for this approach (Keeney, Hasson, & McKenna, 2011). As a consequence, the number of participants in studies employing this technique can vary significantly from under 15, to 100s or even 1,000s. In general, however, a small sample size for homogeneous samples is generally regarded as allowable, and a number of authors suggest that a sample size of between 8 and 12 is adequate (Keeney et al., 2011).

The criteria for the sample of expert entrepreneurs were adapted from research by Sarasvathy (2008, p. 21), who defined an expert entrepreneur as 'a person who, either individually or working as part of a team, had

(1) founded one or more companies,
(2) remained a full time founder/entrepreneur for 10 years or more, and
(3) participated in taking at least one company public' (numbering added by the author).

Target participants were chosen who satisfied the first two criteria and whose company had reached a significant turnover (over £2M) and a substantial number of employees (over 20). Ultimately, the third criterion of company floatation was not applied, as the consensus of the participating expert entrepreneurs was that floatation was not necessarily the only reliable indication of business success, and was not generally regarded as the ultimate goal for every business.

Many other people who do not comply with the criteria set out here may also be argued to be entrepreneurs, or even expert entrepreneurs, but it would be hard to argue that any individual complying with the criteria set out above was not an expert entrepreneur.

A list of nine candidate threshold concepts, together with brief descriptors, was developed by coding the interview transcripts using NVIVO10 software. Thematic analysis was combined with grounded theory and a social constructionist approach. Interview data were treated as stories and narratives through which the interviewees described their world and not as 'potentially "true" pictures of "reality"' (Silverman, 2013, p. 238). The aim was to generate threshold concepts that served as hypotheses, theoretically describing the constructs in every sentence. The interview transcripts were coded according to particular themes, which emerged on reading and re-reading them, line by line. Coding and analysis were conducted hand in hand in a cyclical fashion, recognising that they are related but separate activities (Saldaña, 2009). The process of coding leads from the data to the idea and from the idea to all the data, pertaining to the idea (Richards & Morse, 2007). A large number of themes were developed quickly at first, and then as more transcripts were coded, the number of themes plateaued, indicating that perhaps a complete list had been generated. At the same time, the themes were also gradually grouped together in families from which the candidate threshold concepts emerged. For example, 'Focus' included the themes of 'persuasive', 'prioritisation', 'seeing the big picture', 'stubborn' and 'vision'. Candidate threshold concepts were developed which highlighted patterns in the data and attempted to explain why the patterns were there in the first place.

Once the candidate threshold concepts had been developed, participants were asked to rate each candidate threshold concept (and descriptor) according to *how important they felt it was to thinking as an entrepreneur,* using online survey software (Bristol Online Survey). They were also asked to rank the candidate threshold concepts according to their importance to thinking as an entrepreneur, and also according to how much they differentiated between thinking as an entrepreneur, and not thinking as an entrepreneur. Responses were analysed and slight modifications were made to the descriptors of two of the candidate threshold concepts as a result. In this rating stage, the online questionnaire was sent to 16 of the interviewees (the expert in entrepreneurship education was not invited to participate) asking them to rate each candidate threshold concept in terms of importance to thinking as an entrepreneur. Fifteen responded, three of which were excluded as the respondents did not strictly comply with the definition of expert entrepreneur being used here, to ensure a homogenous sample. The turnovers of the companies founded by the respondents at this stage ranged from £2.4m to £1.3bn and 5 of the 12 had publically floated the companies they had founded.

The third and final stage of the process was conducted via email. The collated perspective of the group was shared from the second stage – however, it seemed inappropriate to ask participants to repeat exactly the same exercise again, with the only difference being knowledge of their own previous response and the group response. Little comment has been made on the required levels of tolerance of the respondents in a Delphi exercise. Repeatedly being asked the same question, albeit with new information regarding how everybody else answered it last time could become tiresome, especially for respondents with strongly held opinions that are relatively fixed and not easily influenced by others, as was likely in this case. It was also difficult to see how any consensus could be claimed that was not in fact unanimity in participant ranking. Consequently, in the final round, participants were asked to indicate if they thought each candidate threshold concept was critical to thinking as an entrepreneur – yes or no. Ten responses were received at this final stage.

Consensus is generally regarded to be broad agreement, a collective opinion and a shared view. Keeney et al. (2011, p. 27) discuss a 'level of consensus' in a Delphi, implying that unanimity is not required. They point out that the definition of an acceptable level of consensus is contentious and is often an arbitrary figure, which is not stated at all in many studies. With this in mind, participants were asked to vote on the candidate threshold concepts in the final round and consensus was defined as >80% agreement.

FINDINGS

An initial set of nine candidate threshold concepts were developed from the 17 interviews conducted (Table 1).

In the rating round, 16 participants were asked to rate these 9 concepts in terms of importance to thinking as an entrepreneur, and rank them in terms of importance and also in terms of how well they differentiated thinking as an entrepreneur from not thinking as an entrepreneur. Fifteen responded; three responses were excluded, as the respondents did not fit with the 'expert entrepreneur' criteria being used (Table 2).

All nine candidate threshold concepts were rated as at least important to thinking as an entrepreneur, by the majority of the participants, but it was difficult to judge whether or not any consensus had been achieved. Agreement was even less apparent in the ranked responses. Table 3 shows the number of respondents ranking each candidate threshold concept in either the top or bottom four. Consensus could be claimed for *Focus* being important to thinking as an entrepreneur (ranked in the top 4 by 10 of the 12 respondents) and *Business Fundamentals* being less important to thinking as an entrepreneur (ranked in the bottom 4 by 11 of the 12 respondents.)

Table 1.   Initial Set of Nine Candidate Entrepreneurship
Threshold Concepts Drawn from Interview Data.

Self-efficacy	Self-efficacy is about thinking 'I can do this' whilst being highly self-aware, self-controlled and conscious of one's own strengths and weaknesses. It is about accepting mistakes as part of learning, and always being interested in knowing more
Focus	Focus is about making choices, having a clear vision and passionately driving towards it. It implies effective prioritisation, appropriate delegation and never switching off. Focus means intense, single-minded determination
Deviance	Deviance is about being unconsciously unconventional, able to resist the pressure to conform or do what family and society expect. It implies a degree of strong mindedness and can sometimes be perceived as being difficult or arrogant
Risk	Risk is regarded as a sign of a potential opportunity, something to be understood – even sought out – rather than necessarily avoided. It implies quick wits, requires discernment and is not reckless
Opportunity	Opportunity is about seeing commercial potential where others do not. It is associated with intuition, making patterns and connections. It implies future orientation and a focus on possibilities for improvement
Impact	Impact is about making things happen and taking action on a grand scale combined with a sense of urgency and a desire to make a difference. It requires courage and implies a degree of compulsion
Work	Work is not a distinct bounded set of activities, but integral to and indistinguishable from living and playing. It implies incredible effort invested by choice which is intrinsically motivated
Team	An effective team is prerequisite to success. Team is about knowing that the team can do more than the collection of individuals combined, not feeling threatened by the capabilities of others, but seeking out others more able than you
Business fundamentals	Having fundamental knowledge in sales and marketing, finance and human resources

Table 2. Participant Rating of Initial Set of Nine Candidate
Entrepreneurship Threshold Concepts.

Importance to Thinking as an Entrepreneur	Not Related	Little Relevance	Some Relevance	Important	Critical
Focus				2	10
Risk				3	9
Opportunity				3	9
Self-efficacy			1	3	8
Impact			1	4	7
Work			2	4	6
Team		1	1	4	6
Business fundamentals		1	5	3	3
Deviance			5	5	2

Table 3. Participant Ranking of Initial Set of Nine Candidate
Entrepreneurship Threshold Concepts in Terms of Importance
to Thinking as an Entrepreneur.

	Top 4	Bottom 4
Self-efficacy	7	4
Focus	10	0
Deviance	4	8
Risk	6	4
Opportunity	6	5
Impact	4	5
Work	4	7
Team	6	4
Business fundamentals	1	11

Participants were also asked to rank the concepts in terms of how well they distinguished between thinking as an entrepreneur from not thinking as an entrepreneur. Table 4 shows the number of respondents ranking each concept in the top or bottom four according to these criteria.

Little consensus was apparent in this ranking exercise either, with the exception of 11 of the 12 respondents ranking *Business Fundamentals* in the bottom 4 in terms of how well it distinguished between thinking as an entrepreneur from not thinking as an entrepreneur.

In the final stage of data collection, participants were asked to indicate if they thought each of the nine concepts were critical to thinking as an entrepreneur. The wording of the descriptors of two of the concepts was modified slightly in response to qualitative feedback. The word 'highly' was omitted from the descriptor of *Self-efficacy* and it became:

> Self-efficacy is about thinking 'I can do this' whilst being highly self-aware, self-controlled and conscious of one's own strengths and weaknesses. It is about accepting mistakes as part of learning, and always being interested in knowing more'.

Table 4. Participant Ranking of Initial Set of Nine Candidate Entrepreneurship Threshold Concepts in Terms of How Well They Distinguish between Thinking as an Entrepreneur from not Thinking as an Entrepreneur.

	Top 4	Bottom 4
Self-efficacy	7	4
Focus	8	2
Deviance	3	6
Risk	8	3
Opportunity	9	1
Impact	5	6
Work	5	6
Team	2	9
Business fundamentals	1	11

Table 5. Participant Voting on Initial Set of Nine Candidate Entrepreneurship Threshold Concepts in Terms Whether They are Critical or Not to Thinking as an Entrepreneur.

Critical to Thinking as an Entrepreneur	Yes	No
Focus	10	0
Self-efficacy	9	1
Risk	9	1
Opportunity	9	1
Impact	9	1
Deviance	7	3
Work	6	4
Team	6	4
Business fundamentals	5	5

The words 'on a grand scale' were omitted from the descriptor of *Impact* and it became:

> Impact is about making things happen and taking action on a grand scale combined with a sense of urgency and a desire to make a difference. It requires courage and implies a degree of compulsion.

Ten responses (from 12) were received (Table 5).

It was judged that consensus had been reached for five of the nine candidate threshold concepts, with at least 9 of the 10 respondents indicating they were critical to thinking as an entrepreneur. These were *Focus, Self-efficacy, Risk, Opportunity* and *Impact*. These are illustrated with verbatim quotes from the interviews below.

The threshold concept of *Focus* is about making choices and perhaps turning away from other attractive opportunities as explained here,

> [...] you realise you know years on, that actually being very focussed and not straying is a key asset ... there's always that desire to break out and try and do more, go off and do other things at the same time as running your business, your core business .... And whilst you might think it's entrepreneurial to go and sort of try to do other things or, or tangential things along the way, actually – don't. (Transcript 13)

In the context of *Focus*, it is important to have a clear vision and passionately, and perhaps stubbornly, drive towards it.

> I think an entrepreneur is somebody who, err, as I said before, has a vision for something that can be, that they can do … erm … and perhaps something that you see a real opportunity and you think, 'I can do that better than somebody else.' I can make a real success of that. I can gather a team of people around me to deliver that and they've got the drive and determination to make it work because failure is not an option. You know, you have to succeed or, you know, the business will, will fold. (Transcript 9)

Effective prioritisation is also an important component of *Focus*,

> I learned how to you know cut through the crap basically and sort of you know just sort of spend time on what was important. (Transcript 15)

as well as the ability to quickly see the big picture:

> One of the things a lot of entrepreneurs are very quick, they're not as some people think, they're not kind of salesmen or somebody trying to do a quick turn or a quick deal or do something very, very quick, you just do it. Most entrepreneurs that I know that are really successful are able to take in the whole world view whether that's the environment that's round and about you, erm, the people that are working for you, the customers, quite a lot of different things, but just to be able to take that whole view into account very, very quickly, erm, and they can see themselves and their business decisions in the context of the local economy, the place in which they work, the market place in which they work, the wider economy, erm, other things going on around about in a different that may influence the consumer. They can see all those different things going on but they get that big world picture very, very quickly. I, I find that that's something that I've got a, a knack of doing and not everybody else can […]. (Transcript 8)

The final aspect of *Focus* is its all absorbing nature.

> Just that incredible sort of consistency of dedication to the whole thing. You know, you just never let it drop, you never relax, you never, you know, you don't ever stop doing what you're trying to do really. It's, it's kind of, it's what drives you sort of thing. (Transcript 5)

The threshold concept of *Self-efficacy* is about being attracted to challenges and thinking 'I can do this' whilst being highly self-aware, self-controlled and conscious of one's own strengths and weaknesses. One respondent summarised it like this,

> […] you don't want an easy ride, because that would be boring. (Transcript 10)

Mistakes are regarded as an important way of learning, and par for the course.

> You've also got to grasp the concept, and this is where I would define a good entrepreneur is somebody who does not recognise failure. And what I mean by that is that you may not succeed, but you see that as something different. So my, what would seem to the world, say, at times my failures, I, I don't see them as fail-, I may be, I may hurt at the time that they happen … and I feel all the pain of failure … but I quickly get engaged in a dialogue that says, 'Well, that's a learning experience'. (Transcript 7)

Self-efficacy is also concerned with self-confidence, almost to the point of arrogance and a level of self-knowledge that is deep enough to acknowledge important limitations, but not so deep as to inhibit risk taking.

> I mean overwhelmingly we tend to look at everything and go 'we could do that better' Doesn't matter what it is actually! (Transcript 14)

The threshold concept of *Risk* is about understanding risk as an inherent part of pursuing any potential opportunity, and something not to be avoided but perhaps even sought out.

So every spare penny we ever had, and in fact quite a lot of money we didn't have, we used to put into growing and scaling up as quickly as possible. (Transcript 14)

I have a high propensity for risk, even to the point where, err, I'm uncomfortable when I'm comfortable. (Transcript 7)

Risk also involves being discerning regarding potential opportunities, but also having faith in your own decisions, trusting your gut and not needing to have all the detail,

But I do think that a very sort of rigid approach and very analytical approach to, to things probably isn't the obvious characteristic of an entrepreneur because they will do, you know, those kind of people will do things logically, they'll do lots of analysis and, again, to use those dreadful phrases, you get paralysis by analysis. You need someone who says, 'Yeah, yeah, I know all of that, but [...]' (Transcript 6)

The threshold concept of *Opportunity* is about seeing commercial potential where others do not.

You join dots. You know, you see connections. You see, you see your own pathways that other people just don't see. (Transcript 7)

Is also involves a strong desire to change the status quo.

There's definitely that desire to change, to want to do things differently and to be the person that thinks they're the ones that can do it. Umm, I think you also have to have a certain level of dissatisfaction about just the general status quo all the time, I guess it ties in to wanting to change things but I get irritated when ... I think I mean I look for solutions to things all the time. (Transcript 14)

Finally, the threshold concept of *Impact* is about making things happen and taking action.

And I think an entrepreneur is someone who – really important – doesn't think about the consequences because if you start to think about it too much, you don't do it, and that is **the most**, for me, defining thing about an entrepreneur. And the second thing – it's strange to say it's second, but I think it's really important – is that you then do it. You don't delay by a day. You don't delay by a week. You just absolutely do it. (Transcript 10)

To summarise, when an individual has understood the threshold concepts of *Focus*, *Self-efficacy*, *Risk*, *Opportunity* and *Impact*, they will also understand what it means to think like an entrepreneur.

CONCLUSIONS

In this chapter, ways in which entrepreneurs think have been explored and, using thematic coding and a Delphi-style survey process with expert entrepreneurs; five threshold concepts have been identified that could be distinctive to entrepreneurship – Focus, Self-efficacy, Risk, Opportunity and Impact. They are bounded and distinct; not simply a list of activities entrepreneurs (and others) may engage in, or competencies that entrepreneurs (and others) demonstrate.

Acknowledging that the term 'entrepreneur' is widely interpreted, expert entrepreneurs were identified as those that had founded a company in which they worked for over 10 years and which had grown to a turnover of at least £2m and employed at least 20 people. Five of the ten entrepreneurs completing all three stages of the research had also taken at least one of their companies public (launched on the stock market).

Although some believe that attempts to stimulate entrepreneurial activities through formal training and education are not likely to have any strong and direct impact on the development of entrepreneurial knowledge (Politis, 2005), research into entrepreneurship from a learning perspective is opening up promising new avenues. Educational initiatives which offer relevant entrepreneurial experience such as venture creation and seek to foster critical thinking, and generative learning through reflection, can have a significant impact on both the motivation and ability of students to develop entrepreneurial knowledge throughout their professional lives. If there is a general consensus that entrepreneurship is learned by doing – then educational initiatives need to be developed that offer students relevant experiences together with structured opportunities to reflect. The identification of entrepreneurship threshold concepts will enable a greater focus on what the most relevant experiences for optimal learning of entrepreneurship in higher education might be. Threshold concepts in any discipline or multidisciplinary subject area are important to educators and trainers in developing enterprising and pedagogical approaches. It is hoped that the application of the threshold concept framework in entrepreneurial learning here will contribute to the process of clarifying what students of entrepreneurship need to learn. These entrepreneurship threshold concepts can be used to set out a structure for the design and (re)development of enterprise and entrepreneurship curricula, as well as enabling more constructively aligned assessments.

ACKNOWLEDGEMENTS

The author would like to thank Emerald Publishing for permission to use Hatt's (2017) article as a basis for this chapter.

REFERENCES

Amos, T., & Pearse, N. (2008). Pragmatic research design: An illustration of the use of the Delphi technique. *Electronic Journal of Business Research Methods*, 6(2), 95–102.

Atkinson, J. W. (1957). Motivational determinants of risk-taking behavior. *Psychological Review*, 64(6, pt. 1), 359–372.

Autio, E. (2007). *Entrepreneurship teaching in the Öresund and Copenhagen regions*. Copenhagen, Denmark: Danmarks Tekniske Universitet.

Baron, R. A. (1998). Cognitive mechanisms in entrepreneurship: Why and when entrepreneurs think differently than other people. *Journal of Business Venturing*, 13, 275–294.

Barradell, S. (2013). The identification of threshold concepts: A review of theoretical complexities and methodological challenges. *Higher Education, 65*(2), 265–276.

Béchard, J.-P., & Grégoire, D. (2007). Archetypes of pedagogical innovation for entrepreneurship in higher education: Model and illustrations. In A. Fayolle (Ed.), *Handbook of research in entrepreneurship education: A general perspective* (Vol. 1, pp. 261–284). Cheltenham & Northampton, MA: Edward Elgar.

Blank, S. (2014). *Steve Blank: 'Entrepreneurship is a calling, not a job.'/Interviewer: N. Zipkin.* Retrieved from www.entrepreneur.com

Bourdieu, P. (1990). *The logic of practice.* Stanford, CA: Stanford University Press.

Carland, J. W., Carland, J., Hoy, F., & Boulton, W. R. (1988). Distinctions between entrepreneurial and small business ventures. *International Journal of Management, 5*(1), 98–103.

Cope, J., 2005. Toward a dynamic learning perspective of entrepreneurship. *Entrepreneurship Theory and Practice, 29*(4), 373–397.

Cousin, G. (2006). An introduction to threshold concepts. *Planet, 17*(1), 4–5. Retrieved from http://www.neillthew.typepad.com/files/threshold-concepts-1.pdf

Cousin, G. (2008). *Strategies for researching learning in higher education: An introduction to contemporary methods and approaches.* Oxford: Routledge.

Cousin, G. (2009). *Researching learning in higher education.* Oxford: Routledge.

Deakins, D., & Freel, M. (1998). Entrepreneurial learning and the growth process in SMEs. *The Learning Organization, 5*(3), 144–155.

Donovan, P. (2017). A threshold concept in managing: What students in introductory management courses must know. *Journal of Management Education, 41*(6), 835–851.

Enterprising Oxford, University of Oxford. (Producer). (2010). *What's the difference between entrepreneurs & small businesses?* Retrieved from http://www.eship.ox.ac.uk/whats-difference-between-entrepreneurs-and-small-business-owners

Entrepreneurs' Forum. (2017). *About us.* Retrieved from http://www.entrepreneursforum.net/about-us

Gartner, W. B. (1988). "Who is an entrepreneur?" Is the wrong question. *American Journal of Small Business, 12*(4), 11.

Gartner, W. B. (1990). What are we talking about when we talk about entrepreneurship? *Journal of Business Venturing, 5*(1), 15–28.

Garud, R., Hardy, C., & Maguire, S. (2007). Institutional entrepreneurship as embedded agency: An introduction to the special issue. *Organizational Studies, 28*(7), 957–969

Gibb, A. (1987). *Enterprise culture — Its meaning and implications for education and training.* Bradford: MCB University Press.

Guba, E. G., & Lincoln, Y. S. (1994). Competing paradigms in qualitative research. In N. K. Denzin, & Y. S. Lincoln, (Eds.), *Handbook of qualitative research* (Chapter 6, pp. 105–117). London: Sage.

Hatt, L. (2017). Threshold concepts in entrepreneurship – The entrepreneurs' perspective. *Education + Training, 60*(2), 155–167. doi:10.1108/ET-08-2017-0119

Hechevarria, D., Ingram, A., Justo, R., & Terjesen, S. (2012). Are women more likely to pursue social and environmental entrepreneurship? In K. Hughes & J. Jennings (Eds.), *Global women's entrepreneurship research: Diverse settings, questions and approaches* (pp. 135–151). Cheltenham: Edward Elgar.

Keeney, S., Hasson, F., & McKenna, H. (2011). *The Delphi technique in nursing and health research.* Chichester: Wiley-Blackwell.

Kolb, D. A. (1984). *Experiential learning: Experience as the source of learning and development.* Englewood Cliffs, NJ: Prentice-Hall.

Land, R., Meyer, J., & Smith, J. (2008). Editors' preface. In R. Land, J. Meyer, & J. Smith (Eds.), *Threshold concepts within the disciplines* (pp. ix–xvi). Rotterdam, The Netherlands: Sense Publishers.

Lazzarato, M. (2012). *The making of the indebted man: An essay on the neoliberal condition.* Amsterdam, The Netherlands: Semiotext(e) Intervention Series.

Linstone, H. A., & Turoff, M. (1975). *The Delphi method: Techniques and applications* (Vol. 29). Reading, MA: Addison-Wesley.

McClelland, D. C. (1961). *Achieving society.* Princeton, NJ: Van Nostrand.

Meyer, J., & Land, R. (2003). Threshold concepts and troublesome knowledge (1) linkages to ways of thinking and practising within the disciplines. In G. Gibbs (Ed.), *Improving student learning theory and practice – 10 years on* (pp. 412–424). Oxford: OCSLD.

Meyer, J., & Land, R. (2005). Threshold concepts and troublesome knowledge (2): Epistemological considerations and a conceptual framework for teaching and learning. *Higher Education*, *49*(3), 373–388. doi:10.1007/s10734-004-6779-5

Meyer, J., & Land, R. (2006). Threshold concepts and troublesome knowledge – An introduction. In J. Meyer & R. Land (Eds.), *Overcoming barriers to student understanding* (pp. 3–18). Oxford: Routledge.

Morris, M. H., Webb, J. W., Fu, J., & Singhal, S. (2013). A competency-based perspective on entrepreneurship education: Conceptual and empirical insights. *Journal of Small Business Management*, *51*(3), 352–369.

Murphy, P. J., Liao, J., & Welsch, H. P. (2006). A conceptual history of entrepreneurial thought. *Journal of Management History*, *12*(1), 12–35.

Nielsen, S. L., Klyver, K., Evald, M. R., & Bager, T. (2012). *Entrepreneurship in theory and practice: Paradoxes in play.* Cheltenham: Edward Elgar Publishing.

Pinchot, G. (1987). Innovation through intrapreneuring. *Research Management*, *30*(2), 14–19.

Pittaway, L. (2005). Philosophies in entrepreneurship: A focus on economic theories. *International Journal of Entrepreneurial Behavior & Research*, *11*(3), 201–221.

Pittaway, L., & Cope, J. (2007). Entrepreneurship education: A systematic review of the evidence. *International Small Business Journal*, *25*(5), 479–510.

Politis, D. (2005). The process of entrepreneurial learning: A conceptual framework. *Entrepreneurship Theory and Practice*, *29*(4), 399–424.

Prahalad, C. (2005). *The fortune at the bottom of the pyramid: Eradicating poverty through profit and enabling dignity and choice through markets.* Upper Saddle River, NJ: Wharton School.

QAA. (2012). *Enterprise and entrepreneurship education. Guidance for UK higher education providers.* Retrieved from http://www.qaa.ac.uk/en/Publications/Documents/enterprise-entrepreneurship-guidance.pdf

Rae, D., & Carswell, M. (2001). Towards a conceptual understanding of entrepreneurial learning. *Journal of Small Business and Enterprise Development*, *8*(2), 150–158.

Richards, L., & Morse, J. M. (2007). *Readme first for a user's guide to qualitative methods* (2nd ed.). Thousand Oaks, CA: Sage Publications.

Robles, L., & Zárraga-Rodríguez, M. (2015). Key competencies for entrepreneurship. *Procedia Economics and Finance*, *23*, 828–832.

Saldaña, J. (2009). *The coding manual for qualitative researchers.* London: SAGE Publications.

Sarasvathy, S. D. (2008). *Effectuation. Elements of entrepreneurial expertise.* Cheltenham: Edward Elgar Publishing.

Schumpeter, J. A. (1934). The theory of economic development: An inquiry into profits, capital, credit, interest, and the business cycle. *Social Science Electronic Publishing*, *25*(1), 90–91.

Senge, P. M. (1990). *The fifth discipline: The art and practice of the learning organisation.* London: Century Business.

Sewell, W. H. Jr. (1992). A theory of structure: Duality, agency, and transformation. *American Journal of Sociology*, *98*(1), 1–29.

Shane, S. A. (2000). *A general theory of entrepreneurship: The individual-opportunity nexus.* Cheltenham: Edward Elgar Publishing.

Silverman, D. (2013). *Doing qualitative research* (4th ed.). London: SAGE Publications.

UNCTAD. (2012). *Entrepreneurship policy framework and implementation guidance.* Retrieved from http://unctad.org/en/PublicationsLibrary/diaeed2012d1_en.pdf

CHAPTER 4

EXPLORING DECISION-MAKING: AN INFORMATION PROCESSING PERSPECTIVE

Marian Evans

ABSTRACT

Adopting a dual processing cognitive perspective, this study explores the decision-making processes past the start-up stage that small entrepreneurial businesses employ to grow. The author examines how entrepreneurs evaluate and make decisions on growth opportunities in their business environment. The author uses cognitive style as a theoretical lens to capture differences in information processing, combining interviews and psychometric questionnaires to analyse cognitive styles. The longitudinal mixed methods approach illustrates the richness of the entrepreneur's decision-making process, which the author tracks over a two-year period. The author determines how intuitive and analytical cognitive styles are used by entrepreneurs and the contribution these styles make to decision-making. The findings show that the two cognitive styles are versatile as entrepreneurs adjust and adapt their cognitive style over time, in keeping with the situational factors of their business environment. The author also finds marked differences between novice and mature entrepreneurs and that experienced entrepreneurs exhibited greater levels of cognitive versatility, which was directly linked to their prior experience. The study has significant implications for future research, which should consider the question how an entrepreneur's cognitive style is dependent on the business context and their prior experience.

Keywords: Entrepreneurship; opportunity evaluation; decision-making; cognitive style; cognitive versatility; dual processing

Creating Entrepreneurial Space: Talking Through Multi-voices, Reflections on Emerging Debates
Contemporary Issues in Entrepreneurship Research, Volume 9B, 45–71
Copyright © 2019 by Emerald Publishing Limited
All rights of reproduction in any form reserved
ISSN: 2040-7246/doi:10.1108/S2040-72462019000009B004

INTRODUCTION

Small business entrepreneurs who have survived the start-up stage face the next challenge of maintaining and growing their business. This is not an easy task given the nature of the small business environment, where decisions are frequently made without adequate information or professional assistance (Barrow, 1998). Yet identifying opportunities necessary to take the business forward is a core process in entrepreneurship (Shane & Venkataraman, 2000), thus, any decisions made during the opportunity identification process will have a significant outcome for future progression and growth.

The focus of this study is to explore the information processes entrepreneurs use when evaluating and making decisions for a business opportunity. We use a cognitive style lens to explore their individual, decision-making frameworks and the evaluation of an opportunity as the context for the decision process. The focus on opportunity identification and implementation has led to a 'glossing over' of the opportunity evaluation stage (Wood & McKelvie, 2015). Wood and Williams (2014) state that the cognitive dynamics and decision-making frameworks used by entrepreneurs to evaluate these opportunities are under researched. In addition, Wright and Stigliani (2013) suggest that understanding how entrepreneurs make decisions on whether or not to grow their business and the internal and external factors that influence this decision is still missing from research. Furthermore, it is important to engage in a deeper understanding of the cognitive styles that entrepreneurs rely on when making decisions.

Taking the well-supported view that entrepreneurship is regarded as a process (Shane & Venkataraman, 2000) and that individuals are heterogeneous in their beliefs (Shepherd, Williams, & Patzelt, 2014), most decision-making studies have adopted the individual as a level of analysis (Barbosa, 2014). Small business entrepreneurs are usually the chief decision makers (Iederan, Curşeu, & Vermeulen, 2009). Therefore, in order to explore and unpack how these decisions are made, we take an information processing perspective that examines the cognitions of novice and mature entrepreneurs. Our focus is on the entrepreneur as the individual unit of analysis.

Entrepreneurs, compared to non-entrepreneurs, are considered to have distinct cognitions (Mitchell et al., 2002, 2007). These cognitions refer to the activities of thinking, knowing and processing information (Armstrong & Hird, 2009). Prior research has indicated that there are differences in the way entrepreneurs process information, considered important for understanding information gathering and processing (Baron, 2009; Lee-Ross, 2014; Sadler-Smith, 2004). Advances in this field and in cognitive neuroscience promote a theoretical dual process approach to cognition, which posits two parallel interactive modes of information processing: rational (analytic) and experiential (intuitive). The rational process is considered to develop through actively seeking knowledge, such as education, whereas the experiential process develops through life experiences (Epstein, 1994). The dual process theory argues that the two systems are most effective in different contexts and can operate simultaneously or sequentially with differing demands (Novak & Hoffman, 2009).

Sadler-Smith (2004) states that the business environment is complex and requires alternatives to the typical rational-intuitive styles needed for successful performance. Decisions in small business are frequently made in the context of uncertain, ambiguous and competitive environments, subject to time pressures, emotional intensity, limited resources and high risk (Baron, 2008; Busenitz & Barney 1997; Clarysse, Brunel, & Wright, 2011). We argue that taking an information processing perspective will contribute towards a better understanding of the relationship between these situational and individual characteristics in decision-making (Barbosa, 2014), by focussing on the cognitions of the individual entrepreneur. We ask the research question 'How do entrepreneurs make decisions when evaluating business growth opportunities and what information processes or cognitive styles influence their decision-making?'

We examined how entrepreneurs evaluated and made these decisions over a two-year time period, using a dual process theoretical approach. This makes a valuable addition to the entrepreneurial cognition literature, as existing studies on opportunity evaluation and decision-making have mostly taken a more rational, rule-based approach. Using cognitive style as the research lens has enabled us to capture the different ways individual entrepreneurs processed information and provided greater insight into the structural changes seen in their cognitions. Understanding how this emerged over time will show how intuitive and analytical cognitive styles are used by the individual, the contribution these styles make to decision-making and their relevance to understanding entrepreneurs and their behaviour. This study also answers a call for mixed methods (Cools & Van den Broeck, 2007, 2008) to enhance and strengthen qualitative findings in the field of cognitive style and decision-making research.

In order to examine the research question, we used a repeated measures approach to explore the richness of the decision-making process. Each entrepreneur was tracked over a two-year period at six monthly intervals, from January 2015 to January 2017. The development of the decision-making process, from the initial perception of the opportunity to final decision, was explored using cognitive style as the research lens. Semi-structured interviews were analysed using cognitive mapping techniques and psychometric questionnaires to assess cognitive style. We have answered the call for more longitudinal, qualitative work in the field of cognitive style and small business growth (Cools & Van den Broeck, 2007) and a mixed method approach to enhance and strengthen qualitative findings (Cools & Van den Broeck, 2008). We argue that this approach makes a valuable contribution to the research agenda on entrepreneurial decision-making (ESDM) by 'combining established methods in new ways' (Shepherd et al., 2014, p. 28).

In this chapter, we first examine relevant literature and debates in the field of cognitive style and decision-making, followed by a description of the research sample and methodology. Key findings from the study are described next and illustrated, followed by a final discussion, which outlines the limitations of this research study. Here, we also make several recommendations for future research.

ENTREPRENEURIAL COGNITIONS

Studies have shown that the role of entrepreneurial cognition has an important part to play in the entrepreneurial process (Grégoire, Corbett, & McMullen, 2011; Wright & Stigliani, 2013). According to Sánchez, Carballo, and Gutierrez (2011), two main lines of enquiry, cognitive structures and cognitive processes, are representative of the two streams. Cognitive structures are mental models used by entrepreneurs to make sense of their information. These have shown that successful and mature entrepreneurs think differently from less successful and novice entrepreneurs, through the application of more refined, complex and adaptive scripts (Gustafsson, 2006; Westhead, Ucbasaran, & Wright, 2009). On the other hand, cognitive processes are associated with opportunity recognition and decision-making, which are critical processes in the life of a small business entrepreneur.

COGNITIVE STYLE

Cognitive styles are defined as the stable attitudes, preferences or habitual strategies that determine an individual's mode of perceiving, remembering, thinking and problem solving (Messick & Bazerman, 1976). The development of this research stream has had a roller coaster ride, from the early 1950s mass popularity of style types to the fragmented field of the 1970s, as well as a more recent view held by many cognitive scientists that style research has reached an impasse (Kozhevnikov, 2007). Its fall from popularity has resulted in a decline of cognitive style used in research, yet paradoxically, 'investigators in numerous applied fields have found that cognitive style can be a better predictor of an individual's success in a particular situation than general intelligence or situational factors.' (Kozhevnikov, 2007, p. 464)

Despite criticisms, style research has made important contributions towards management, organisational development, education and other applied fields (Armstrong, Cools, & Sadler-Smith, 2012). As a key determinant of individual and organisational behaviour (Sadler-Smith & Badger, 1998), styles interact with the external environment and can be modified in response to situational demands and previous life experiences (Allinson & Hayes, 1996). Entrepreneurs might be versatile in their use of style, depending on the context and demands of the decision-making task (Hodgkinson & Sadler-Smith, 2003). This is an interesting line of enquiry, which we explore in our research study.

However, more recently there have been major advances in understanding individual differences of cognitive functioning and how cognitive style relates to complex cognitive tasks, such as problem solving, decision-making behaviour, conflict, strategy development, group processes and learning. An attempt to bring together the wide variety and types of styles as a unifying theory, rather than a two factor model of cognitive style (comprising of separate analytical and intuitive dimensions), has been an ongoing debate that has divided the field of cognitive style research in recent years. Conceptualising intuition and analysis as two ends of a single continuum suggests that an increase in one mode is at the expense of the other, implying that individuals are 'either or' and thus cannot be operating both systems together (Hodgkinson & Sadler-Smith, 2003). This does not support dual process theory application.

Importantly, the ability for an individual to 'switch more readily between analytic and intuitive processing strategies' (Hodgkinson & Clarke, 2007, p. 246), known as cognitive versatility or a 'versatile style' (Sadler-Smith, 2009) is important for this research. More recently, Lee-Ross (2014) suggested that intuition and rational styles were complementary and used simultaneously in decision-making, where a rational style may not be dominant in decision-making scenarios, but present alongside intuitive thinking. These findings indicate the importance of taking a dual process approach. We argue that cognitive styles have an adaptive function and mediate the relationship between the individual and their environment (Kozhevnikov, 2007). Cognitive styles act as heuristics and can be identified at each level of information processing, from perceptual to metacognitive (Kozhevnikov, 2007). Hierarchical models have multiple levels and dimensions; for example, Leonard, Scholl, and Kowalski (1999) and Nosal (1990) classify styles that encompass perception, memory and thought. We consider that a multidimensional approach embraces the cognitive processes entrepreneurs use when evaluating and making decisions for an opportunity.

ENTREPRENEURIAL COGNITIONS AND DECISION-MAKING

Decision-making is seen as a multi-staged process which has been conceptualised in many different ways (Gibcus, Vermeulen, & Radulova, 2008). There are many theoretical models of decision-making, which outline the process from a variety of perspectives. It is complex and iterative, involving the decision maker, the decision process and ultimately the decision outcome. As previously stated, small businesses are very different from larger enterprises. A typical characteristic of strategic decision-making in small and medium enterprises is the entrepreneurial owner-manager as the key decision maker (Curşeu, 2008). This makes the decision-making process more difficult to understand, as it is heavily influenced by the individual's characteristics and cognitive processes, as well as the growth patterns in their environment. Evaluating a decision requires the individual to access and configure the necessary resources (Wiklund & Shepherd, 2003) and apply their cognitive processes to determine whether or not the opportunity is feasible. Therefore, individuals may use certain cognitive processes in their search for opportunities, which may differ from the way they process and evaluate information when compared to managers in large organisations (Busenitz & Barney, 1996).

Reviewing the decision literature suggests that ESDM frequently takes place in conditions of high uncertainty, time pressures and emotionally charged contexts (Shepherd et al., 2014). Decision-making topics associated with entrepreneurship were categorised by Shepherd et al., (2014) in their review, citing opportunity assessment decisions and characteristics of the entrepreneurial decision maker as primary activities associated with ESDM. They note that although there has been theoretical progress in understanding how entrepreneurs make different types of decisions, as well as different decisions in different contexts overall, the complexities and dynamics of ESDM have not been fully captured. We would agree that this is important for our line of enquiry. Additionally, a focus should be placed on the way an individual's style may change over time and how this influences the decision-making process. This supports our approach where the entrepreneur is the individual unit of analysis for a cognitive, time-based study.

However, we point out that decisions are seldom made in isolation. The impact of social cognition (Wood & McKelvie, 2015) implies that entrepreneurs may be influenced by other contributions in the decision process. There is a growing research stream that demonstrates the importance of team cognitions in the entrepreneurial process. Vaghely and Julien (2010) argue that the unit of analysis can be both the entrepreneur and the social network, depending on whether the scholar's views on the nature of opportunity is socially constructed or created by the knowledge of the entrepreneur. We believe that the information processing perspective is an appropriate approach for exploring an entrepreneur's cognitions in context, but recognise that the external environment may also be a contributing factor in the decision process.

The literature also shows that the strategic decision process has been well researched in larger businesses, but with less attention paid to individual entrepreneurs (Gibcus et al., 2008). Furthermore, time constraints, costs or abilities to process information (Lunenburg, 2010) have meant that the entrepreneur frequently makes decisions where rationality is limited. Curşeu (2008) argues that ESDM is somewhat different to strategic decision-making and proposes a dual process model that considers the differences between small business entrepreneurs and managers of larger enterprises. This model also recognises that entrepreneurs have the overall responsibility for their strategic choices, as well as an increased relevance of personal factors and constraints imposed by the high level of complexity in the decision situation (Curşeu, 2008). Furthermore, as entrepreneurs are involved in making strategic choices, often involving high-stake decisions that are influenced by an uncertain and complex environment, the cognitive component underlying entrepreneurial actions makes for a special category of decision makers (Curşeu, 2008).

Finally, we argue that there is still a lack of research on how cognitive processes influence and guide the entrepreneur as they make their decisions, especially post start-up. We have identified this as a gap in the literature. Additionally, the diversity of empirical research in the field of entrepreneurship is problematic for developing understanding (Shepherd et al., 2014), which is noticeable when examining the decision-making literature. Fragmentation has made it difficult to identify future research opportunities and very little is known about how an entrepreneur's evaluation and decision-making cognitions change over time. Furthermore, the lack of success of both rational and bounded rationality models in the field of managerial decision-making (Langley, Mintzberg, Pitcher, Posada, & Saint-Macary, 1995; Nutt, 1999) has led to a search for new approaches and perspectives (Sinclair & Ashkanasy, 2005). More recent developments in cognitive neuroscience and psychology emphasise the development of dual process models, which considers both analysis and intuition in the decision-making process. We therefore propose an integrated, dual process model for our theoretical framework that includes both the entrepreneur's cognitions and their external business environment. This is discussed in the next section, 'Theoretical Framing: A Conceptual Model'.

THEORETICAL FRAMING: A CONCEPTUAL MODEL

To underpin our conceptual framework, we use the Cognitive-Experiential Self-Theory (CEST), described by Epstein, Pacini, Denes-Raj, and Heier (1994, 1996). The theory posits that two parallel, interactive modes of information processing, rational (analytic) and experiential (intuitive), are effective in different contexts. These can operate simultaneously or sequentially with differing demands (Novak & Hoffman, 2009). Although this theory is one of several dual process theories, it has an extensive body of supporting research. CEST theory emphasises the importance of automatic learning as a fundamental aspect of the experiential system. More recent dual process theories share similar features to CEST, for example, Sloman's (1996) model refers to the two modes of information processing as rule-based and associative and has similar content to Epstein's (2003) model. Smith and DeCoster (2000) likewise identify the two modes as associate and rule-based and propose their own model. After an extensive review of the dual process models (see Evans & Stanovich, 2013), we decided that CEST was the most appropriate model for this research, citing three main reasons.

Firstly, based on CEST, Sadler-Smith (2009) proposed a duplex model of cognitive style used during decision-making, comprising of a separate intuitive and analytical mode. Averaged out over a variety of tasks and over time, Sadler-Smith (2009) stated that most individuals have a predisposition for one or other of the modes. 'The extent to which an individual is able to deploy the intuitive or analytic mode in ways that are contextually appropriate is termed cognitive versatility' (Sadler-Smith, 2009, p. 14). In addition, Sadler-Smith proposed that the duplex model has a hierarchical structure comprising of a specialised level (stable preferences) and flexible level (use of both). Thus, styles may be brought to bear simultaneously and are not mutually exclusive (Lee-Ross, 2014; Sadler-Smith, 2004). Entrepreneurs may be versatile (Hodgkinson & Sadler-Smith, 2003) in their use, depending on the context and demands of the decision-making task.

Secondly, both information processing modes have separate but shared considerations for the research question. The rational system, with its focus on logical and analytical reasoning, is important for processing information where data collection and analysis are required. Likewise, the experiential system for intuitive processing is also important for contributions that past experience and learning bring to the decision process. Empirical research on intuition is a growing trend. Consideration of intuition in cognition research is important, as according to the CEST model, intuition and analysis interact competitively, cooperatively and collaboratively (Hodgkinson & Sadler-Smith, 2018). As this study looks at how decisions are made over a period of time, both rational and intuitive thinking must be explored, as well the interactions between the two systems.

Thirdly, as stated previously, CEST has been used extensively in research and dual process theories are currently a hot topic in cognitive psychology. This dual process approach is represented across different fields and research streams and provides a well-respected, theoretical foundation for the research study. Examples of its use in the field of cognitive style and decision-making are wide ranging (see e.g. Cools, Van den Broeck, & Bouckenooghe, 2009; Dane et al., 2012; Gallén, 2006; Hough & Ogilvie, 2005; Khatri & Ng, 2000; Kirton, 1994; Sadler-Smith & Burke-Smalley, 2015; Yang, Wang, & Zhang, 2012). We propose that CEST is the most appropriate dual process model to use as a framework for our research question.

Finally, the Rational-Experiential Inventory (REI) (Pacini & Epstein, 1999) is an acceptable and recommended measure for interpreting two different thinking-style scales (Hodgkinson et al., 2009; Sadler-Smith, 2016). This was designed to assess preferences for information processing that distinguish between the two cognitive styles; a rational style emphasises a conscious, analytical approach and an experiential style, emphasises a pre-conscious, affective intuitive approach. The use of the REI as an assessment tool supports the CEST dual processing model. Hodgkinson and Sadler-Smith (2003) proposed the use of the more 'tenable' dual process conceptualisation, which allows for the representation of distinct constructs and a typology of cognitive styles based on the REI (Gore & Sadler-Smith, 2011; Hodgkinson & Clarke, 2007). We believe the use of a smaller number of key style dimensions with 'better established theoretical underpinnings and more robust psychometric properties' (Akinci & Sadler-Smith, 2012) is more appropriate as an assessment. We also used the Cognitive Style Indicator (CoSI) (Cools & Van den Broeck, 2007), which assesses the individual preferences for information processing styles, knowing, planning and creating. In this respect, we are addressing the multidimensional and multilevel nature of contemporary cognitive style models.

To summarise, the study's framework (see Fig. 1) shows the cognitive environment of the individual (the entrepreneur's thinking and decision-making processes), sourced from CEST (Epstein et al., 2003), the ESDM model (Curşeu, 2008) and the duplex model of style (Sadler-Smith, 2009). Within this internal structure lies the concept of intuitive expertise, as tacitly held knowledge acquired through previous experiences and which aids the process of intuiting through pattern matching (Baron, 2006; Sadler-Smith, 2016). The external business environment shows four concepts, data sources for information collection and analysis, social networks, teams and experience and feedback, derived from the literature review. We consider these are influential factors in the decision process.

METHODOLOGY

For this study, we used a mix of both qualitative and quantitative methods to capture the decision process. We used two different style assessments for

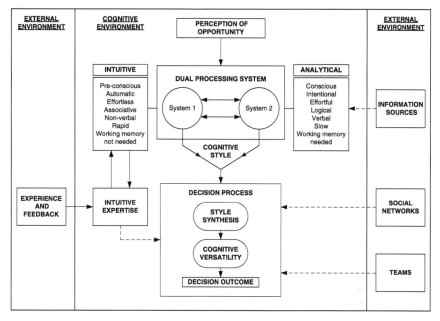

Fig. 1. Conceptual Framework. *Source*: Author.

information processing styles, the REI and the CoSI, to provide a benchmark assessment at the start of the study and at six monthly intervals thereafter, for comparison. We also conducted semi-structured interviews after each style assessment, to explore the decision process and the factors that influenced this. This qualitative approach provided rich, in-depth data of the entrepreneur's cognitive processes in their own decision situations, as well as addressing the 'how' and 'why' questions for detecting relationships between external factors and style in the decision-making process. There is a lack of qualitative studies on cognitive style (Cools & Van den Broeck, 2008), so this study will address a gap in methodology. In addition, a major criticism of style research has been inappropriate measurement and lack of rigour in psychometric testing (Peterson, Rayner, & Armstrong, 2009). We consider a mixed methods design will use the strengths of both methodologies, providing a fresh perspective and alternative approach.

RESEARCH SAMPLE

Eleven entrepreneurial companies were selected using purposive sampling to meet certain criteria; they were managed by the principal founder/s of the business with a minimum of three years of experience, they were a small to medium

Table 1.   Case Study Demographics at T0 (Baseline).

Entrepreneur	Gender and Age	Year Established	Business Background Details	Number of Employees
01	Male, 26 years	2010	Computer numerical controlled (CNC) machining and engineering, bought into established business	12
02	Male, 56 years	1985	Lighting design and manufacture	14
03	Female, 35 years	1975, started role in 2011	Display screens and design manufacture, family business	40
04	Male, 53 years	2003	Touch foil design and manufacture	30
05	Female, 51 years	1990	Embroidered clothing design and manufacture	18
06	Male, 57 years	1998	Model prototyping and manufacture	17
07	Female, 56 years	1989	Design, print manufacture and mailing	23
08	Female, 51 years	2010	Trailer design and manufacture	13
09	Male, 49 years	1992	Pneumatic and electronic design and manufacture	12
10	Male, 63 years	1979, new business 2013	CNC machining and engineering	10
11	Female, 52 years	2013	CNC machining and engineering	10

enterprise with 10–49 employees at the start of the study and they were trading in the manufacturing sector. Manufacturing was chosen as we are familiar with this sector and have regional access to small businesses. A brief background for each entrepreneur is shown in Table 1. The sample had a mix of experience including four novice, six mature and one intermediate entrepreneur. Novice entrepreneurs had less than five years of experience at the start of the study, whereas mature entrepreneurs had more than 20 years of experience. Those in-between this range were named intermediates. We asked each participant for the year that they began their role as owner-manager/director and used this as a start measure for the study. The sample was obtained through personal and business networks.

DATA COLLECTION

We identified a growth opportunity at the start of the study (see Table 2). We collected data from January 2015 to January 2017, over five time points (T0–T4), using in-depth, semi-structured interviews and style assessments. We asked participants at T0 about their background and growth intentions, what business opportunities they were considering and how they thought through their decision process. We used a guide of prewritten questions to initiate dialogue and asked the participants questions on aspects that arose during the interview. Our aim was to allow a free-flowing dialogue on decision-making processes and

Table 2. Identified Growth Opportunity.

Entrepreneur	Identified Opportunities for Growth
01	Machine purchase to increase production and capacity of existing site
02	Lighting design and overseas office for global distribution
03	Design screen product for internet sales with internal restructuring of company
04	New business strategy to develop existing global networks
05	Factory build to merge office and manufacturing on existing office site
06	Internal growth strategy to meet customer demands
07	New business strategy with appointment of senior management team
08	Relocation to new business premises for growth
09	Development of new design for manufacture and supply
10	New machine purchase and strategy to increase customer base
11	Business partner of entrepreneur 10

evaluation of the opportunity. Subsequent interviews followed a similar framework, where we asked participants about more recent decisions, progress and items of interest that had been noted from the previous interview. The interview T4 finalised any analysis queries and provided an up-to-date progress report on the opportunities we had tracked. The style assessments were completed at the start of each interview. A pilot study was carried out before the first wave of interviews, to check the first set of questions. Interviews were audio-recorded and transcribed and lasted between 45 and 120 minutes.

DATA ANALYSIS

The study focussed on understanding how entrepreneurs evaluated and made decisions on a growth opportunity and the information processes that influenced this decision-making process. A review of the entrepreneurial cognitions and decision-making literature partly informed the analysis. Transcripts were analysed according to two main themes; the factors that influenced the decision-making process when evaluating the opportunity and the use of analytical and intuitive styles in the individual's cognitive processes.

We used a mixed methods methodology. For the qualitative strand, we used interviews and thematic coding; for the quantitative strand, the REI and CoSI style assessments. We chose the CoSI (Cools & Van den Broeck, 2007) because it addressed the theoretical debate between use of bipolar or multidimensional cognitive styles and the dominant/auxiliary combinations for potential synthesis. The CoSI is a self-report questionnaire of 18 items, taking about 10 minutes to complete, which was useful for practical application in real settings. The REI (Pacini & Epstein, 1999) is considered a valid and reliable instrument for measuring both analytical and intuitive styles. Both styles were used to provide a benchmark assessment at the start of the study and as an ongoing assessment of style over the two-year period to determine any changes in information processing and any external environmental factors that influenced their decisions.

QUALITATIVE STRAND

To prepare for the qualitative strand, we first used a pilot study for the interview questions. This pretested questions ready for the first wave and checked that interview protocols were appropriate for the interview conditions. Subsequent interviews for the first wave used the same set of questions. Each wave of interviews asked a new set of semi-structured questions. This ensured consistency between each interview wave. We arranged for each wave of interviews to be completed within a month, although in a few situations, due to cancelled appointments, this became six weeks. Interviews were recorded with the participants' permission and transcribed. All transcripts were read thoroughly prior to coding. We used Nvivo10 software for coding; T0 coding was partly guided by themes, identified from the literature review and T1 and T2 identified emergent codes and established themes. T3 reviewed existing patterns and any new emergent themes. T4 was conducted as a brief face-to-face or telephone interview on final decision outcomes and progress of the opportunity.

Interviews were cross-analysed after each wave to aggregate findings and strengthen results. We coded the decision-making process first, exploring how entrepreneurs made their decisions whilst evaluating the opportunity and next, cognitive style for analytical, intuitive thinking and cognitive versatility. The analysis looked for changes of style across time to demonstrate versatility and potential relationships between external influences and the entrepreneur's cognitions during evaluation and decision-making. The decision process was also descriptively coded to identify decision-making concepts and the relationship between concepts and the external environment.

COGNITIVE MAPPING FOR THE DECISION PROCESS

In order to provide a visual method to illustrate the complexities of the decision process, we used an ideographic approach to decision-process mapping, derived from cognitive mapping techniques used by Curşeu (2008) and Cossette (2000). A cognitive map is a 'representation of the perceptions and beliefs of an individual about his own subjective world' (Klein & Cooper, 1982, p. 63) and provides an in-depth and detailed knowledge of the thought flow of the individual. It also allows a holistic and discursive representation of the individual concepts and links in the decision process.

Maps identified the thought process that took place during decision-making, using concepts and themes derived from the qualitative analysis T0–T3. The cognitive maps were discussed with the participant at T3 for validation, linking identification and feedback. Some minor changes were made with layout. The final map was reviewed again at T4. The written protocols used were based on concept elicitation from qualitative analysis, refinement and relationship identification. Concepts were derived from the coding data, using the participant's language and illustrated the thought process (Gómez, Moreno, Pazos, & Sierra-Alonso, 2000). We compared these across case. Several adjustments were made where concepts were similar or expressing the same idea, as understood by the researcher.

Maps and concepts were analysed to establish relationship connections based on Gómez et al.'s (2000) taxonomy (causal, associative, chronological and structural) and Cossette's (2002) analysis techniques. This allowed us to view any key relationships between concepts.

STYLE AND VERSATILITY

Transcripts were examined to see whether intuitive and analytical thinking was present, coding words such as 'feeling', 'intuitive' or 'gut' for an intuitive style or 'facts', 'analysis', 'check', for an analytical style. Where both types were used in the explanation coding for 'versatility' was applied. The styles were compared at each time point to determine any variation and if so, analysed further for influences that may have prompted this change. Cross-case analysis was also carried out to look for similarities, differences and relationships between style, experience and time.

QUANTITATIVE STRAND

The quantitative segment was used to establish a baseline assessment and corroboration for triangulation. We measured intuitive and analytical styles at the start of each interview to establish the participant's cognitive style using the CoSI and REI self-report instrument measures. Results from these psychometric assessments were used to produce descriptive statistics for triangulation. According to Denzin (1978), two categories of triangulation were appropriate for this study: data triangulation (self-report measures and interview) and methodological triangulation (software-based inferences and descriptive self-report assessments). Data triangulation also combined analysis across time points and both case and cross-case analysis to increase the validity of the overall findings.

FINDINGS

Research suggests that entrepreneurs may be partly differentiated by the cognitions used in evaluating and exploiting opportunities (Busenitz et al., 2003) and that entrepreneurs are heterogeneous in their individual characteristics (Shepherd et al., 2014). We discuss our findings based firstly on the map analysis and secondly from the cognitive style analysis that shows entrepreneurs can be differentiated by their cognitions and that these differences are dependent on experience and context.

COGNITIVE DECISION-PROCESS MAPS

Cognitive mapping illustrates the mental representations required by the decision maker for complex environments (Curşeu, 2008). Our cognitive maps supported this observation, but all entrepreneurs did not exhibit the same process.

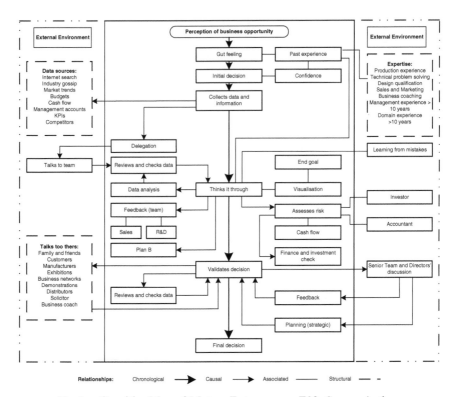

Fig. 2. Cognitive Map of Mature Entrepreneur E02. *Source*: Author.

Firstly, we noticed that mature entrepreneurs, for example, entrepreneur E02 (see Fig. 2), commenced with a gut feeling based on past experience. This gave rise to an immediate initial decision, where data and information collection were used for a brief analysis prior to reflective thinking. This pattern was evident in entrepreneurs E04, E05, E06, E07 and E09. All these participants had a minimum 20 years of experience as directors of their businesses. Both analytical and intuitive thinking processes were evident in all cases, prompting us to consider the notion of versatility.

Similarly, the intermediate entrepreneur E04 (see Fig. 3) with 12 years of experience also demonstrated a similar pattern. Visualisation associated with creativity and experiential thinking was used to support this process; 'I can play out a lot of things [in my head] without having to write them down' (E04, T1). Visualisation is associated with creative thinking and intuition.

We noticed that in marked contrast and showing a completely different pattern, mature entrepreneur E10 began with a gut feeling, followed by a complex and iterative process that involved data collection and reflection before making an initial decision. Despite 36 years in business, his decision process was very similar to that of a novice. We suggest this was due to a previous bad experience associated with business failure and loss of confidence which prompted the use of a dominant analytical style for cross checking and validation. This illustrates that

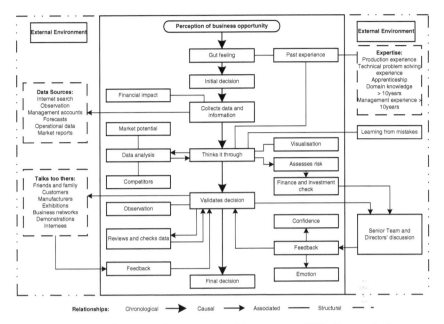

Fig. 3. Cognitive Map of Intermediate Entrepreneur E04. *Source*: Author.

crisis situations and failure may lead to the conscious activation of an analytical style, overriding any previous intuitive response.

Secondly, novice entrepreneurs followed a more analytical process and only used a gut feeling if they had some previous experience or knowledge that was relevant, or were making an easy, quick decision with no strategic consequences. The novice's cognitive map, for example, E03 (see Fig. 4), showed a different thought flow. The process began with a gut feeling followed by an assessment of risk and finance that triggered data collection and analysis. This was only bypassed, if there was a recognised gut feeling based on some previous market experience. However, this feeling was still checked out by data collection and analysis. The thinking through involved talking to others and the team to gain knowledge, as well as to listen to options, therefore suggesting this was used as an information source. Data analyses were performed after this as an elaborate process of checking different data sets before a final decision was made. Validation of the decision involved conversations with the team and other directors for checking and feedback. The process was highly analytical and a series of 'stepping stones' (E03, T0). Yet, surprisingly, there was some evidence of an intuitive style seen as a gut feel or check of whether the decision still 'felt right'. We suggest that these were the early stages of the development of domain experience, which makes up the highly contextual preexisting schemas developed in the long-term memory of System 1 over time, called intuitive expertise. We also noted that by year two of the study, some developing links between concepts, notably the use of past experience and team feedback increased the complexity of the mental structure, which helped decision effectiveness.

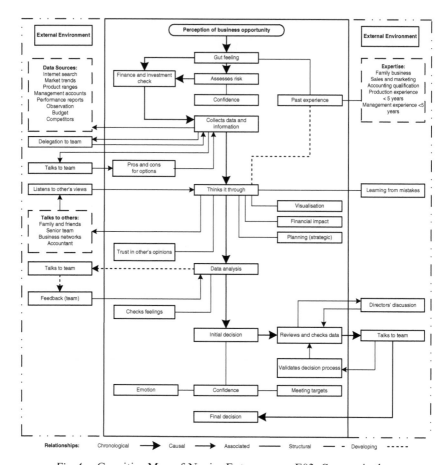

Fig. 4. Cognitive Map of Novice Entrepreneur E03. *Source*: Author.

Additionally, novice map structures were less complex but more focussed on analytical tasks, such as financial analysis, pros and cons for options, data collection for back up evidence and cross-checking thoughts and feelings. Novice entrepreneur E11 was the exception here. With only two years of business experience, her cognitive map was very analytical, relying on data collection and analysis, plus cross checking, before an initial decision was made. Yet, curiously, her initial response to the opportunity was based on her gut. When asked about this she stated,

> I think the intuitive thinking comes out first really ... and then you check it out ... it's definitely you feel it, then you check it. (E11, T4)

This suggests that her previous business experience was generating an intuitive reaction, but the lack of domain expertise was overriding this response. This is in line with dual process theory, whereby the rational system can control or discount the influence of the experiential system, but to do this, it has to be aware of the experiential system, first experienced here as a gut feel.

Thirdly, we observed that mature entrepreneurs quickly made a decision on a gut feeling, then validated that decision by cross checking with networks, both internal and external to the business. In addition, a relationship between talking to others and the individual was present in all maps but was different depending on the level of experience. For mature entrepreneurs, it was a key concept in their validation process. In contrast, novices used this for gleaning knowledge and information, as part of their thinking through process. We suggest that conversations with both external and internal networks play an important part in the process and is a potential area for further research. Risk and confidence were also observed as important concepts of the decision process for both mature and novice entrepreneurs but were positioned at different stages in the thought flow. Again, we suggest that this is related to experience. Data and information collection illustrated the use of similar sources, common to all participants. This is not surprising, given the types of information required for evaluation and the availability of the internet. All entrepreneurs referred to past experience in their long-term memory and the value of learning from mistakes as a means of helping them to make decisions. In addition, over the study we noticed that the acquisition of expertise, or domain experience, was seen to subtly change the pattern of thinking over time in novice entrepreneurs. This was seen as a developing link in the novice maps (see Fig. 4, shown as a dotted line). Novices also commented on the value of this for future decision-making.

To summarise, we observed an iterative thinking flow between the information processing modes of the entrepreneur and the external environment, seen in all maps. However, there were some interesting differences in the thought flow between the novice and mature entrepreneurs. Curşeu (2008, p. 82) argued that the 'most proximal factor to decisional outcome is the cognitive representation developed in the working memory space', which is the 'result of interplay between the functioning of System 1 and System 2'. This interplay refers to the notion of cognitive versatility, where both processing modes are used simultaneously and are complementary, as seen in our findings. We suggest that this development of versatility is key to effective decision-making. This is discussed in the next section, 'Cognitive Style Differences in the Decision-Making Process'.

COGNITIVE STYLE DIFFERENCES IN THE DECISION-MAKING PROCESS

Cognitive style assessments were taken at each time point; the higher the assessment score, the greater the preference was for that style. Individuals could also be high on more than one style at any one time. Less experienced entrepreneurs had a higher analytical style score. Over time, novice entrepreneurs showed an increase in their intuitive style score. We also observed that findings from the qualitative data suggested both styles were used together in the decision process, where reference to both analysis and intuition (as a feeling) were made. This supported the notion of cognitive versatility.

[...] we need to do this, this is going to work, I can see big areas for it and then after I've had that feeling I will then do my research, so that's where my analytical comes in [...]. (E03, T1)

I do tend to jump around a bit, so I'll start to have a think about it and then I'll be checking that in my head and thinking about that and how I feel about that and then I might go back and think well I need to support that with something and I write about it so no, it's probably this, jump forwards and then jumps back. (E08, T0)

We compared REI (intuitive/analysis) and CoSI (knowing/planning/creative) style results at each time point to show variation over time. Fig. 5 shows that the novice entrepreneur's (E03) analytical style (knowing, planning (CoSI) and rational (REI)) decreased over time points, with a move towards a higher score for the intuitive style. Qualitative data inferred that this change was due to experience.

I think as the years are going by I'm feeling more confident in the decisions that I'm making, which is going on my experience. Where it's gone wrong, if I'm getting that feeling, then it's following, it's so you are saying you're more able to make that quick gut feeling, you are using previous experience. (E03, T2)

Findings also emerged from the data showing that style preference was influenced by the decision maker's context (see Table 3, for E08). This novice entrepreneur was relocating her business to a new site, previously in a shared business space. Quantitative results also supported this (see Fig. 6), resulting in a higher knowing and planning (analytical) in T1 and a higher creative style (intuitive) in T2, before a return to planning in T3. This suggests a relationship between style and changing circumstances.

As we found in the maps, the use of previous past experiences emerged as a significant part of the decision-making process and where lacking, novices replaced their lack of experience by advice from other more experienced individuals. This was very evident in the novice cognitive maps and interview data.

Once I've got to the stage where I think I've got it figured out in my head I will generally go and talk to someone else because other people, especially people with an outside perspective, have a nasty habit of seeing things that I haven't seen. (E01, T0)

I feel I need to have a team around me to listen to them and from them gain knowledge to make a decision. (E03, T0)

Table 3.   Style Change Over Time Points for Novice Entrepreneur 08 from Interview Data.

Time Point	Excerpt from Interview Transcript on Relocation Move
T0	'Yes, it's become more analytical really, yes as a reassurance to myself that the decision I have made intuitively is valid, my little safety blanket'
T1	'I think it needs to be more planning ... because creativity is not always about the detail, is it is sometimes if you haven't got the detail you make mistakes ... I didn't think I worked that way, I still don't think I normally work that way, I appear to be [planning ...]'
T2	'I'm quite creative so it doesn't really lend itself to that ... for example, this moving, I told you how much analysing and research and checking and double checking that I did, but not since them ... no, it was only relevant for what was going on then'
T3	'No, I think I do more and more planning, I still think I'm in planning [style]'

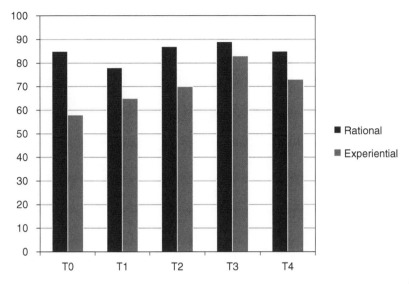

REI assessment scores

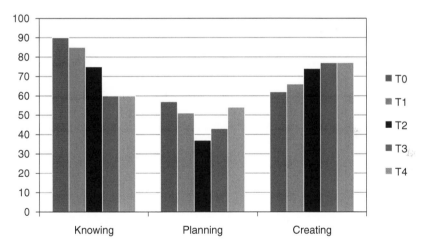

CoSI assessment scores

Fig. 5.   Changing Styles of Novice Entrepreneur E03 Over Time Points T0–T4.
Source: Author.

More experienced entrepreneurs used past domain experience in their decision process and inferred that business is a learning process.

> I think intuitive decisions, the technical things draw on my experience you know. I think that comes into play, whereas from running a business, from where is the business going, how do direct it I haven't necessarily got that, I learn that bit along the way. (E05, T1)

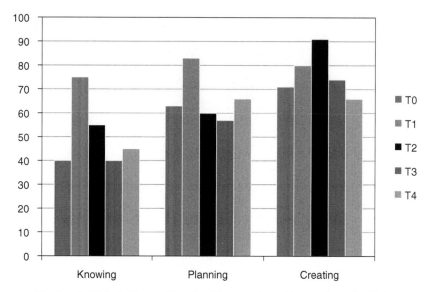

Fig. 6.   CoSI Style Scores Showing Changes Over Time Points T0–T4 for
            Novice Entrepreneur E08. *Source*: Author.

STYLE VERSATILITY IN THE
DECISION-MAKING PROCESS

In accordance with Sadler-Smith's (2009) duplex model, entrepreneurs with a
versatile style use both analytical and intuitive styles interchangeably. We coded
the transcripts to see if this versatility emerged from the rich interview data.
Table 4 shows some coded examples from two other case studies, E07 and E04.
Phrases in bold highlight an analytical style, those in italics highlight an intuitive
style. Sometimes, a reference was made to versatility directly; this is underlined.

This coded data tell us that both analytical and intuitive style were inter-
changeable in the decision process. In addition, both an intuitive style (as a gut
feel) and an analytical style (as analysis and information collection) were seen in
the decision maps. The cognitive style data also showed high scores for more than
one style. Collectively, this suggests that individuals can be high on more than
one style at a given time, supporting the notion of style versatility in the process.

DISCUSSION

Our study provided a rich mix of information of the decision-making process
and cognitive styles of 11 entrepreneurs in the context of a small business manufacturing environment. Our analysis showed that entrepreneurs' decision-making is very complex and influenced by both cognitive and environmental factors.

Cognitive mapping was used to view the entrepreneur's cognitions, which
allowed us to interpret the complexity of the decision-making process. Firstly,

Table 4. Examples of Versatility Taken from the Qualitative Data Extracts for Entrepreneurs 07 and 04 over Three Time Points.

Entrepreneur	Interview T0	Interview T1	Interview T2
07	'I'd say a <u>mixture of</u> *intuition, gut* and **facts**, a good mix'	'I spend a lot of time thinking but I don't sit in the corner and just think if that makes sense *it's like thoughts come, they just roll in nice and easy* and then you just **validate it'**	'Yes, but you are <u>using the intuitive with the analytical</u> because why did I start doing the **analytical** in the first place, ... Using <u>both of them, because one is actually feeding the other'</u>
04	'*I tend to use the intuitive*, it's stronger than *the analytical, I do intuitive before I do analytical'*	'<u>*I'd sort of double between,*</u> because I do a lot of stuff up here in terms of, *if I absorb some facts that I would have been processing, a lot of facts in my head'*	'I still think what probably happens is *that I take over information and then check, a bit of intuitiveness* (comes) into that decision-making process'

analysis of the structure and content of the entrepreneur's thinking showed that novice or less experienced entrepreneurs used a dominant analytical approach, before making their final decision. This has been shown previously, where novices were more prone to analytical decision-making than experts (Gustafsson, 2006). However, risky and key financial decisions also prompted a more analytical approach for experienced entrepreneurs, suggesting that these business factors are critical determinants in the decision process, which is not surprising, given the limited resources that small businesses have available.

Secondly, the decision maps showed that an individual's cognitive process was not a series of rational steps. Both intuitive and analytical thinking was evident in the entrepreneur's cognitive processing. Surprisingly, this was seen in all cognitive maps but to a lesser degree in novice entrepreneurs. Agor's research (1989) identified three different approaches using intuition in the decision-making of senior executives and some similarity was noted in our findings across all cases in this study. The commonest pattern that emerged included both intuitive feelings and analysis for checking, similar to Agor's (1989) 'eclectic' type. For the entrepreneur to make decisions in a complex, real-world environment suggests that both styles are beneficial for decision-making. Even the less-experienced entrepreneurs used 'gut feelings', at times, associated with having 'done this before'. This infers that the application of past experience in the decision-making process is significant and therefore the relationship between these two styles in the decision process is a critical question for model development (Sinclair & Ashkanasy, 2005). Interestingly, the number of concepts seen in the maps was similar for both novice and mature structures. The key difference noted was the order of how the concepts were linked to others and their order in the thought flow. There were less connections in a mature entrepreneur's map, which suggests the use of simplifying heuristics with experience. The functioning of System 1 as intuitive expertise leads to simplified representations. Feedback from the participants indicated that the cognitive maps helped them to utilise the benefits of both types of processing style more effectively and highlighted a need in some instances to have less reliance on a gut feel or a 'modify later on' approach.

Thirdly, cognitive versatility was seen more in mature entrepreneurs than novices. Style preference changed according to context, supporting Sinclair and Ashkanasy's (2005) findings. Baseline CoSI assessments (T0) showed the creative style (intuitive) score was higher than the analytical score in most cases, that is, entrepreneurs are more intuitive than non-entrepreneurs (Armstrong & Hird, 2009). However, although the dominance of each style in the decision process could not be statistically determined, nevertheless, changes in style dominance were evident, in both data sets, within case and across time points, suggesting that it is not a stable characteristic, but varies in response to contextual factors. Dutta and Thornhill's (2008) study showed that growth intentions were revised upwards or downwards, depending on the competitive conditions at the time, so it is reasonable to assume that given a downturn in business, experienced entrepreneurs would then show a more dominant analytical style in their decision-making. This was seen post-Brexit referendum vote across some case studies, regardless of experience, suggesting that an analytical style is the 'default' processing mode. In times of crisis or recession, this could have a negative effect on the evaluation of a growth opportunity at the very time when the business needs growth to stabilise.

Findings also indicated that an entrepreneur could be high on more than one style, supporting Lee-Ross's (2014) suggestions that intuitive and rational styles were not independent and may be brought to bear simultaneously during the decision-making process. Style assessments showed that the entrepreneur was high on both analytical and intuitive styles across time points. Novice entrepreneurs demonstrated a move towards a more intuitive style over the duration of the study, indicating the importance of intuitive expertise in the process. If this expertise could be taught or learned through business social networking or mentoring programmes, then, arguably, the entrepreneur will become more versatile at an earlier stage in their development. It is often difficult for small business owners to find time to attend networking and business events, but this is a fruitful source of expertise and experience that would help to develop domain experience and business knowledge, required when reflecting on the decision and validating any opportunities.

The ability of an individual to apply both style modes and exhibit movement from one style to another, depending on contextual factors, supports the notion of style versatility (Sadler-Smith, 2009). Thematic analysis and cognitive mapping techniques demonstrated that the more experienced entrepreneurs used both modes, illustrating the importance of using a dual process model to further understanding of the decision process (Dane & Pratt, 2007; Stanovich & West, 2000).

These movements between processing modes, or style versatility, indicate the importance of exploring the decision process over a period of time. Lee-Ross (2014) argued that the rational style might not be dominant in decision-making scenarios but still present alongside intuitive thinking the process, and this study suggests that this is correct, as even novice entrepreneurs used a gut feeling at times. Likewise, the novices showed a move towards an intuitive style, that is, they showed a preference for intuition over time as they acquired more experience.

Our findings showed that the synthesis of both intuitive and analytical styles in the decision process, combined with expertise from many years of acquiring domain experience provided the entrepreneur with cognitive versatility to adapt accordingly to the decision-making context, without the need for over analysis. As the entrepreneur gained experience and feedback, this allowed him/her to use domain schemas to interpret and short cut information processing and identify key cues from the environment that aided intuitive thought. Kahneman and Klein (2009) suggested that expertise develops in a high-validity environment where cues can be evoked without explicit validation resulting in an intuitive judgment. Dane et al., (2012) showed the existence of a cognitive basis for domain-specific expertise. The development of the intuitive style in novices and use of past experience from learning would suggest this is correct. In today's fast-moving environment, the ability to operate both styles in accordance with contextual factors and task demands is advantageous. Intuitive expertise takes approximately 10 years to develop (Sadler-Smith, 2009). Therefore, a longitudinal study would provide additional insight into this process. Helping novice entrepreneurs develop intuitive skills and expertise through practice and feedback from coaching and mentoring would support this process.

Finally, an important relationship between past experience and versatility emerged from the data. Past experience, as a structural relationship, was seen in all cognitive maps. Less experienced entrepreneurs sought advice from other more experienced individuals, tapping into internal and external expertise to help them make decisions. More experienced entrepreneurs used past experience to kick-start their evaluation and decision process. The use of past experience for developing expertise was seen in both data sets across time points. Experienced entrepreneurs, when operating outside their domain experience, asked questions, using their external networks. This implies entrepreneurial learning and expertise is a continuous process and fundamental to decision-making. The importance of providing and maintaining network and business support for small business entrepreneurs cannot be overlooked, as this helps to provide rich experiences that are needed to support cognitions and versatility for decision-making.

LIMITATIONS OF THE STUDY AND RECOMMENDATIONS FOR FUTURE RESEARCH

There are several limitations to this study. Firstly, the study was in the manufacturing sector, undertaken when trading was positive and environmental conditions were mostly stable. This meant that variations in style were only noticeable where the growth opportunity resulted in a clearly observable process change; for example, internal restructuring or relocation. However, the two-year study has provided sufficient evidence to demonstrate that entrepreneurs exhibit versatility, which is influenced by situational factors and decision context. The data from T3 interviews and assessments do suggest however that competitive conditions may prompt a return to an analytical style, although further style assessments are needed to show this is significant.

Secondly, interview data was collected from the participant, whereby their decision process was discussed retrospectively. This meant that there was a hindsight bias present, which may skew results. However, the interviewer ensured that the questions covered both past, present and future decisions on the growth opportunity. Cognitive style assessments were used for triangulation to minimise the hindsight bias and within-case checks of the interview data for any anomalies. Style assessments could be improved further by leaving an interval between questionnaire and interview to avoid such influences.

Finally, the time points were kept at six monthly intervals to minimise disruption for the participant. However, small business entrepreneurs are subject to immense pressures, so invariably cancellations or interruptions minimised the availability for quality discussion, which had an impact on some of the data collected and the time frame. In addition, in some cases a decision had been made by the next visit and the entrepreneur had 'moved on', presenting challenges for continuity and understanding the process to final decision. Despite contact with each participant between time points, we were not always aware of progress until the next visit. Although time consuming, more frequent visits would help to track progress and capture more subtle, dynamic changes of style that would improve our theory building.

Overall, the study demonstrates that cognitive style is a still suitable lens for entrepreneurial cognition research. Future research should explore the role of experience and versatility in the decision process, as we have shown that these are important factors to be considered and account for key differences between novices and mature entrepreneurs. A longitudinal study of five years or more would allow relationships between changes of style and external influences to be examined in more detail and illustrate when certain situations prompt certain styles. This would be very beneficial for practitioners who are involved in training and mentoring programmes, as well as helping individuals to understand their own decision-making process for reflective practice and learning development.

REFERENCES

Agor, W. H. (1989). *Intuition in organizations: Leading and managing productively.* Newbury Park, CA: Sage Publications.

Allinson, C. W., & Hayes, J. (1996). The cognitive style index: A measure of intuition-analysis for organisational research. *Journal of Management Studies, 33*, 119–135.

Akinci, C., & Sadler-Smith, E. (2012). Intuition in Management Research: A Historical Review. *International Journal of Management Reviews, 14*(1), 104–122.

Armstrong, S. J., Cools, E., & Sadler-Smith, E. (2012). Role of cognitive styles in business and management: Reviewing 40 years of research. *International Journal of Management Reviews, 14*(3), 238–262.

Armstrong, S. J., & Hird, A. (2009). Cognitive style and entrepreneurial drive of new and mature business owner-managers. *Journal of Business Psychology, 24*, 419–430.

Barbosa, S. D. (2014). Revisiting entrepreneurship research from a decision-making perspective. In A. Fayolle (Ed.), *Handbook of research on entrepreneurship. What we know and what we need to know* (pp. 389–426). Cheltenham: Edward Elgar.

Baron, R. A. (2006). Opportunity recognition as pattern recognition: "How entrepreneurs connect the dots" to identify new business opportunities. *Academy of Management Perspectives, 20*, 104–119.

Baron, R. A. (2008). The role of affect in the entrepreneurial process. *Academy of Management Review, 33*(2), 328–340.

Baron, R. A. (2009). Effectual versus predictive logics in entrepreneurial decision-making: Differences between experts and novices. Does experience in starting new venture change the way entrepreneurs think? Perhaps, but for now caution is essential. *Journal of Business Venturing, 24*, 310–315.

Barrow, C. (1998). *The essence of small business (Essence of management)* (2nd ed.). Upper Saddle River, NJ: Prentice Hall.

Busenitz, L. W., & Barney, J. B. (1997). Differences between entrepreneurs and biases and heuristics in strategic decision-making. *Journal of Business Venturing, 12*(1), 9–30.

Busenitz, L.W., Page West 111, G., Shepherd, D., Nelson, T., Chandler, G.N. & Zacharakis, A. (2003). Entrepreneurship Research in Emergence; Past Trends and Future Directions, *Journal of Management, 29*, 285.

Clarysse, B., Brunel, J., & Wright, M. (2011). Explaining growth paths of young technology-based firms: Structuring resource portfolios in different competitive environments. *Strategic Entrepreneurship Journal, 5*(2), 137–157.

Cools, E., & Van den Broeck, H. (2007). Development and validation of the cognitive style indicator. *The Journal of Psychology, 141*(3), 359–387.

Cools, E., & Van den Broeck, H. (2008). Cognitive styles and managerial behaviour: A qualitative study. *Education and Training, 50*(2), 103–114.

Cools, E., Van den Broeck, H., & Bouckenooghe, D. (2009). Cognitive styles and person-environment fit: Investigating the consequences of cognitive (mis)fit. *European Journal of Work and Organisational Psychology, 18*(2), 167–198.

Cossette, P. (2002). Analysing the thinking of F. W. Taylor using cognitive mapping. *Management Decision, 40*(1/2), 168–182.

Curşeu, P. (2008). The role of cognitive complexity in entrepreneurial strategic decision-making. In P. A. M. Vermeulen & P. L. Curşeu (Eds.), *Entrepreneurial strategic decision-making* (pp. 68–86). Cheltenham: Edward Elgar.

Dane, E., & Pratt, M. G. (2007). Exploring intuition and its role in managerial decision-making. *Academy of Management Review, 32*(1), 9933–9954.

Dane, E., Rockmann, K. & Pratt, M. G. (2012). When should I trust my gut? Linking domain expertise to intuitive decision-making effectiveness. *Organizational Behaviour and Human Decision Processes, 119,* 187–194.

Denzin, N. K. (1978). *The research act: A theoretical introduction to sociological methods.* New York, NY: McGraw-Hill.

Dutta, D. K., & Thornhill, S. (2008). The evolution of growth intention: Towards a cognition-based model. *Journal of Business Venturing, 23*, 307–332.

Epstein, S. (1994). Integration of the cognitive and the psychodynamic unconscious. *American Psychologist, 49*, 709–724.

Epstein, S. (2003). Cognitive-experiential self-theory of personality. In T. Millon, M. J. Lerner, & M. J. Hoboken (Eds.), *Handbook of psychology: Personality and social psychology* (pp. 159–184). Hoboken, NJ: John Wiley and Sons.

Epstein, S., Pacini, R., Denes-Raj, V., & Heier, H. (1996). Individual differences in intuitive-experiential and analytical-rational thinking styles. *Journal of Personality and Social Psychology, 71*, 390–405.

Evans, St. B. T., & Stanovich, K. E. (2013). Dual process-theories of higher cognition: Advancing the debate. *Perspectives on Psychological Science, 8*(3), 223–241.

Gallén, T. (2006). Managers and strategic decisions: Does cognitive style matter? *Journal of Management Development, 25*(2), 118–133.

Gibcus, P., Vermeulen, P. A. M., & Radulova, E. (2008). The decision-making entrepreneur: a literature review. In P. A. M. Vermeulen & P. L. Curşeu (Eds.), *Entrepreneurial strategic decision-making* (pp. 11–40). Cheltenham: Edward Elgar.

Gómez, A., Moreno, A., Pazos, J., & Sierra-Alonso, A. (2000). Knowledge maps: An essential technique for conceptualization. *Data and Knowledge Engineering, 33*(2), 169–190.

Gore, J., & Sadler-Smith, E. (2011). Unpacking intuition: A process and outcome framework. *Review of General Psychology, 15*(4), 314–316.

Grégoire, D. A., Corbett, A. C., & McMullen, J. S. (2011). The cognitive perspective in entrepreneurship: An agenda for future research. *Journal of Management Studies*, *48*(6), 1443–1477.

Gustafsson, V. (2006). *Entrepreneurial decision-making. Individuals, tasks and cognitions.* Cheltenham: Edward Elgar.

Hodgkinson, G. P., Sadler-Smith, E., Burke-Smalley, L. A. & Claxton, G. (2009). Intuition in Organizations: Implications for Strategic Management. *Long Range Planning*, *42*(3), 277–297

Hodgkinson, G. P., & Clarke, I. (2007). Exploring the cognitive significance of organizational strategizing. A dual process framework and research agenda. *Human Relations*, *60*(1), 243–255.

Hodgkinson, G. P., & Sadler-Smith, E. (2003). Complex or unitary? A critique and empirical re-assessment of the Allinson–Hayes cognitive style index. *Journal of Occupational and Organizational Psychology*, *76*, 243–268.

Hodgkinson, G. P. & Sadler-Smith, E. (2018). The Dynamics of Intuition and Analysis in Managerial and Organizational Decision Making. *Academy of Management Perspectives, 32*(4), 473–492.

Hough, J. R., & Ogilvie, D. T. (2005). An empirical test of cognitive style and strategic decision outcomes. *Journal of Management Studies*, *42*(2), 417–448.

Iederan, O. C., Curşeu, P., & Vermeulen, P. A. M. (2009). Effective decision-making: The role of cognitive complexity in strategic decisions. *Studia Psychologica*, *51*(4), 293–304.

Kahneman, D. K., & Klein, G. (2009). Conditions for intuitive expertise: A failure to disagree. *American Psychologist Association*, *64*(6), 515–526.

Khatri, N., & Ng, H. A. (2000). The role of intuition in strategic decision-making. *Human Relations*, *53*(1), 57–86.

Kirton, M. J. (Ed.). (1994). *Adaptors and innovators: Styles of creativity and problem solving.* New York, NY: Routledge.

Klein, J. H., & Cooper, D. F. (1982). Cognitive maps of decision-makers in a complex game. *The Journal of the Operational Research Society*, *33*(1), 63–71.

Kozhevnikov, M. (2007). Cognitive styles in the context of modern psychology: Towards an integrated framework of cognitive style. *Psychological Bulletin*, *33*(3), 464–481.

Langley, A., Mintzberg, H., Pitcher, P., Posada, E., & Saint-Macary, J. (1995). Opening up decision-making: The view from the black stool. *Organisational Science*, *6*(3), 260–279.

Lee-Ross, D. (2014). Entrepreneurial thinking: A study of cognitive styles in small businesses. *The Internal Journal of Design Management and Professional Practice*, *8*(2), 1–16.

Leonard, N. H., Scholl, R. W., & Kowalski, K. B. (1999). Information processing style and decision-making. *Journal of Organisational Behaviour*, *20*(3), 407–420.

Lunenburg, F. C. (2010). The decision-making process. *National Forum of Educational Administration and Supervision Journal*, *27*(4), 1–12.

Messick, D., & Bazerman, M. (1996). Ethical leadership and the psychology of decision-making. *Sloan Management Review*, *37*(Winter), 9–22.

Mitchell, R. K., Busenitz, L., Bird, B., Gaglio, C. M., McMullen, J. S., Morse, E. A., & Smith, J. B. (2007). The central question in entrepreneurial cognition research. *Entrepreneurship Theory and Practice*, *31*, 1–27.

Mitchell, R. K., Busenitz, L., Lant, T., McDougall, P. P., Morse, E. A., & Smith, J. B. (2002). Toward a theory of entrepreneurial cognition: Rethinking the people side of entrepreneurship research. *Entrepreneurship Theory and Practice*, *27*, 93–104.

Nosal, C. S. (1990). *Psychologiczne modele umysłu.* [Psychological models of mind.] Warsaw, Poland: PWN.

Novak, T. P., & Hoffman, D. L. (2009). The fit of thinking style and situation: New measures of situation-specific experiential and rational cognition. *Journal of Consumer Research*, *36*(1), 56–72.

Nutt, P. C. (1999). Investigating the success of decision-making processes. *Journal of Management Studies*, *45*(2), 425–455.

Pacini, R., & Epstein, S. (1999). The relation of rational and experiential information processing styles to personality, basic beliefs, and the ratio-bias phenomenon. *Personality and Individual Differences*, *76*, 972–987.

Peterson, E. R., Rayner, S. G., & Armstrong, S. (2009). Researching the psychology of cognitive style and learning style: Is there really a future? *Learning and Individual Differences*, *10*, 518–523.

Sadler-Smith, E. (2004). Cognitive style and the management of small and medium enterprises. *Organisational Studies*, *25*, 155–181.

Sadler-Smith, E. (2009). A duplex model of cognitive style. In L. F. Zhang & R. J. Sternberg (Eds.), *Perspectives on the nature of intellectual styles* (pp. 3–28). New York, NY: Springer.

Sadler-Smith, E. (2016). The role of intuition in entrepreneurship and business venturing decisions. *European Journal of Work and Organizational Psychology*, *25*(2), 212–225.

Sadler-Smith, E., & Badger, B. (1998). Cognitive style, learning and innovation. *Technology Analysis and Strategic Management*, *10*(2), 247–266.

Sadler-Smith, E., & Burke-Smalley, L. A. (2015). What do we really understand about how managers make important decisions? *Organisational Dynamics*, *44*, 9–16.

Sánchez, J. C., Carballo, T., & Gutierrez, A. (2011). The entrepreneur from a cognitive approach. *Psicothema*, *23*(3), 433–438.

Shane, S., & Venkataraman, S. (2000). The promise of entrepreneurship as a field of research. *The Academy of Management Review*, *25*(1), 217–226.

Shepherd, D. A., Williams, T. A., & Patzelt, H. (2014). Thinking about entrepreneurial decision-making: Review and research agenda. *Journal of Management*, *41*(1), 11–46.

Sinclair, M., & Ashkanasy, N. M. (2005). Intuition: Myth or a decision-making tool? *Management Learning*, *36*(3), 353–370.

Sloman, S. A. (1996). The empirical case for two systems of reasoning. *Psychological Bulletin*, *119*, 3–22.

Smith, E. R., & DeCoster, J. (2000). Dual-process models in social and cognitive psychology: Conceptual integration and links to underlying memory systems. *Personality and Social Psychology Review*, *4*(2), 108–131.

Stanovich, K. E., & West, R. F. (2000). Individual differences in reasoning: Implications for the rationality debate? *Behavioural and Brain Sciences*, *23*, 645–665.

Vaghely, I. P., & Julien, P. A. (2010). Are opportunities recognised or constructed? An information perspective on entrepreneurial opportunity identification. *Journal of Business Venturing*, *25*(1), 73–86.

Westhead, P., Ucbasaran, D., & Wright, M. (2009). Information search and opportunity identification; the importance of prior business ownership experience. *International Small Business Journal*, *27*(5), 659–680.

Wiklund, J., & Shepherd, D. A. (2003). Aspiring for and achieving growth: The moderating role of resources and opportunities. *Journal of Management Studies*, *40*, 1919–1942.

Wood, M. S., & Williams, D. W. (2014). Opportunity evaluation as rule-based decision-making. *Journal of Management Studies*, *50*(4), 573–602.

Wood, M. S., & McKelvie, A. (2015). Opportunity evaluation as future focused cognition: Identifying conceptual themes and empirical trends. *International Journal of Management Reviews*, *17*, 256–277.

Wright, M., & Stigliani, I. (2013). Entrepreneurship and growth. *International Small Business Journal*, *31*(1), 3–22.

Yang, X., Wang, D., & Zhang, J. (2012). Impacts of cognitive style and strategic reference point on decision-making choices of managers. Presented at 2102 19th international conference on management science and engineering (pp. 320–326), Dallas, September 20–22, 2012.

CHAPTER 5

FACILITATION OF LEARNING IN TRANSFORMATIVE LEARNING CIRCLES: ENABLING ENTREPRENEURIAL MINDSETS THROUGH CO-CREATION OF KNOWLEDGE

Martin N. Ndlela, Åse Storhaug Hole, Victoria Konovalenko Slettli, Hanne Haave, Xiang Ying Mei, Daniella Lundesgaard, Inge Hermanrud, Kjell Staffas and Kamran Namdar

ABSTRACT

The need for developing new entrepreneurial ways of thinking and acting has been in the agenda for the Organisation for Economic Co-operation and Development and the European Union countries. In line with their agenda, the Nordic Council of Ministers has been preoccupied with the development of entrepreneurial mindsets among the adult population. Seeking to meet the urgent need for developing entrepreneurial thinking, the Nordic Network for Adult Learning, together with the Nordic Council of Ministers, has elaborated and tested a Scandinavian model for stimulating entrepreneurial mindsets through the transformative learning circles. Based on the study of the TLC pilot project, this chapter explores the process of facilitation of entrepreneurial

Creating Entrepreneurial Space: Talking Through Multi-voices, Reflections on Emerging Debates
Contemporary Issues in Entrepreneurship Research, Volume 9B, 73–93
Copyright © 2019 by Emerald Publishing Limited
All rights of reproduction in any form reserved
ISSN: 2040-7246/doi:10.1108/S2040-72462019000009B005

learning. The literature on entrepreneurial learning and education emphasises on the importance of facilitation; however, this issue is yet to be addressed in-depth. This chapter seeks to fill in this gap and contribute to our understanding of the role that facilitators play in the entrepreneurial and transformative learning processes. Drawing on the social constructionist approach to learning, this chapter discusses how facilitators and learners (entrepreneurs) become co-creators of knowledge and learning experiences.

Keywords: Entrepreneurial mindset; entrepreneurial thinking; entrepreneurial learning; facilitation; knowledge co-creation; transformative learning

INTRODUCTION

Entrepreneurial learning has gained much interest from the researchers and policymakers over the last decade. The Organisation for Economic Co-operation and Development and the European Union (EU) underline that entrepreneurial learning is to become one of the key elements both in the formal education and in vocational training. According to the EU 'Europe 2020' strategy, more 'entrepreneurial learning experiences should be encouraged' (Fayolle, Pittaway, Politis, & Toutain, 2014). Nordic countries are a part of this trend (see e.g. Christensen & Lelinge, 2016). The traditional Nordic welfare state system is currently facing a number of challenges due to multifaceted processes of globalisation, which are reconfiguring the dynamics of production, labour market, demographic developments, welfare expenditure and social inclusion among others. Seeing the importance of meeting the present challenges and securing the wellbeing of the Nordic states, the Nordic Council of Ministers expressed a need for new – entrepreneurial – ways of thinking and action to be developed. Assuming that 'entrepreneurship is first and foremost a mindset' (European Commission, 2003), the Nordic Council of Ministers, together with the Nordic Network for Adult Learning (NVL), initiated some steps towards promoting an entrepreneurial mindset among the adult population. Beyond engagement in starting new enterprises, the entrepreneurial mindset refers to a range of skills and abilities to seek, identify and realise potential in different social and organisational settings (Namdar, 2015). The social nature of an entrepreneurial mindset in modern economy is argued to be 'the need of the day' (Assudani & Kilbourne, 2015). Täks, Tynjälä, and Kukemelk (2016) suggest that a person with an entrepreneurial mindset should possess the following set of skills; the ability of identifying opportunities, creative problem solving, negotiating, thinking strategically, networking, making decisions in the face of uncertainty, becoming resilient to failures, lifelong learning skills, etc.

In the context of the Nordic countries, developing the entrepreneurial mindset for social entrepreneur receives a particular emphasis. Social entrepreneurship may be defined as an activity of individuals or groups aiming to identify gaps in the social system, as an opportunity to serve marginalised groups, and further, addressing these needs in entrepreneurial ways (Gurrieri, Lorizio &

Stramaglia, 2014). Social entrepreneurship suggests that entrepreneurship may be aimed at benefiting society rather than merely maximising individual profits (Tan, Williams, & Tan, 2005). This form of entrepreneurship thus focusses on the benefits that society in general may reap. It is entrepreneurship that combines commercial enterprises with social impacts (Emerson & Twersky, 1996), or innovating for social impacts (Dees, 1998) and as a catalyst for social transformation. The transformative learning circles (TLC) project presented in this chapter was premised within catalysing for social transformation.

Drawing on the notions of social entrepreneurship (Dees, 1998), transformative learning (Mezirow, 1997, 2003), reflective practitioner (Schön, 1987), principles of participative/experiential and action-based learning (Wang & Chugh, 2014; West & Choueke, 2003), knowledge co-creation (Regeer & Bunders, 2009) and the role of critical incidents for entrepreneurial learning (Cope & Watts, 2000), the NVL, with the support of the Nordic Council of Ministers, has elaborated an adult learning model. The purpose of the TLC model was to develop entrepreneurial mindset for social and business entrepreneurship. The model and study programmes for enabling entrepreneurial mindsets are currently one of the most nascent topics under discussion in the education circles (see e.g. Assudani & Kilbourne, 2015; Christensen & Lelinge, 2016; Fayolle & Gailly, 2008; Higgins, Smith, & Mirza, 2013; Middleton & Donnellon, 2014; Pantea, 2016; Rahman & Day, 2015). Practitioners and researchers are trying to 'crack the code' of the entrepreneurial education that would bring the desired results. Meanwhile advocating for a conversational, dialogical approach to developing entrepreneurial mindsets, the researchers underline the importance of facilitation of the learning processes. That is, the role of the instructor or coach that evolves to being a facilitator and co-explorer (Assudani & Kilbourne, 2015). Recent studies have touched upon the issue of facilitation of entrepreneurial learning; however, our knowledge about this issue is still scarce. This chapter seeks to contribute to the understanding about the facilitation of entrepreneurial and transformative learning and the role of facilitators. In particular, the chapter illustrates how facilitators take on different roles and employ a mix of handbook and innovative-participatory styles towards facilitation. The principle of co-creation sets the fundamental framework for facilitation to occur, and results in co-creation of knowledge and learning experiences. The following sections present an overview of the key literature in the area, the description and analysis of the case study, and concluding remarks.

KEY LITERATURE

In this section, we present a frame of reference pertinent to this study. First, we address the role of networks as educators. Then, we provide a brief review of what literature on entrepreneurial learning says about the facilitation of learning processes. Further, the notion of facilitation and facilitation styles are discussed. The section is finalised by addressing the concept of co-creation in the learning context.

Networks and the Entrepreneurial Mindset

The role of networks in influencing and shaping entrepreneurial strategies and mindsets is recognised in a number of research on entrepreneurship (Brown & Rose, 1993; Casson, 2010). At the same time, it is acknowledged that networks are a complex phenomenon, as they are organised and structured in different ways, use different ways of relationships, both formal and informal and bring together different mixture of organisations or individuals. There are many different types of networks with different structures and purposes. These networks can be commercial, social, educational, local businesses and serve different purposes, be it finance, knowledge or information. In their research, Brown and Rose (1993) note that networks have a profound influence on entrepreneurial behaviour. They argue that networks – based frequently on common values and attitudes born of localities, religious groupings, educational, business or familial contacts – help to counteract uncertainty in business activity (p. 6). Casson (1993) also argues that by reducing the transaction costs, networks represent viable alternatives to the firm. Furthermore, networks serve to reduce risk in an uncertain world (Brown & Rose, 1993). In a network, different sectors, organisations or individuals put their resources together in an endeavour to spur new ways of thinking and thereby shaping entrepreneurial mindset. Literature on entrepreneurial networks often underlines that participants in the network benefit from the exchange of information, know-how and knowledge externalities. Hoang and Antoncic (2003) note that one of the key elements of the network for the entrepreneurial process is the easy access to advice, information and problem solving, which enables actors to identify new opportunities and ideas. They view relationships as the medium through which actors gain access to a variety of resources held by other actors.

Gurrieri et al (2014, p. 6) argues that

> in a network the co-existence of contacts, exchange relationships and the consequently high level of social links permits the circulation of many sentiments as well as information that can be acquired by the involved entrepreneurs.

Literature on networks also emphasises the issue of social capital. Social capital is connected with voluntary cooperation and trust (Gurrieri et al, 2014). Trust in an entrepreneurial network often evolves over time as network participants meet and interact. Trust between partners is cited 'as a critical element that enhances the quality of the resource flows' (Hoang & Antoncic, 2003, p. 166). Network content, governance, structure, size and communication patterns have an impact on resource flows. Understanding the role of networks in facilitating learning is crucial for our study of the Nordic TLC, moreover on the facilitation of learning.

Facilitation of Learning Processes in the Entrepreneurial Education

A number of studies addressing entrepreneurial learning suggest that the role of the instructor/teacher/course leader shifts from being a traditional lecturer and transmitter of knowledge to acting as a facilitator of learning processes, collaborator and a co-explorer in the class (Assudani & Kilbourne, 2015; Higgins et al., 2013; Täks et al., 2016). This is in line with the practice-based view of knowledge and learning. One of the major facilitation premises is encouraging dialogical inquiry rather than conducting a monologue. The facilitator of entrepreneurial learning has to provide freedom and create opportunities to liberate students' creativity, and grant them personal space for learning and acting (Täks et al., 2016). In addition, it is important to set aside time for students' reflection and evaluation, which are a part of the learning process. Taking on the facilitator role allows the instructor to assist students in exploring the content of their interactions, capturing where the students show similar patterns and experience paradoxes (Assudani & Kilbourne, 2015). Ramsgaard and Christensen (2016) argue that facilitators of learning processes act as designers of learning spaces, where the boundaries of what is expected from the learner are challenged. Furthermore, Rahman and Day (2015) suggest that the facilitation role of the lecturer concerns facilitating the involvement of the other dominant entrepreneurial role models.

Such an approach is the one where the instructor acts as the facilitator, views students not as passive knowledge recipients, but as the carriers of unique knowledge, and experiences equally participating in the process of knowledge co-creation. This view supports the understanding of learning as meaning seeking based on the socio-constructivist learning theories (e.g. Higgins et al. 2013). According to this view, the student is placed in the centre of the learning process – as opposed to the traditional teacher-focussed view on learning as reproducing (Täks et al., 2016).

Understanding Facilitation

Kitson, Harvey, and McCormack (1998, p. 152) describe facilitation as 'a technique by which one person makes things easier for others.' The concept originates from the Latin word *facilis*, which means 'easy' or 'to make easier' (Solem & Hermundsgård, 2015). This notion of 'making easier' is also reflected in the Oxford English Dictionary (1989 as cited in Solem & Hermundsgård, 2015); ... to make easier, to promote, to help forward; to lessen the labour of .... The notion of facilitation draws on several disciplines and perspectives like psychology, group-psychology, pedagogy and learning theories, organisation and leadership theories. In their conceptualisation of facilitation, Harvey et al. (2002) argue that the concept can be understood both as a task-oriented, practical approach, with the purpose of doing for others, or, on the other side, as a holistic approach, with the purpose of enabling others. They outline a model with a continuum, consisting of a task-oriented approach on one side and a holistic-oriented approach on the other side. Facilitation of learning can appear along this continuum, depending on the context and purpose. A holistic approach requires a flexible facilitator role, and this approach is the best for adult learning. They do not draw any conclusion on this, as they argue that more research is required.

Ravn (2011) suggests that the multidisciplinary approach has contributed to seeing facilitation as a practice and a skill, rather than a scientific approach to learning and knowledge exchange in groups. The guiding principles of facilitation are not new, awareness of the importance of involvement and democratic participation in group-processes stem from ancient times. Research on group dynamics goes back to the 1930s. For example, contributions by Lewin, Lippitt, and White (1939) have been of great importance to the field of facilitation. From pedagogy, the theories of learning by doing (Dewey, 1969) and experiential learning (Kolb, 1985) have influenced the development of the concept.

The International Association of Facilitators (IAF) has since 1994 worked to develop a platform of facilitation, framing the core competences of a facilitator. These core competences are as follows:

(1) Create cooperative relations.
(2) Design and facilitate group-processes.
(3) Create and maintain a supportive climate.
(4) Guide the group to acceptable results.
(5) Build and maintain professional knowledge.
(6) Be a role-model for a positive and professional attitude (IAF).

According to Heron (1999), there are three approaches to facilitation, or more precisely, three grades of involvement towards the group you are facilitating. A *hierarchic approach* means that the facilitator is in charge, has control, makes decisions and manages the relational issues. A *cooperative approach* advocates for the sharing of power with the participants, and the invitation of participants to design the processes. The third approach is a *democratic style* that seeks to develop the independence of the participants. The group is given responsibility for both planning of the agenda, the process and the summing up. Facilitation styles can also be named as 'handbook style', 'innovative style' and 'laissez-faire'. These styles are in many ways parallel, if not similar to Heron's categories. The facilitator can either use one of the approaches, or a combination of the three. Which style should be adopted by the facilitator will depend on several factors such as the competence and maturity of the group, the competence and personality of the facilitator, the problem at stake and the situation.

Rogers (1989) states that the personal qualities and attitudes of the facilitator are more important than any methods they employ. He suggests that methods and strategies would be ineffective unless the facilitator demonstrates a genuine desire to 'create a climate in which there is freedom to learn' (Rogers, 1983, p. 157). Rogers (1989) further describes the essential personal qualities of a facilitator as, being real, demonstrating pricing, acceptance and trust, and practising empathic understanding.

Co-creation and Learning

Co-creation is a relatively new term in education and learning (Ng & Forbes, 2009). Depending on the context and usage, co-creation can be defined in various ways. For the purpose of this chapter, it is relevant to define co-creation as an approach to collaboration and innovation, which seeks to bring together people with diverse backgrounds in co-creating sustainable and meaningful solutions for new learning experiences or environments for learning. Co-creation itself can be described as a learning journey that requires two or several parties to adopt new practices and processes (Akhilesh, 2017). In a co-creation approach, participants or students are addressed not as receivers of information, but as shapers of knowledge (Marquard M., n.d.). Co-creation, which is also called engagement, is arguably directly related to the performance outcomes of an organisation (Van Doorn et al., 2010). Payne, Storbacka, and Flow (2009) further argue that an environment that facilitates co-creation to occur can lead to better outcomes for individual learners and educators in terms of knowledge and skills value as well as positive outcomes to the overall organisational learning. Such a definition of co-creation can be understood as the active involvement of end-users in various stages of the production process (Prahalad & Ramaswamy, 2000; Vargo & Lusch, 2004). Furthermore, co-creation can also be considered as experiential learning. Experiential learning is a learner-centred approach, where the learner is actively involved in a series of learning processes and sees the learner from the cognitive, emotional and physiological outlook (Akhilesh, 2017; Kolb, 1984).

DESCRIPTION OF THE CASE STUDY

In this chapter, we undertake an in-depth exploration of the facilitation of entrepreneurial learning and the role of facilitators in the course of a TLC pilot project. The entrepreneurial case study used in this chapter draws from the work of the NVL's network for entrepreneurial learning and innovation. In 2013, the NVL created a network with a special focus on entrepreneurship, entrepreneurial mindsets, innovation and learning. The network's main objective was to enhance entrepreneurship and entrepreneurial learning in the Nordic region. The network also sought to develop and try new pedagogical approaches and methods. A pilot project on the TLC was initiated in 2015, with the establishment of three Nordic circles around the themes of rehabilitation in workplaces; entrepreneurship, innovation and education; and integration. The project brought together participants from Denmark, Finland, Island, Norway and Sweden. These had diverse national, linguistic and professional backgrounds in research, consulting, public service and educational institutions. The basic premise behind the organisation of the TLC pilot project was that diversity, combined with a high degree of participant-involvement and cooperation across various disciplines, sectors and general individual attitudes can help promote innovation, entrepreneurial learning and entrepreneurship (NVL, 2017). Furthermore, it was hoped that this diversity would stimulate the co-creation of knowledge and solutions. The circles worked on diverse themes within general social entrepreneurship, ranging from for-profit business, education, to migration and integration issues. The circles also emphasised on the enhancement of entrepreneurial actions, co-creation and facilitator competences.

The TLC held between three and five physical meetings each coupled with a number of digital meetings between the physical meetings. A log system was utilised to document activities, experiences and reflections before, during and after the meetings. The logs included a set of guiding principles, key questions to reflect on and some indicators. The logs were designed to capture the experiences, reflection and learning outcomes at individual or group levels. Reflection refers to the systematic, intentional and disciplined meaning-making process that moves a learner from one experience into the next with deeper understanding of its relations and connections to other experiences (Hibbert, 2013; Lindh & Thorgren, 2016). The log system hence aimed at capturing new insights and experiences of the participants. In the general individual learning logs, participants could describe what they have done in order to bring about change on themselves or their organisations, and the guiding principle they have applied, and also document any transformational indicators as well as what they or their organisations have leant. The participants could also register a critical incidence pertaining to individual or organisational transformation. Critical incidents are actions, thoughts or things that have happened that have had a transformative effect on the person who reports them. They are highly significant events in a developmental or change process. Critical incidents can give rise to new awareness, a different perspective, or novel modes of action (Cope & Watts, 2000, p. 113). Even though critical incidents are primarily subjective in nature, they can provide important indications about the kind of circumstances or experiences that can be conducive to inner transformation in any individual. It has been argued that one's reaction to critical events initiates and accelerates learning (Lindh & Thorgren, 2016) and enhances entrepreneurial learning (Cope, 2003). Cope (2003) suggests that learning and adaptation is stimulated by critical events, incidents and crises. Lindh and Thorgren (2016) also note that the individual's awareness of his/her emotions, thoughts and action enables critical event recognition, and reaction and reflection on this event results in among other things, a task-specific mindset. Critical reflection can thus enhance entrepreneurial learning.

Methodologically, this chapter draws upon data generated between August 2016 and March 2017, when the authors followed the meetings of three Nordic TLC. Observation method was used to gain insights into the various dynamics of circle meetings, both physical and digital meetings. Through this method, we observed how the facilitators facilitated the meetings, interaction patterns during the circle meetings, communication, roles and the use of learning aids in the meetings. In-depth interviews were conducted with three circle facilitators in order to gain insights into their facilitation styles, choices and challenges. Focus group discussions were also held with learning circle participants, in order to solicit their views and experiences with the learning model and spaces.

In the literature to-date, the two dominant approaches to the study of knowledge are 'the epistemology of possession' and 'the epistemology of practice' (Cook & Brown, 1999). The epistemology of possession views knowledge as a cognitive entity, a resource to be accumulated, captured and transferred across the TLC participants. This perspective builds on an objectivist idea that explicit knowledge can exist and can be shared relatively easily, building on an assumption regarding language; that there is a direct equivalence between words and the things they mean. From this perspective, learning can take place more or less from the first few meetings.

The practice-based view of knowledge and the epistemology of practice, however, underlines the idea that knowledge or knowing is socially constructed (Hislop, 2013) and emphasises the symbolic meanings of words, objects and so on. It can be seen as a shift from viewing knowledge as an entity to viewing knowledge or 'knowing', as some writers prefer – as something inseparable from human activity (Orlikowski, 2007). From this perspective, a sense of truth and learning across a network of people is discovered, made known, reinforced and changed by interactions. The epistemology of practice is related to the replacement of individual learning theory with the social learning theory, coincident with the social constructivist turn in social science and educational studies (Berger & Luckmann, 1966; Brandi & Elkjær, 2011). From this perspective, the TLC meetings will be more successful if the participants spend more time together while talking and representing their entrepreneurial activities as authentic as possible. Learning is from this perspective consequently dependent on mutual knowledge interests, and their mutual development of language and trust within the group.

Facilitation in the TLC

Facilitation is an integral part of the TLC project. In this part, we present data from our material that shed light over the facilitation process and the role of the facilitator in the TLC.

Facilitation Competences

The learning circles and its members are diverse when it comes to experience and competences. Some of the participants work as professional change-leaders and therefore were especially concerned with the subject. Reflections upon and development of facilitation experience have therefore been a matter of discussion in one circle, while in the two other circles facilitation has been more of a method for the circle-leaders.

The competences of the facilitator consist of knowledge, attitudes and skills. From the discussions about facilitation in the learning circles, it was highlighted that the facilitator needs to have knowledge about adult learning and facilitating methods. Furthermore, facilitators must have the ability to be both a participant and a facilitator, and be able to manage the balance between leading and participating. Important is also the ability to build trust and create a learning environment that supports learning processes. Both participants and facilitators have shared the responsibility of creating a climate of trust, but the facilitator has a special responsibility for stimulating and maintaining this. A climate of trust appeared to be the basic prerequisite for learning and co-creation in the groups. All three circles in the network seemed to have succeeded in this. It also involved adjusting the facilitation to the situation, the group, the themes, the agenda and goal for the meeting. The supportive climate in the circle meetings appeared to have enabled the participants to adopt an entrepreneurial approach to their development projects at home, see new perspectives and co-create new ideas with others. To achieve that, the participants must be challenged to break up patterns and create new ones. To encourage others to challenge themselves means to meet others in a respectful and humble way, focussing on tolerance, mutual respect, trust and openness.

Facilitation Design
How the facilitators organised their work in this project depended much on the structure of the circles meetings and, to some extent, the organising of the log. Through the project period, the circles had between three and five physical meetings and three and five digital meetings. The facilitators organised their work in a cycle of a three-step structure: *before, during* and *after* the meetings.

Before the meeting – The facilitators did preparations by reading the members' logs, especially the critical incidents log to generate themes for discussion. The circle members were invited to contribute to the agenda of the next meeting. Most circle members were, according to the facilitators, deeply involved with their day-to-day work, so they often needed extra encouragement from the facilitator to come forward with suggestions.

During the meeting – During the sessions, we observed that the facilitators used different tools and various methods of sharing information and leading discussions. This could be cartoons, notes, postcards, the reflecting team-method or different kinds of liberating structures work models (e.g. 1–2–4–all). One of the facilitators brought his own critical incidents as a start-up for discussion in the circle meetings. By doing this, the facilitator also undertook the role of being a peer in the group, instead of undertaking the leader-role of the group. Another approach was to work with the members to share the group's learning needs and learning strengths at the end of the session. As a result, some of these suggestions were put on the agenda for the next meeting.

We also noted the use of a reflective team approach in one of the circles. One of the participants conducted an interview with the circles' facilitator, while two other participants had the task of observing and three others were taking notes and reflecting over the situation. After the interview, they had a discussion where both reflectors and observers shared their views on the outcome and the quality of the discussion. One of the participants summed up the discussions by collecting and putting post-it notes into relevant categories on the whiteboard. This discussion, reflection and writing gave a background for the next step, the groups' co-creation of 'the body of facilitation' on the following day. On the following day, the participants were given the challenge of suggesting important skills, attitudes and competences of a facilitator. The participants wrote post-it notes, and these were collected and placed on the whiteboard. In doing so, they co-created 'the body' – a 'Michelin-man' type of structure with head – heart – belly – arms and legs, as a metaphor to visualise the central characteristics of the facilitator. Each part of the body represented the attitudes, competences and skills: *head*: knowledge and cognition; *heart*: feelings and attitudes; *belly*: feelings, emotions, energy, enthusiasm and motivation; and *arms* and *legs:* skills and methods. This example illustrates the nature of discussions in the TLC meetings.

The process of discussion and dialogue used by the TLC could be referred to as Collaborative Transformative Learning (Namdar, 2012), in keeping with the nature and aim of the TLC, or as deliberative discussion (Burkhalter, Gastil, & Kelshaw, 2002). The ultimate purpose of such a process is to help a group of people discover or create new modes of action that will bring about transformation. Primarily, the discussion aimed at transformation needs to help formulate a common *discursive field*. Discursive field refers to a broader enveloping context within which discussions, decisions and actions take place. A shared discursive field is necessary for a group of people attempting to learn about transforming their organisations, as it provides a mutual analytical and creative framework within which diverse narrations can become co-creative.

Janiszewski Goodin and Stein (2008) identify three central elements in deliberative discussion: dialogue, questioning and active engagement. Deliberation for transformative learning requires not only a set of cognitive methods, but also, perhaps even more importantly, certain attitudes. Active engagement needs to be based on a non-egoistic reach for higher-level systemic relevance, as well as a genuine desire to co-create with a number of other agents. The significance of questioning can be seen in what Collier (1994) calls *explanatory critique* that is used to unravel the real nature of societal institutions and cultural phenomena, including various ideas, beliefs and interpretations pertaining to these, and thereby contribute to the dialectic processes of promoting societal good, such as social justice and individual emancipation. Explanatory critique is not only used to reveal errors and inconsistencies in cognitive reasoning, but it can also expose false consciousness and what Bhaskar (1986) calls 'defective and unfulfilling being'.

There exists a wealth of commentaries about the mechanisms and benefits of dialogical learning. In relation to the TLC, it can be summarised analogically to what Delanty (2009, p. 67) calls the *third culture*, as discussion aiming at arrival at new insights and solutions emerging 'out of the critical dialogue of standpoints' and consisting of 'a transcendence of difference and diversity'. Against this background, diversity was considered and proclaimed, from the outset, as a vital resource, rather than an impediment, in the work of the TLC. Participants of one of the TLC emphasised on the importance of an atmosphere of trust that was created in their Circle, and that enabled them to let go of their previously held notions, and to publicly expose themselves to totally new ways of thinking and acting emanating either from themselves or from other Circle members.

After the meeting – The members' learning logs were also a source of learning and reflection. In one of the groups, they made notes on notepads instead of using the meeting learning logs or the individual learning logs. This group also developed a simplification of the log system for use on mobile phones to make it easier to write reflections on logs (Table 1).

Both preparations and after-meeting work are important for a good result in the learning circles. However, the most important is what is going on in the circle meetings. This was well documented by the members. The materials indicated that the members expressed their satisfaction with the process of the learning circle and the implementation of the process. The experience and outcome

Table 1.   The Overview of the Circles' Work during and in-between
the Meetings.

Before the Meetings – Preparations	During the Meetings – Both Physical and Online	After the Meetings
• Using the participants critical incidents log • Group members are invited to contribute to the agenda of the next meeting	• Facilitator bring in own critical incidents for initiating the discussion • Using tools and various methods of sharing information and leading discussions. • Cartoons, notes, postcards, reflecting team-method, 1–2–4–all • Identifying learning strengths and learning needs	• Writing meeting evaluation log with some contribution from the participants • Using the individual learning logs

have been different depending on the participants' anticipation and also what each individual has obtained in the process related to the project that they were brought in. The learning circle has been a space for giving to and harvesting from the others in the group. It has been a place for filling up with new energy, where the participants both can share experience and be challenged, within a friendly space.

It was clear that the facilitators differed in how they used the log procedure. The Entrepreneur group did not use the logs explicitly, since they used to work very result-oriented and pragmatic, the focus seldom originated directly from the logs. The facilitator set the agenda hierarchically since there were no individual logs to proceed from. Therefore, the logs were more or less a protocol of what has been going on, rather than the driving force of the process since there were no problem in finding issues to discuss in a pragmatic way, and the participants seemed happy that way. This has implications on the role of the facilitator: to adapt to the group practice. However, the practical work during sessions originated from the intended intention of the logs, it just was not as explicit as in the two other groups. In the Island group, there was a long process just to understand how to use the logs, which made the facilitator to adapt more to Herons cooperative approach, gradually giving the participants more and more influence of the process as the understanding rose. First, the discussion started more or less from presenting their topics and explaining how to fit the issue at hand in the log procedure, the better the understanding, the more of the democratic style of facilitation was noted. It was also clear that this group adapted the actual log procedure and considered it a great tool in their daily work after, as it was intended during the circle work. Several of them claimed receiving an understanding of the facilitation process, attributed to the work in the group focussing on the log procedure, and could use that in their own practice at their work place.

Facilitation Roles and Style

Our material shows that the facilitator' role is constituted by different approaches and styles. The facilitators in our study appeared to have somewhat different styles, but we find that they were also able to do some variations and changing between the styles. We have also identified the tendency to use a combination of different approaches. One way of facilitating is when the facilitator is being on the outside looking into the group. Another way is to facilitate the whole group. A third alternative is to integrate in the group, that is, being part of the group participating on the same level (as peer) and working with the group. One way of doing this is bringing in their own critical incidents for the group to start a discussion. To what extent the facilitator has to be the driving force depends on the participants, the situation, number of participants and participants' competence (Interview – facilitator).

All three facilitators in the three circles emphasised on building a safe climate in their groups. Both participants and facilitators indicated that they trusted each other, and both expressed that they felt safe to be challenged. This view confirms Hoang and Antoncic's (2003) postulations that trust between partners is a critical element in networks and it enhances the quality of the resource flows. The emphasis on empowering the participants also meant that the facilitators shared the responsibility for evolving the learning processes with the circle members. What then is the role of the facilitator? The driving force? Being the glue of the group? The juggler? The facilitators took the responsibility of creating the frames around the work. This also meant being a driving force for the processes of the group when necessary. They have found a way of managing the diversity of the group, with both practitioners and academics. This was done by being able to manage diversity by making approaches depending on the people they were managing. This may be compared to acting like a juggler, balancing the different inputs and staging during the different parts of the process. It also meant empowering participants, through working with people making them able to share what they have on their mind.

'Set the energy free of the individuals in the group' (Interview – facilitator).

Facilitation has been described as working as 'the glue of the group'.

'Trust is the basic – and you have to feed the process. The participants have to bring something into the process' (Interview – facilitator).

This meant that the learning process in the circles depended not only on the facilitation, but also on the ongoing contribution from the members of the group. To be willing and share experiences, the participants must learn to know each other. If they know each other, they can easily reflect upon each other's experiences. The stronger the relationship, the easier it is to reflect together (Interview – facilitator).

Despite the different styles and roles conduct, some common values seemed to be strong in the facilitation. All of the facilitators shared the attitude that it is important to facilitate in a democratic way, to secure everybody's participation and engagement. In terms of styles, we identified mainly two different facilitator styles in the TLC project: a *handbook style* where the facilitator has a more of an 'instrumental' approach to the process, and an *Innovative-participatory* approach where the facilitator tends to make a point of blending in and work with the group as a member. These findings are partly in line with two of Heron's (1999) approaches, the cooperative and the democratic approach. The facilitators were more or less structured, non-hierarchal; they felt responsible for the processes of the group, and they all made a point of the importance of group democracy.

Facilitators applied their facilitating efforts to what the group requires. The reason for this may be that the facilitators themselves to some extent had chosen their group members, and that they were adjusting their way of facilitating to what works with the group members. As stated earlier, facilitating also has to do with the facilitators' personal attitudes and qualities, which also is something that will influence the approach. Likewise, it is our belief that there has been a development and learning process that has influenced and changed the facilitators' approach in the course of the TLC pilot project. We find that the facilitators, in spite of difference in styles and approaches, had common values that are characterised by democratic and low hierarchical approach, where ability to create trust and empower the circle members were crucial to promote the learning processes. As long as they shared the same democratic values, securing everybody to develop and learn, the approaches to facilitation can vary. It is important, however, to use the guidelines and the logs as tools for reflecting and learning.

Our conclusion is that the facilitators have had an important role in the TLC. Although we have seen that there is a shared responsibility in the circles for developing a climate of trust, the facilitator contributes by taking a special responsibility for this, by being a role model. We have also seen that there is shared responsibility in the circles both for individual learning and learning on the group-level, but the facilitator brings in fuel into the processes by guiding and being a driving force in developing transformational entrepreneurship. The facilitators contributed significantly to the continuity of the transformative learning processes.

Participant's Perceptions
'The best facilitation is often when you don't see it, like it's invisible' (Interview – participant).

From the participant's point of view, we observed that they appeared to appreciate the work of their circle's facilitators. Facilitating is seen as an important and necessary factor for supporting the learning-processes of both individuals and the learning circles. This is a sound approach when working with adult learning, where working to support reflection and co-creation is important.

> When facilitation is at its best you hardly notice it. But if the facilitator is too much a leader of the group, it can be very bad, and a hinder to participant's learning processes (Interview – participant).

Too much facilitation can hinder the learning process. A good facilitator would be able to find and manage the balance between leading and participating.

Challenges Faced by the Facilitators
Facilitators' major challenges were connected to the following areas: the participants' work with the individual logs, a sense of responsibility for the learning outcomes and facilitation of the digital meetings. The first type of challenge experienced by the facilitators was connected to log writing. In one of the groups, only a few participants wrote individual logs. One facilitator attributed this to

the abstract language used in the instructions to log writing. More training in log writing and using the guidelines could have been helpful in the beginning of the project. However, in another group, the logs were not seen an obstacle. The logs were successfully implemented and these enabled the facilitator to manage the preparations and facilitation of the circle meetings.

The second challenge pertains to facilitators feeling great responsibility for the learning processes of the participants. They all have made great efforts in preparing for the meetings and supporting the learning processes during the meetings. 'Preparation for the meetings is a great mental challenge' (Interview – facilitator). Reflection after the meetings is of great importance: 'Did I light the fire?' (Interview – facilitator). Taking notes and reflecting by writing logs after the meetings have been a necessary method to gather the threads, and catching up. Because of the heterogeneity of participants, the progression of learning outcomes had been more explicit and clear for some of the participants than others. 'It has been challenging to secure everybody's learning outcome' (Interview – facilitator). The balance between leading and being a peer can be challenging, but all three facilitators have been aware of this, and have adjusted their styles to the progression groups. In spite of this, they indicated that their main challenge was finding this balance, and reflecting upon this in the meeting learning logs and during the interviews.

Thirdly, conducting the digital meetings was seen as a challenge often due to unforeseen technical problems with connectivity and sound quality. Another challenge was the issue of language used. As mentioned before, the participants were drawn from different Nordic countries and thus no Scandinavian language could be used as a common lingua franca. Subsequently, English became the main language of choice for the meetings.

Co-creation of Knowledge in the TLC

In the pilot project, it can be argued that co-creation is the fundamental framework of the TLC, meaning that the entire process of the TLC is in fact part of a co-creation process. Some respondents explicitly mentioned co-creation as a foundation of their TLC. – 'We have from the beginning said that our circle is about co-creation and facilitation'. Furthermore,

> it was a kind of strategic frame because you could have different strategies for different arenas of … so we could actually have several approaches, several drawing made in co-creation. (Focus group discussion)

While other respondents did not specifically mention the term co-creation in the interviews, the co-creation process extends to cover the entire TLC pilot project. Co-creation also occurred when the term was not specifically used or mentioned. In some instances, the respondents may have been describing a process, which is a typical example of a co-creation process within their circle meeting without realising the co-creation aspect of it. When co-creation was particularly mentioned, the respondents described the working process and solving challenges by working together with other participants – 'I think this was a great example of how we could make co-creation based on a specific issue and find ways to solve this' (Interview – participant). Other comments include new perspectives and new ways of handling issues, co-creation in practice, and 'the feeling of co-creation, being able to be part of something that's happening here' (Interview – participant). An example of a more institutional change:

> We have worked a lot with co-creation at my work. Through the TLC we have experimented with, adjusted and thought about new ways of promoting co-creation – concretely through a multicultural network across our departments and voluntary organizations. We have over 100 participants and it has been a great success. The departments have not collaborated before, but we are using the same openness and ideas of co-creation as in TLC and it has been a good thing for everybody involved. (Interview - participant)

Essentially, this approach to solving problems and challenges requires various inputs from all circle participants, as co-creation is a collaborative effort (Akhilesh, 2017). The respondents also mentioned the importance of seeing how other circle participants would have solved similar problems or challenges. This is also considered as a co-creation learning process.

Prerequisites for Co-creation
Factors for co-creation include resources, process and outcome. Although the entire process of the TLC had co-creation as the fundamental framework, respondents also highlight that the co-creation process still needs to be facilitated, as it does not happen on its own. The overall role of the facilitator was discussed in the previous section 'Facilitation Roles and Styles'. In terms of co-creation, the facilitator plays a key role in assisting the learners with an environment, which allows co-creation to occur. This may include creating an environment for sharing and learning, and focussing on the right objectives (Akhilesh, 2017).

In addition to facilitating, in order for co-creation to occur, the respondents also mentioned some other preconditions, which should exist. These include the participants, their priorities and expectations of the TLC. As discussed, trust and respect were mentioned as key factors for co-creation to occur. Trust allows circle members to be comfortable to share their experiences.

> We do not co-create when we see someone who I think is going to steal my stuff or are going to abuse what's coming up or really looking to keep me down. (Interview – participant)

Huhtilainen and Savitskaya (2012) argue for instance that such a learning and sharing experience is not dependent on formal business commitment or contract, but rather on the faith that the collaborators have in each other. Hence, trust is a crucial prerequisite in order to co-create learning experiences. Other prerequisites mentioned by the respondents include: (i) feeling secure, (ii) equality, (iii) understanding each other's context, (iv) willingness to share, (v) possibilities to share, (vi) curiosity and (vii) interest (Focus group discussion). Conversations in the focus group discussions indicated that these prerequisites were present in each group, thus enabling a good and open co-creative dialogue.

Co-creation Results – Visible and Tangible, Immediate Versus Long Term
In an attempt to describe co-creation as something unique and different than other types of learning processes, many respondents highlighted that co-creation

is what makes the results tangible and visible. While one of the most rewarding outcomes of co-creation are the results, which are visible and tangible, respondents also argued that results of a co-creation process might not be immediately visible as it can be a long-term process (Akhilesh, 2017). It is not always easy to identify what has been co-created, as the results can crystallise much later. Co-creation can also occur on several levels. On which levels co-creation occurs depends on the participants in the circles and their goals.

One of the main goals of the TLC was for learning and co-creation to occur beyond the pilot project. Some respondents managed to initiate some spin-off projects because of the TLC. Examples include new methods, tools, new approaches and processes such as the approaches used for newcomers (immigrants). Challenges and solutions discussed in the TLC translated into tangible changes at workplaces.

Barriers to Co-creation

While co-creation plays an important role in learning, knowledge sharing and innovation, there are also several limitations to co-creation. For instance, co-creation is a long-term process as discussed above because it requires the building of knowledge and expertise of the appropriate group of people and their collaboration and willingness to learn and share (Akhilesh, 2017). Hence, it is a collaborative effort, which does not exist in a vacuum. Although the fundamental framework of the TLC is co-creation, the results also indicate that there were some barriers to co-creation within certain circles. The various opinions and approaches to problem solving contribute to co-creation; however, various ideas and priorities may also hinder co-creation. The respondents were also conscious of the fact that if the circle members are too homogenous or they get too comfortable with each other, it can also hinder co-creation as explained.

Another barrier to co-creation pertains to the choice of documentation platforms used by the participants as well as the log writing process as discussed. Another example given by some respondents relates to the use of platforms like Google accounts – 'all should have a google account but not all wanted that' (Interview – facilitator). The documentation structure to some extent affected the co-creation processes. This is not surprising as it can be challenging to build the right infrastructure and processes for co-creation to occur (Akhilesh, 2017).

CONCLUSION

According to Heron (1999), there are three approaches to facilitation: a hierarchic approach, a cooperative approach and a democratic approach. In addition, facilitation styles can be named as a handbook style and an innovative-participatory approach. Harvey et al. (2002) identify different approaches to facilitation: a task-oriented approach on one side and a holistic approach on the other side of a continuum. We find support for a holistic approach to facilitation in our study. A holistic approach corresponds to an innovative-participatory approach. A 'handbook approach', which to some extent corresponds to a task-oriented approach, can also be of great value, depending on the context and the purpose of the meetings. We consider the holistic approach, which requires flexibility of the facilitator role, to be the most relevant facilitation style to support entrepreneurial learning. This approach supports the co-creation of knowledge and promotes critical reflection in the groups. The facilitators in our study differ on their approaches to facilitation depending on the maturity of the groups and the agenda of the meetings. We found this flexibility to be of great importance and a strength in this pilot project. The facilitators in our study shared common democratic values characterised by a mutual respect, trust, openness and inclusiveness. A democratic and low hierarchical approach aided the creation of trust by empowering the circle members. An ability to create a learning environment of tolerance, trust and openness appears to be crucial in promoting the entrepreneurial learning processes. This finding is in line with practice-based learning theory where real and authentic entrepreneurial practice needs to be discussed (Hislop, 2013). This learning climate enables the participants to feel empowered and take responsibility both for their own development and the development of others. Sharing of the same democratic values and a holistic approach to facilitation seemed to be central elements in the Nordic approach to entrepreneurial learning in the TLCs.

The co-creation of knowledge identified in our study contributes to new ideas and entrepreneurial mindset as well as individual learning. It can be argued therefore that the creation of the network, and the diversity of the participants, can potentially enhance an entrepreneurial mindset spurning geographical, cultural and professional boundaries. The TLC pilot project created the space for experimenting with new pedagogical models of entrepreneurial learning. However, inculcating an entrepreneurial mindset is a process that takes time and the participants must not only develop trust across each other which current literature stress, but also develop trust in their methods for learning such as log writing. If not, the participants will not use them.

Furthermore, the facilitators must be conscious of the differences among the participants in the group when facilitating. It is important to facilitate the discussion in such a way that everyone participates and takes responsibility. Importantly, in well-educated and resource-rich groups, the participants would have many things to share and contribute to the discussion and learning. Putting this issue on the agenda can itself be a means to facilitate the group. Focussing on the importance of both the democratic values and methods shared by all in this pilot project, we point at the importance of developing a climate of tolerance and trust to support entrepreneurial learning. Suggestions for further research including studying more in detail how skills, attitudes and competences of the facilitator affect the development of such learning climates.

ACKNOWLEDGEMENTS

We would like to extend our sincere gratitude to the NVL and the Nordic Council of Ministers for allowing us to observe and conduct interviews during their TLC pilot project.

REFERENCES

Akhilesh, K. B. (2017). *Co-creation and learning: Concepts and cases.* New Delhi, India: Springer.

Assudani, R., & Kilbourne, L. (2015). Enabling entrepreneurial minds: Using appreciative inquiry as a pedagogical tool for uncovering self-awareness and for generating constructivist learning. *Journal of Entrepreneurship Education, 18*(1), 65–73.

Berger, P. L., & Luckmann, T. (1966). *The social construction of reality.* New York, NY: Anchor Books.

Bhaskar, R. (1986). *Scientific realism and human emancipation.* London: Verso.

Burkhalter, S., Gastil, J., & Kelshaw, T. (2002). A conceptual definition and theoretical model of public deliberation in small face-to-face groups. *Communication Theory, 12*(4), 398–422.

Brandi, U., & Elkjaer, B. (2011). Organizational learning viewed from a social learning perspective. In M. Easterby-Smith & M.A. Lyles (Eds.), *Handbook of organizational learning and knowledge management* (Vol. 2. pp. 23–41). Chichester: John Wiley & Sons.

Brown, J., & Rose, M. B. (Eds.) (1993). *Entrepreneurship, networks and modern business.* Manchester: Manchester University Press.

Casson, M. (1993). Entrepreneurship and business culture. In J. Brown & M. B. Rose (Eds.), *Entrepreneurship, networks and modern business* (pp. 30–54). Manchester: Manchester University Press.

Casson, M. (2010). *Entrepreneurship: Theory, networks, history.* Cheltenham: Edward Elgar Publishing.

Christensen, J., & Lelinge, B. (2016). The importance of the meeting in relation to entrepreneurial learning-two learning environments within a Swedish context: A research circle and a school musical. *ESR Journal, 1*(1), 1–19.

Collier, A. (1994). *Critical realism: An introduction to Roy Bhaskar's philosophy.* London: Verso.

Cook, S. D., & Brown, J. S. (1999). Bridging epistemologies: The generative dance between organizational knowledge and organizational knowing. *Organization Science, 10*(4), 381–400.

Cope, J. (2003). Entrepreneurial learning and critical reflection discontinuous events as triggers for 'higher-level' learning. *Management Learning, 34*(4), 429–450.

Cope, J., & Watts, G. (2000). Learning by doing—An exploration of experience, critical incidents and reflection in entrepreneurial learning. *International Journal of Entrepreneurial Behavior & Research, 6*(3), 104–124.

Dees, J. G. (1998). *The meaning of social entrepreneurship.* Kansas, MO: Kauffman Center for Entrepreneurial Leadership.

Delanty, G. (2009). *The cosmopolitan imagination: The renewal of critical social theory.* Cambridge: Cambridge University Press.

Dewey, J. (1969). *Experience and education.* New York, NY: Macmillan.

European Commission (EC). (2003). *Green paper: Entrepreneurship in Europe.* Brussels, Belgium: EC.

Emerson, J., & Twersky, F. (1996). *New social entrepreneurs: The success, challenge and lessons of non-profit enterprise creation. A progress report on the planning and startup of non-profit businesses.* San Francisco, CA: Roberts Foundation Homeless. Economic Development Fund. Retrieved from http://www.mass.gov/hed/community/funding/economic-development-fund-edf.html.

Fayolle, A., & Gailly, B. (2008). From craft to science: Teaching models and learning processes in entrepreneurship education. *Journal of European Industrial Training, 32*(7), 569–593.

Fayolle, A., Pittaway, L., Politis, D., & Toutain, O. (2014). Entrepreneurial learning: Diversity of education practices and complexity of learning processes. *Entrepreneurship & Regional Development, 26*(3–4), 1–3.

Gurrieri A.R., Lorizio M., Stramaglia A. (2014) Entrepreneurship and Network. In: Entrepreneurship Networks in Italy. SpringerBriefs in Business. Springer, Cham. 1–15.

Harvey, G., Loftus-Hills, A., Rycroft⊠Malone, J., Titchen, A., Kitson, A., McCormack, B., & Seers, K. (2002). Getting evidence into practice: The role and function of facilitation. *Journal of Advanced Nursing, 37*(6), 577–588.

Heron, J. (1999). *The complete facilitator's handbook.* London: Kogan Page.

Hibbert, P. (2013). Approaching reflexivity through reflection: Issues for critical management education. *Journal of Management Education, 37*(6), 803–827.

Higgins, D., Smith, K., & Mirza, M. (2013). Entrepreneurial education: Reflexive approaches to entrepreneurial learning in practice. *The Journal of Entrepreneurship, 22*(2), 135–160.

Hislop, D. (2013). *Knowledge management in organizations: A critical introduction.* Oxford: Oxford University Press.

Hoang, H., & Antoncic, B. (2003). Network-based research in entrepreneurship. A critical review. *Journal of Business Venturing, 18*, 165–187.

Huhtilainen, L., & Savitskaya, I. (2012). Contract process capabilities in co-creation settings. *ISPIM conference proceedings* (pp. 1–16), Manchester. Manchester: The International Society for Professional Innovation Management.

Janiszewski Goodin, H., & Stein, D. (2009). The use of deliberative discussion to enhance the critical thinking abilities of nursing students. *Journal of Public Deliberation, 5*(1), 1–18.

Kitson, A., Harvey, G., & McCormack, B. (1998). Enabling the implementation of evidence-based practice: A conceptual framework. *Quality in Health Care, 7*, 149–158.

Kolb, D. A. (1984). *Experiential learning: Experience as the source of learning and development.* Engle Wood Cliffs, NJ: Prentice Hall.

Lindh, I., & Thorgren, S. (2016). Critical event recognition. An extended view of reflective learning. *Management Learning, 47*(5), 525–542.

Lewin, K., Lippitt, R., & White, R. K. (1939). Patterns of aggressive behavior in experimentally created "social climates". *The Journal of Social Psychology, 10*(2), 269–299.

Marquard, M. Co-creating learning areas. Unpublished document from NVL (Nordic Network for Adult Learning)

Mezirow, J. (1997). Transformative learning: Theory to practice. *New directions for adult and continuing education, 1997*(74), 5–12.

Mezirow, J. (2003). Transformative learning as discourse. *Journal of Transformative Education, 1*(1), 58–63.

Middleton, K. W., & Donnellon, A. (2014). Personalizing entrepreneurial learning: A pedagogy for facilitating the know why. *Entrepreneurship Research Journal, 4*(2), 167–204.

Namdar, K. (2012). *In quest of the globally good teacher: Exploring the need, the possibilities, and the main elements of a globally relevant core curriculum for teacher education.* Doctoral dissertation, Mälardalen University, Sweden.

Namdar, K. (2015). *Fostering transformative entrepreneurship through transformative learning circles.* A position paper for the NVL Network, the Nordic Council of Ministers.

Ng, I., & Forbes, J. (2009). Education as service: The understanding of university experience through the service logic. *Journal of Marketing for Higher Education, 19*(1), 38–64.

NVL (2017) Verksamhesplan. Retrieved from http://nvl.org/Content/ Verksamhetsplan-2017-4. Accessed on June 29, 2017.

Orlikowski, W. J. (2007). Sociomaterial practices: Exploring technology at work. *Organization Studies, 28*(9), 1435–1448.

Pantea, M.-C. (2016). On entrepreneurial education: Dilemmas and tensions in non-formal learning. *Studies in Continuing Education, 38*(1), 86–100.

Payne, A., Storbacka, K., & Flow, P. (2008). Managing the co-creation of value. *Journal of the Academy of Marketing Science, 36*(1), 83–96.

Prahalad, C. K., & Ramaswamy, V. (2000). Co-opting customer competence. *Harvard Business Review, 78*(1), 79–87.

Rahman, H., & Day, J. (2015). Involving the entrepreneurial role model: A possible development for entrepreneurship education. *Journal of Entrepreneurship Education, 18*(1), 86–95.

Ramsgaard, M. B., & Christensen, M. E. (2016). Interplay of entrepreneurial learning forms: A case study of experiential learning settings. *Innovations in Education and Teaching International, 55*(1), 55–64.

Ravn, I. (2011). Facilitering. *Ledelse af møder der skaber værdi og mening.* (Facilitation. Management of meetings that create value and meaning.) København, Denmark: Hans Reitzels Forlag.

Regeer, B. J., & Bunders, J. F. (2009). Knowledge co-creation: Interaction between science and society. *A transdisciplinary approach to complex societal issues.* Den Haag, the Netherlands: Advisory Council for Research on Spatial Planning, Nature and the Environment/Consultative Committee of Sector Councils in the Netherlands [RMNO/COS].

Rogers, C. R. (1983). *Freedom to learn for the 80s.* London: Charles E. Merrill Publishing Company.

Rogers, C. R. (1989). The Interpersonal Relationship in the Facilitation of Learning. In C. R. Rogers, V. L. Henderson, & H. Kirschenbaum (Eds.), *The Carl Rogers reader* (pp. 304–322). London: Constable.

Schön, D. (1987). *Educating the reflective practitioner.* San Francisco, CA: Jossey-Bass.

Solem, A., & Hermundsgård, M. (2015). *Fasilitering.* Oslo, Norway: Gyldendal.

Tan, W. L., Williams, J. N., & Tan, T. M. (2005). Defining the 'social' in 'social entrepreneurship': Altruism and entrepreneurship. *International Entrepreneurship and Management Journal, 1*(3), 353–365.

Täks, M., Tynjälä, P., & Kukemelk, H. (2016). Engineering students' conceptions of entrepreneurial learning as part of their education. *European Journal of Engineering Education, 41*(1), 53–69.

Van Doorn, J., Lemon, K. N., Mittal, V., Nass, S., Pick, D., Pirner, P., & Verhoef, P. C. (2010). Customer engagement behaviour: Theoretical foundations and research directions. *Journal of Services Research, 13*(3), 253–266.

Vargo, S. L., & Lusch, R. F. (2004). Evolving to a new dominant logic for marketing. *Journal of Marketing, 68*(1), 1–17.

Wang, C. L., & Chugh, H. (2014). Entrepreneurial learning: Past research and future challenges. *International Journal of Management Reviews, 16*(1), 24–61.

West, P., & Choueke, R. (2003). The alchemy of action learning. *Education + Training, 45*(4), 215–225.

CHAPTER 6

BUSINESS SUPPORT AS REGULATORY CONTEXT: EXPLORING THE ENTERPRISE INDUSTRY

Oliver Mallett

ABSTRACT

This chapter examines the interactions of formal and informal forms of small and medium-sized enterprise (SME) business support, characterised as interactions within an 'enterprise industry'. An analysis of the interactions revealed in the existing literature for different forms of business support develops a new conceptual framework for understanding those varied forms of external influence targeted at SMEs that constitute and extend a 'patchwork quilt' of provision. This chapter focusses on how different forms of support and advice interact, the centrality of state influence and how such interactions can be considered part of a firm's regulatory context. This conceptualisation allows the consideration of both business support and state regulations to move beyond conceptions of positive or negative impacts on factors such as firm growth. Instead, it establishes a conceptual lens for considering how the different forms of external influence can shape the practices and attitudes of SMEs and their owner-managers. Policy makers and organisations within the enterprise industry seeking to develop effective forms of support or regulation should not consider such activities in isolation or in simple, decontextualised positive or negative terms.

Keywords: Business support; advice; regulation; regulatory context; policy; enterprise industry

Creating Entrepreneurial Space: Talking Through Multi-voices, Reflections on Emerging Debates
Contemporary Issues in Entrepreneurship Research, Volume 9B, 95–113
Copyright © 2019 by Emerald Publishing Limited
All rights of reproduction in any form reserved
ISSN: 2040-7246/doi:10.1108/S2040-72462019000009B006

INTRODUCTION

This chapter examines the interactions of formal and informal forms of small- and medium-sized enterprise (SMEs) business support by reading across the different literatures and debates that relate to different areas of business support. SME business support involves the external provision of services aimed at assisting SMEs in maintaining or improving effective business operations. A high-profile review of these services in the UK concluded that there has been significant growth in their provision; yet, it lacks a clear rationale, is overly complex, has low awareness and take-up, and lacks the evaluation and evidence of impact (Richard, 2008).

The different sources and types of business support provision can be grouped together as an 'enterprise industry' (Bennett, 1998; Greene, Mole, & Storey, 2008; MacDonald & Coffield, 1991; Ramsden & Bennett, 2005); that is, the organisations involved in the provision of services (support and advice) or influence (advocacy) relating to SMEs, whether new or established (cf., the 'entrepreneurship industry' defined by Hunt & Kiefer, 2017, p. 233, as 'the goods and services explicitly intended for opportunity discovery and development by current and prospective entrepreneurs'). The enterprise industry is constituted by organisations and actors, including membership, professional services and advocacy organisations, that undertake roles in relation to SMEs on full-time or less frequent bases and that have created a 'patchwork quilt' of provision (Storey, 1994, p. 304). This chapter focusses on how different forms of support and advice interact and how such interactions can be considered parts of a firm's regulatory context. This allows consideration of both business support and alleged constraints, such as state regulations, to move beyond conceptions of positive or negative impacts on factors such as firm growth. Instead, it will establish a conceptual lens for considering how the different forms of external influence can shape the practices and attitudes of SMEs and their owner-managers.

SMEs employ significant numbers of people in the world's major economies and, in contemporary international debates, are presented as the likely saviours of economies struggling to build sustainable growth. For example, SMEs are acknowledged to create jobs, although many SMEs fail and thus they also account for a high proportion of job losses (see Anyadike-Danes, Hart, & Du, 2015). Rainnie (1985, p. 145) observed that small firms have been cast in political discourse as simultaneously the 'small furry animals' of the economy, needing support and assistance, and the 'shock troops' that will return the economy to prosperity (see also, Matthias, 1969, p. 13). This continues to carry resonance today with these firms being targets for forms of support and advice, and for a wide range of government interventions and initiatives in order to achieve ambitious economic goals (Wapshott & Mallett, 2018). The prominence of such debates and the literature focussed on different forms of business support within the UK make this country an interesting case on which to focus the present chapter. Having such a focus (albeit one embedded in wider political contexts such as, at time of writing, the European Union) allows understanding of a specific national context to focus the analysis of interactions between different sources of influence.

For the purposes of this chapter, SMEs will be defined as those firms employ-ing less than 250 people, therefore including medium (50–249 employees), small (10–49 employees) as well as micro businesses (1–9 employees, OECD, 2005). This broad definition, widely used among academics and policy makers, is necessary when reviewing a range of literature that may become confused if one were to focus on particular, more discrete groupings of businesses. Nonetheless, irrespec-tive of which definition is adopted, one of the biggest barriers to understanding the influences on SMEs is the heterogeneity of these firms in how they manage the challenges presented by their external and internal environments (Burrows & Curran, 1989; Rainnie, 1991). Perhaps, as a result, the provision of business sup-port for SMEs has been criticised for failing to engage with the diverse needs of a wide range of heterogeneous firms, reflected in low-levels of take up (Curran, 2000) and low satisfaction (Bennett, 2008). This may be due to the independence and desire for autonomy that is frequently used to characterise entrepreneurs and SME owner-managers (Curran, 2000). However, it is difficult to evaluate such provision (Curran, 2000; Storey, 2005) and, to fully understand SME support, it is important to consider the range of support available alongside other forms of influence and guidance that may be both formal and informal. This chapter sug-gests that a valuable focus in considering the eclectic mix of formal and informal support, advice and advocacy provided by the enterprise industry is in terms of a broadly conceived *regulatory context*.

Baldwin, Cave, and Lodge (2012) present three ways of thinking about regula-tion. The first is as a specific, formalised set of commands or rules set out by an official body; for example, state regulations directing firms to pay a minimum wage or meet minimum product standards. The second constitutes less direct forms of state influence that are designed to influence the behaviour of individuals or organisations. This second understanding of regulation includes tax incentives or subsidies designed to encourage or discourage behaviours such as business start-up. However, regulation can also be defined more broadly in relation to a regula-tory context which relates to 'all forms of social or economic influence: includes all mechanisms affecting behaviour, state-based and from other sources' (Baldwin et al., 2012, p. 3). That is, forms of regulatory influence including but also beyond that of the state, such as corporations, professional or trade bodies, voluntary organisations and, therefore, the enterprise industry. Such a regulation need not be deliberate or designed but can be incidental to other objectives.

Adopting the idea of a regulatory context, this chapter will argue that this con-ception is valuable for understanding external influences on SMEs, including sup-port and advice services, and particularly for how they interact. The chapter will consider five key areas of SME support and advice: government support; mem-bership organisations such as the Chambers of Commerce; educators such as universities; professional advisors such as accountants; and large businesses and supply chains. The chapter will then briefly discuss state regulation as potentially transcending the common, negative characterisation of 'red tape' and, instead, as providing a form of business support. The chapter will then conclude by discuss-ing the value of understanding the different forms of SME support and advice that constitute the enterprise industry as part of a regulatory context.

SME BUSINESS SUPPORT

This chapter argues for the overlap, interdependency and potential contradiction of different forms of external influence on SMEs, suggesting this as a vital means of understanding SME support and traditionally viewed forms of constraint on an SME's ability to operate or to grow, such as state regulation. However, in order to map out key areas of the literature, it is still useful to begin with apparently distinct areas of support and advice, especially that provided by governments, membership organisations, educators, professional services and large businesses.

Government Support

A key source of SME support in many economies is that provided or subsidised by the government under the auspices of enterprise policies, in the UK running to annual costs of £8 billion (Greene et al., 2008), including £2.5 billion focussed specifically on business support services through the direct provision of advice as well as grants and subsidies that relate to non-governmental support providers (BERR, 2008). What Storey (2005, p. 474) defines as SME policies are 'public policies [...] which use taxpayers' funds to directly or indirectly target primarily or exclusively SMEs'. Such policies commonly seek to address one or more of three types of information imperfection representing a market failure: ignorance of the benefits of business start-up; ignorance of the value of external expert advice; financial institutions over-valuing the risks of smaller businesses, creating a funding gap. Storey explains there may also be a case for government intervention where social returns exceed private returns (e.g. in particular industries or in response to societal challenges such as unemployment or social exclusion) such that private firms will not see the value in providing certain forms of SME support. However, as Storey (2005) remarks, it is often unclear whether the motivation for government subsidies and support relates to these externalities or perceived information imperfections.

Nonetheless, 'EU countries have [...] introduced an almost bewildering range of policies to assist smaller enterprises' (Storey, 2005, p. 486). This has covered a range of different areas responding to SME needs including finance, markets/demand, administrative burdens, premises, new technology and skilled labour and government agendas, including entrepreneurial skills, entrepreneurial awareness, competitiveness, special groups and regional issues. Although such support is popular across the OECD countries, the types of market failure identified and addressed in these SME support services vary (Mole, Hart, Roper & Saal, 2008). This leads to the government provision of support, subsidies and signposting as well as, in their role as powerful economic agents, governments creating opportunities for SMEs and disadvantaging them, for example, through bureaucratic procurement processes.

The social benefits of start-ups and SME growth are widely assumed to make such government intervention worthwhile. However, this can ignore problems such as very few high growth firms being responsible for job creation and the difficulties in identifying and supporting these businesses, with government attempts to do so making repeated failures such as almost exclusively targeting increases in the number of *de novo* firms (Mason & Brown, 2013; Shane, 2009; Wapshott & Mallett, 2018). Where self-employment is presented as an answer to social problems such as marginalisation and exclusion, this also has problems since those best equipped to benefit from SME support are often those least in need such that government investment in the area can risk becoming subsidies for the well-off and well-positioned (see e.g. Mallett & Wapshott, 2015a, 2015b). Further, it can be difficult to ensure a distinctive offering from what is currently available from the private sector (Smallbone, Baldock, & Burgess, 2002) and there may be negative impacts of intervention, such as creating perverse incentives but also restricting innovation, for example, due to excessive clustering (Molina-Morales & Martínez-Fernández, 2009).

Whereas the social benefits of start-ups or SMEs may be contestable, a key assumption underlying government business support remains the perception that there is a market failure that government needs to address. In addition to 'hard' business support such as loan guarantee schemes, subsidised loans or capital grants, this also leads to 'soft' business support including advisory assistance, sharing best practice and signposting (Ramsden & Bennett, 2005; Wren & Storey, 2002). However, Bennett (2008) suggests that if there was a market failure (e.g. in the 1980s), it is not apparent anymore (see also Greene et al., 2008). Mason (2009) analyses supposed market failures around funding for SMEs and how governments have attempted to intervene to address this, for example, in terms of loan guarantee schemes, capital participation schemes and supporting the informal venture capital market, all of which have significant limitations. For Mason (2009, p. 550), 'supporting the informal venture capital market has [...] been largely an act of faith by governments' rather than one based on robust empirical evidence.

An alternative or additional rationale for government support for SMEs is to offset the alleged damage created by state regulation, for example, in terms of compliance costs for resource-constrained firms. The assumption is that government imposes many of the burdens facing SMEs (e.g. Bolton, 1971; Priest, 1999) necessitating SME business support, perhaps, therefore, with a responsibility on government (e.g. Bannock & Peacock, 1998). Dennis (2011) analyses the balance between state-imposed impediments and supports for SMEs such that the different forms of balance produce different environments he classifies as compensating, competing (market oriented), limiting (few resources for support) or nurturing. The nurturing policy approach is where the state offers support while cutting forms of state regulation classified (especially, within neoliberal, free market discourse) as 'red tape' and identifying them as the most popular in developed countries, including the UK. For example, in the comparative analysis of Capelleras, Mole, Greene, and Storey (2008), they identify that England, in comparison to Spain, has both lower levels of state regulation affecting new and small firms as well as greater take up of public sector start-up support.

In the balance between impediments and support, Dennis (2011) suggests that it is the former that tend to have wider implications and to be more powerful, perhaps because of the challenges in effectively targeting and delivering support-ive SME policy (Bridge, 2010). Further, the heterogeneity of SMEs and the vari-ety of contexts and challenges they may face are such that what presents a form of support for one firm might represent an impediment for another. Particular pieces of guidance or advice, and how they are interpreted, will affect busi-nesses in different ways (benefiting one but potentially proving dysfunctional for another) owing to differences in firm size, age and sector (Arrowsmith, Gilman, Edwards, & Ram, 2003; Hart & Blackburn, 2005), competitive conditions and the responses of others in the firm's external and internal environments (Harris, 2000; Kitching, 2006). Discussing unitary effects of external influences such as state provision of (or subsidies for) support and advice is therefore too crude. As dis-cussed below, the relatively indiscriminate nature of impediments or constraints also means that where alleged constraints (e.g. state regulations) are removed or reduced, the positives may be lost as well as any negatives. It is, therefore, vital to develop a fuller picture for forms of support as well as constraints on SMEs, how they interact and how their effects may vary. A useful starting point are those organisations that seek to influence government but also frequently deliver government-backed support or initiatives.

Membership Organisations: Chambers of Commerce

The enterprise industry has, since the 1980s, undergone unprecedented growth (Greene et al., 2008; MacDonald & Coffield, 1991). This can be seen in terms of the number of membership organisations, support and networking groups based on a variety of forms of association along lines of common interest (Bennett, 1998). Those such as the Federation of Small Business (FSB), founded in 1974, very quickly recruited 30,000 members and, more recently, alternatives such as Enterprise Nation, founded in 2005, now claim to have over 70,000 members. These are large memberships, yet they represent a small proportion of the over 5 million SMEs in the UK (5.7 million, Department for Business, Energy & Industrial Strategy, BEIS, 2017, a lower number in the 1970s but still far exceed-ing the membership of the FSB).

Such organisations follow, to some degree, the footsteps of the Chambers of Commerce which have a much longer history (in the UK for over 250 years) and been extensively studied by Robert Bennett. Bennett (2011, p. 4), in a voluminous history of the Chambers, defines them in terms of five key characteristics:

> they seek to act as voices of the local business community; are voluntary (hence expressing inde-pendent, grass-roots local needs/desires); represent general interests (not individual interests of a firm or sectors); are locally rooted in a specific business community or an area; and their voice is derived from and legitimized by a deliberated process in an open and transparent way (such as consultation required by a memorandum and articles of association).

Bennett (1995) studied the choices involved in membership of these organ-isations, identifying the crucial element of the specificity of perceived benefits attracting members, requiring the limiting of access to more general benefits derived from the organisation's activities. Member-specific benefits include the local contact networks offered by the Chambers of Commerce that serve as a means of meeting potential clients or suppliers (including business support services such as accountants or coaches) and provide status in the community and often emphasise on business referrals on behalf of network members. Newer forms of such organisations, such as Enterprise Nation, with less sectoral or regional specificity and more online forms of engagement, have the potential to offer lower membership fees, partly due to infrequent and discontinuous engagement with services, but meaning that if businesses materially benefit they receive an excellent cost/benefit ratio.

Advocacy roles relate to efforts by membership organisations to act as 'a voice for small businesses', lobbying government on behalf of their members but, in theory, also on behalf of many non-members and in competition (or alliance) with other types of organisation such as think tanks (Arshed, 2017). Many Chambers of Commerce have also contracted with government to provide additional services for a fee. Bennett (1995, p. 258) notes that 'This income is of considerable significance and does give UK chambers a public role that is higher than any other UK business organisation'. However, such public-sector income is usually so constrained that it provides little financial support to their other activities.

The interactions between different forms of support is demonstrated by approaches whereby, instead of providing alternative support structures, government subsidises existing providers. This is broadly what happened in England where, partly due to its particular franchise systems, Business Link was seen by some commentators as essentially a nationalisation of business support services (Priest, 1999). Michael Heseltine, the government minister who led the creation of Business Link, has stated that he had wanted the Chambers of Commerce to lead but that they generally were not up to a sufficient standard to compete internationally (Forte, 2011). Heseltine and others identified a lack of joined up support provision to be remedied using a 'one stop shop' approach that would utilise the expertise of the Chambers of Commerce, Training and Enterprise Councils and Local Authorities through a Business Link franchise system. In effect, this represented an attempt to rationalise the early development of the enterprise industry.

Bennett and Robson (2004) analysed the different types of franchise holders operating Business Link and found a very variable service, highlighting the importance of understanding the different sources of business support, including the Chambers of Commerce, local government and the private sector, and how they interact. Such forms of government intervention in the activity of the enterprise industry also require new regulatory frameworks to safeguard taxpayers' money and, in theory, SMEs will ultimately benefit from such a state regulation through checks and assurances on the support providers.

The increasing prominence of the Chambers of Commerce, alongside other providers of support and advice, as subsidised by government with schemes such as the recent Growth Voucher initiative and, in the age of austerity cuts, increasing reliance on the enterprise industry to provide support to start-ups and SMEs, not only promotes their activities, but can also significantly constrain them (Bennett, 1995). For example, with the creation of Local Enterprise

Partnerships (LEPs), the Chambers of Commerce were again central to their establishment (Bentley, Bailey, & Shutt, 2010). However, while policies such as setting up LEPs appear more localised and flexible, they are driven by top-down, centralised targets and bidding processes. One of the key changes from Regional Development Agencies to LEPs was a greater focus on LEPs bidding for funding, which effectively constrained their activities and focussed their strategies along heavily regulated, centrally planned lines (Bentley et al., 2010). It is therefore crucial to understand the ways in which the public and private sectors are interlinked in their influence on SMEs.

Educators: Universities

Universities are an important source for the education and preparation of a graduate workforce and are beginning to place more emphasis on the promotion and support of entrepreneurship (Culkin, 2006). Sanderson (1972) describes how universities (in England but representative of broader trends) began to move away from traditions of anything 'applied' being looked down upon and resisted. The perceived economic needs of the country created pressures for change, often pushed by state intervention such as setting certain requirements for state funding. This has prompted calls for universities to develop their role, for example, in terms of collaboration with business (Wilson, 2012) and their 'third mission', which has broadened to include wider activity to foster engagement and support for SMEs and regional development (Pugh, Hamilton, Jack, & Gibbons, 2016). The Wilson (2012) report on UK university-business collaboration argues for the benefits of mutual collaboration between universities and businesses in the context of universities as a 'national resource' (p. 13). The less profit-oriented nature of universities, their third mission and their engagement with government sources of funding lead them to be focussed on the supposed social benefits of entrepreneurship and small business but potentially also to address perceived market failures.

Culkin (2016), in a review of Higher Education Institution (HEI) activity supporting entrepreneurship, identifies that HEIs can be a focus of financial resources and government action, as, for example, seen in the case of England's University Enterprise Zones, which included 'a new £15 million pilot scheme [that] will allow universities to push through local growth plans and support entrepreneurship and innovation' (Department for Business, Innovation & Skills, BIS, 2015). However, summarising criticisms of HEI engagement, Thorpe and Rawlinson (2014) argue that HEIs, and in particular business schools, fail to adequately engage with businesses and that 'students are poorly prepared for practical management, roles in small and medium-sized enterprises (SMEs), and entrepreneurship' (p. 381). Further, the limited forms of support provided by HEIs are often decontextualised and inattentive to the needs of heterogeneous small firms (Devins & Gold, 2002).

Powell and Houghton (2008) present a case study of a university project using networking and action learning to address poor take up of traditional business support by SMEs and low levels of business engagement with HEIs. This evidences success for peer-to-peer action learning supported by the HEI and reflects a common SME preference for events (e.g. networking and group based) rather than consultancy (Prochorskaite, 2014). A potential avenue for government funding is through HEIs and the relationship between government, universities and small firms is seen as particularly important by some commentators (e.g. Wilson, 2012). For example, Mallett, Richter, Whitehurst and Sear (2016) present research on a government-funded programme through which an HEI capitalised on its reach, reputation and resources to bring together managers from large businesses and small businesses seeking to develop their managerial capabilities. In this way, different sources and forms of support from government (funding), HEI (expertise and facilitation) and large businesses (expertise and experience) interact to develop a successful SME support programme.

Pugh et al. (2016) argue that HEIs can (and should) broaden their activities, for example, including

> designing and running programmes to support entrepreneurship, innovation and business growth; engaging with policy-makers at the local, regional and/or national levels; acting as regional animateurs, engaging with businesses and communities in their localities for economic and wider social benefit. (p. 1358)

Although much of the academic literature focusses on enterprise education and more traditional activities, HEIs may be potentially well equipped to engage with other forms of SME support. Understanding how different forms of support can productively interact may be the key to utilising the unique resources and expertise of HEIs.

Professional Services: Accountants

State regulation encourages and, in some circumstances, requires contact with external advisers such as accountants and solicitors. This relates to how to comply with state regulations and requirements such as how to file tax returns and extends to more general support and advice. Accountants are one of the more popular and impactful sources of business advice due to perceived legitimacy, long-term relationships and the development of trust, in contrast to less familiar sources such as government provision (Bennett & Robson, 1999; Mole, 2002; Scott & Irwin, 2009). Gooderham, Tobiassen, Døving and Nordhaug's (2004) study of small firms in Norway found that the 'quality, rather than the longevity, of the relationship between firm and authorised accountant is an important antecedent of the degree to which small firms use accountants as business advisers' (Abstract). This makes sense where businesses tend to stick with the same accountants, even if they are unhappy with them (Marriott & Marriott, 2000). The advice received can extend far beyond traditional areas of accounting.

In Jarvis and Rigby's (2012), study they focussed on human resource and employment advice, finding extensive advice and support ranging from signposting to sharing their own experiences to accompanying their clients to employment-related meetings. Jarvis and Rigby's findings illustrate the development of perceived expertise through previous encounters with clients as well as internal experience of, for example, HR-related issues. This experience was supplemented by online resources and templates and some forms of training, especially in relation to state regulation. However, the degree to which such limited expertise could be tailored to the ends of different clients is unclear. Perhaps, as a result, there were some concerns, especially among the smallest accountancy firms, about giving advice in areas in which they lacked expertise (e.g. reputational damage and litigation). Perhaps, as a result, the accountancy firms, especially where mid-sized, employed HR-qualified staff or entered into partnership with HR specialists.

Assessing accountancy around the turn of the century in the context of deregulation and increasing IT use, Marriott and Marriott (2000) interviewed small firm owner-managers about the information they receive from their accountants. At a basic level, Marriott and Marriott found a desire among business owners to better understand the financial information in order to aid their business. Further, these owner-managers were positive about the move to 'management accounting' services where more strategic and easily understood and acted-upon information is provided by the accountant. Therefore, partly in response to government deregulation, accountants began to extend their provision to small firms in terms of providing information and advice that impacts upon the strategic direction and decision making of the business. This provides an interesting example of interaction where support and advice is developed from a basis of ensuring compliance with state regulation and where, especially with deregulation, this support and advice moves into gaps that emerge, extending the form of influence.

Large Businesses and Supply Chains

Larger businesses are not necessarily an obvious source of SME support, but they do exert powerful influences on SMEs. Rainnie (1989) has argued that small firms that find themselves dependent on larger organisations, or otherwise are subject to their influence indirectly, have very limited scope for determining management action. Moreover, the constraints operating on these dependent small firms serve to limit scope for employees to contest the ways they are managed and negotiate better terms and conditions of employment. Further, large businesses, especially those conceptualised as anchor institutions because of their involvement with and support for local communities (Smallbone, Kitching, Blackburn, & Mosavi, 2015) can provide formal forms of business support.

Beaumont, Hunter and Sinclair (1996), writing about businesses of various sizes, suggest how supply chain relationships can exert influence on employment relationships and practices both directly and indirectly. Direct influence might include contractual requirements (e.g. Investors in People accreditation), whereas indirect influence refers to relationships in which

> increased customer demands for improved supplier performance, increasingly supported by the results of auditing instruments, necessitate the supplier organization making internal changes to their management systems and techniques, and their working practices/arrangements in order to meet the increased expectations and demands of customers. (p. 13)

For example, the client may require cost-savings that indirectly require their suppliers to change work practices and train their staff as a consequence of these changes.

Large firms also, in their wider engagements and large-scale local employment, inevitably develop informal influence, support and guidance, for example, in developing the skills and expertise of owner-managers or other employees they come into contact with (Wapshott & Mallett, 2015). An increasing part of the emphasis placed on corporate social responsibility has related to social purpose issues, including small firm development (Luetkenhorst, 2004). In the case of small firm support, Smallbone et al. (2015) highlight that much learning and development in these firms takes place on an ad hoc, informal and experiential basis. It may, therefore, be derived from 'participation in working activities and from interaction with suppliers, customers, employees and others' (p. vii). In addition to formalised interactions, these are the informal and indirect elements of the SME support environment that supplements and perhaps supplants government and other national initiatives. Large firm requirements for their supply chains can be considered as a key element in the regulatory context but cannot be separated from potentially positive and supportive forms of influence on practices within the SMEs they engage with.

The sources of support, advice and influence discussed above are not intended to be exhaustive. The importance and prevalence of informal, often localised advice accessed by many SMEs from other elements of the enterprise industry, such as business angels, solicitors and bankers, in addition to other influences such as customers, family, friends and employees (Bennett, 2008) is often overlooked. Nonetheless, what this brief overview has sought to demonstrate is that the complexity highlighted in the influence of large firms can be extended to other forms of business support which can be usefully considered in terms of a regulatory context. Before outlining the value of this conceptualisation, it is also worth considering traditional state regulation.

REGULATION AS SUPPORT?

Business regulation represents an attempt by governments and other bodies to influence or control organisational practices, for example, in maintaining open markets and in areas such as protecting employee rights. In this context, state regulation is frequently considered as disproportionately over-complicated, unnecessary and burdensome for SMEs (Edwards, Ram, & Black, 2004). These discussions, in political discourse and many academic studies, focus on the negative effects of regulation, for example, in constraining the growth of firms and supporting loud calls for deregulation (Mallett, Wapshott, & Vorley, 2018). However, the complexity of the effects of state regulation on these firms, which can take dynamic, direct and indirect forms, merits further consideration (Atkinson, Mallett, & Wapshott, 2016; Kitching, Hart, & Wilson, 2015; Kitching, Kašperová, & Collis, 2015).

Perceptions of state regulations and how these shape, among other things, business processes, management practices and investment decisions, are important. Perceived impacts by regulatory requirements on strategic choice, for example, in terms of how much control a business may have in setting its preferred goals and path to growth, can have real constraining impacts. For example, a belief in the dangers of state regulation may prevent a business owner from wanting to grow their business for the fear of state interference. Further, state regulations requiring particular rates of pay, working conditions or other employee rights perform a vital social function but, at the same time, may make it more difficult for owner-managers in competitive environments to compete on price or manage their labour force in the way they believe would most benefit their operational requirements.

As discussed already, state regulation can also have other, indirect effects on SMEs in terms of the support services they encourage engagement with, whether in terms of legal advice, accountancy or mediation. For example, Gooderham et al. (2004) highlight how, while some SMEs will access business support and advice through their accountant, there is a large amount of variability driven by factors such as strategic intent. Where regulatory compliance encourages engagement with forms of external advice, this may overcome potential market failures where SME owner-managers have not valued such sources of advice and support (Storey, 2005). In this way, market failures are overcome not by government subsidies or provision but through their regulatory actions. Traditional discussions of SMEs and forms of state regulation as 'red tape' are at odds with such a focus, since they tend to discuss state regulation in isolation.

This support and advice will constitute not only formalised interactions, but also the overlooked informal and indirect elements of the SME support environment that supplements and perhaps supplants government and other national initiatives. The relevance of forms of business support, for example, have an important influence on how state regulation effects SMEs. As highlighted by Atkinson et al. (2016), in different firms the ways that state regulation is interpreted, enacted, ignored and negotiated produces a variety of unpredictable interactions between the formal rules and the informality associated with routines developed through owner-manager prerogative, external influence and employee negotiation. For Kitching (2016) 'external support networks play a – or perhaps *the* – pivotal role in shaping employer understandings of legal obligations to employees'. Providers of external support, such as the accountants discussed above, mediate the understanding and effects of state regulation within the firms for which they provide guidance and advice. Further, Kitching highlights the importance of informal forms of support, for example, including seeking advice in interpreting state regulation and advice from family members who are also business owners, accountants, solicitors or other relevant occupations.

State regulation can have significant, direct positive effects, for example, in protecting smaller businesses in terms of their property rights or from unfair business practices from their larger and better resourced competitors. But state regulation can have other positive effects more akin to the forms of influence categorised as business support. For example, Baldock, James, Smallbone, and Vickers (2006) studied health and safety regulation in relation to small firms and identified that sales-turnover growth was significantly correlated with undertaking compliance-related improvements, especially in relation to visits from inspectors. It is possible that particular actions taken to ensure compliance with state regulation, such as the introduction of clear policies or the formalisation of practices, could help to develop management skills and support SME performance or growth (Scott, Roberts, Holroyd, & Sawbridge, 1989). It is in this way that state regulations have the potential to constitute a form of business support. However, very little research has examined this (Mallett et al., 2018).

RETHINKING THE REGULATORY CONTEXT

The brief overview of SME support, provided in this chapter, suggests the importance of considering forms of SME support and constraint in a more holistic way than tends to inform debates in this area. To achieve this, it suggests conceptualising the different influences on SMEs as mutually overlapping, interdependent and potentially contradictory and not in simple binary, positive or negative terms. This final section of the chapter will consider this reconceptualisation in terms of a regulatory context that relates to 'all forms of social or economic influence: includes all mechanisms affecting behaviour, state-based and from other sources' (Baldwin et al., 2012, p. 3). That is, it presents a conceptualisation of the forms of influence derived from the enterprise industry and from the state as part of a general regulatory context with both positive and negative effects.

This proposed approach is not to discourage an emphasis on one type of approach over another but rather to place the different approaches to SME support in a broader context. Gibb (2000) highlights the potential implications of government policy that seeks to influence a particular type of external environment. In Gibb's analysis, the political discourse surrounding SMEs and entrepreneurship promotes particular ways to be an entrepreneur in the pursuit of growth and particular sources from whom to seek support and assistance (such as accountants and bankers), who reinforce these assumptions and instil forms of dependency. In this way, the different forms of advice and guidance (together with traditionally conceived forms of constraint such as state regulation) need to be considered together and in terms of the influence they exert on SMEs. This may have productive effects, but it may also dissuade or discourage different forms of SME activity such as giving less status to lifestyle businesses that fail to pursue business growth. Verduyn and Essers (2017) describe an example in which support providers can give guidance to migrant entrepreneurs that (perhaps inadvertently) reinforces us-them divisions even while attempting to integrate people into Western forms of entrepreneurship, limiting any emancipatory potential in terms of how this is experienced, for example, by women ethnic minority entrepreneurs who do not 'fit' with this discourse.

Gibb (2000) describes how state policy has tended to focus on support for SME development, creating support structures, which often involve subsidised programmes of training, finance and counselling. This reinforces an image of SMEs being in need of assistance from an enterprise industry of advisers, consultants and accountants as opposed to less formal, less commercially oriented forms of support within a firm's operating environment, such as personal networks as well as, potentially, HEIs. As a result, smaller businesses become customers and government intervention is focussed upon the market that is subsequently created. Later work by Ram et al. (2013) suggests that such a subsidised industry creates vested interests where many intermediaries are constantly having to ensure they win government funding to secure their own futures. Much of the activity undertaken in this domain is based on assumptions or myths that reflect and reinforce particular world views in relation to SMEs (Gibb, 2000) that can be considered to regulate their behaviour in terms of perceived legitimacy and the support and advice provided that may shape the development of these businesses.

Without regard for the robust research evidence and a deeper understanding of external influences on SMEs that may contest these myths, such perspectives and practices continue to create ignorance about the issues facing these businesses. The prominence of specific myths of mischaracterisations (Wapshott & Mallett, 2018) is partly reinforced and reproduced by the centrality and influence of the state in many forms of SME influence. Curran (2000) suggests that despite significant growth in publicly funded SME business support, the evaluation of policies in this area has tended to lag behind their proliferation, suggesting, perhaps, that the benefits of such initiatives are taken as an act of faith rather than rigourous judgement. Curran identifies three important methodological concerns when evaluating government policy and support: additionality (reliably attributing outcomes to the specific programme), which needs to be offset against the deadweight (outcomes which would have resulted anyway), and displacement (firms not involved in the programme are negatively impacted). The difficulty of overcoming these measurement problems presents a significant challenge and potential limitation to evaluations of SME policy and support (see also, Devins, 1999). This further highlights the necessity to unpick and understand different forms of influence and their interactions in developing a more holistic approach, conceptualised in this chapter as a regulatory context.

CONCLUSION

This chapter offers two core contributions. Firstly, forms of influence on SMEs can be seen through too restrictive a lens if they are considered as 'positive' business support and 'negative' state regulation. There are a variety of overlapping, interacting influences on SMEs, many of them indiscriminate or poorly targeted. Some forms of advice or guidance may be positive for one firm and negative for another, with similar differences in the way state regulation is experienced. Kitching et al. (2015) provide the excellent example of SMEs being granted less regulatory burden by being able to file abbreviated accounts but, as a result, experiencing powerful knock-on effects such as making it more difficult to access finance from potential lenders less able to assess a firm's performance and potential risk. The different sources of overlapping, interacting influence derived from both the state and the enterprise industry are best understood as a regulatory context that will be experienced in different ways and at different times among the incredibly heterogeneous SME population of a given economy.

Secondly, central to many of the overlaps and interactions identified in this chapter, and shaping many of the forms of influence on SMEs, is government. This can be seen from direct provision to the subsidisation of forms of support to encourage SMEs to engage with forms of consultancy, the funding for initiatives delivered by membership organisation and HEIs to the push towards professional services firms to meet compliance with state regulations and accounting requirements. LEPs represent a particularly interesting case where, at a local level, different organisations including, potentially, local businesses, membership organisations, local government, HEIs and other regional stakeholders collaborate together to develop the region's economy (including support for SMEs). However, the provision developed by these organisations has been identified as constrained by a reliance on state funding, which requires bidding processes and conformity to centralised state targets (Bentley et al., 2010). This suggests that at the heart of the enterprise industry, and shaping much of its activity, is central government and the £8 billion a year invested, directly and indirectly, into a wide variety of activities under the heading of enterprise policy.

Offering support while cutting state regulation is an example of the contradiction at the heart of free market neoliberalism: policies designed to lessen one form of government intervention (state regulation) while spending large amounts of government money on other forms of intervention (the enterprise industry). Deregulation is rarely a straightforward matter of ending particular compliance activities. In many economies, new state regulation is constantly being introduced together with the replacement of existing state regulation (Aalbers, 2016). Considering the overlap, interaction and potential for contradiction between SME support and state regulation, this also represents an example of reregulation. Reregulation involves the pressures for compliance moving from one source to another, such as accountants or large businesses, in terms of codes, rules or standards such that

> there is a multiplicity of regulatory sites, spaces and actors whose relationships define the pattern and efficacy of regulation [and] notions of "deregulation" often involve the movement of regulatory function between actors. (MacKenzie & Martínez Lucio, 2005, p. 500; cf., Aalbers, 2016)

There is therefore not necessarily a clear reduction in, for example, compliance costs or the reluctance to grow a business due to the complexity and the apparent bureaucracy of a multitude of organisations. The overall 'burden' of influence from the regulatory context remains consistent.

This is important where governments, researchers or organisations attempt to evaluate or conduct some form of cost-benefit analysis on SME support activity or state (de)regulation. For example, in the UK, government programmes have attempted to improve state regulation by aiming to 'remove or simplify existing regulations that unnecessarily impede growth' (HM Government, 2011, p. 3). This involved assessing regulations in terms of their costs to support a 'one in one out' approach (later one in two out) such that any new regulation was accompanied by a 'deregulatory measure (an "OUT"), which relieves business of the same net cost as any "IN" ' (HM Government, 2011). This chapter suggests that policy makers seeking to develop effective forms of support or state regulation should not consider such activities in isolation or in simple positive or negative terms.

The various forms of business support and advice, together with specific commands and rules, are ultimately about influencing SMEs and can be understood as part of Baldwin et al.'s (2012) broader definition of a regulatory context. This overview of literature across different forms of influence on SMEs develops understanding of the enterprise industry, the central role of the state and of businesses' regulatory context in terms of understanding how different forms of influence, advice and support interact. This may partially account for perceived market failure and low take-up of these services where SME owner-managers often want independence and are wary of bureaucracy (Curran, 2000). Understanding the regulatory context of SMEs, in this way, should also develop insights for policy makers keen to develop an effective entrepreneurship ecosystem (Mason & Brown, 2014). This chapter has therefore sought to make a contribution to our understanding of business support relevant to academics, practitioners and public policy.

ACKNOWLEDGEMENTS

This chapter was supported by funding from the Institute for Small Business and Entrepreneurship, Research and Knowledge Exchange fund.

REFERENCES

Aalbers, M. B. (2016). Regulated deregulation. In S. Springer, K. Birch, & J. MacLeavy (Eds.), *Handbook of neoliberalism* (pp. 591–601). London: Routledge.

Anyadike-Danes, M., Hart, M., & Du, J. (2015). Firm dynamics and job creation in the United Kingdom: 1998–2013. *International Small Business Journal, 33*(1), 12–27.

Arrowsmith, J., Gilman, M. W., Edwards, P., & Ram, M. (2003). The impact of the National Minimum Wage in small firms. *British Journal of Industrial Relations, 41*(3), 435–456.

Arshed, N. (2017). The origins of policy ideas: The importance of think tanks in the enterprise policy process in the UK. *Journal of Business Research, 71*, 74–83.

Atkinson, C., Mallett, O., & Wapshott, R. (2016). 'You try to be a fair employer': Regulation and employment relationships in medium-sized firms. *International Small Business Journal, 34*(1), 16–33.

Baldock, R., James, P., Smallbone, D., & Vickers, I. (2006). Influences on small-firm compliance-related behaviour: The case of workplace health and safety. *Environment and Planning C, 24*(6), 827–846.

Baldwin, R., Cave, M., & Lodge, M. (2012). *Understanding regulation.* Oxford: Oxford University Press.

Bannock, G., & Peacock, A. T. (1989). *Governments and small business.* London: Sage.

Beaumont, P. B., Hunter, L. C., & Sinclair, D. (1996). Customer-supplier relations and the diffusion of employee relations changes. *Employee Relations, 18*(1), 9–19.

BEIS. (2017). *Business population estimates 2017.* Retrieved from https://www.gov.uk/government/statistics/business-population-estimates-2017

Bennett, R. (1995). The logic of local business associations: An analysis of voluntary chambers of commerce. *Journal of Public Policy, 15*(3), 251–279.

Bennett, R. (1998). Business associations and their potential contribution to the competitiveness of SMEs. *Entrepreneurship & Regional Development, 10*(3), 243–260.

Bennett, R. (2008). SME policy support in Britain since the 1990s: What have we learnt? *Environment and Planning C: Government & Policy, 26*(2), 375.

Bennett, R. (2011). *Local business voice: The history of Chambers of Commerce in Britain, Ireland, and Revolutionary America, 1760–2011*. Oxford: Oxford University Press.

Bennett, R., & Robson, P. (2004). Support services for SMEs: Does the 'franchisee' make a difference to the Business Link offer? *Environment and Planning C: Government and Policy, 22*, 859–880.

Bentley, G., Bailey, D., & Shutt, J. (2010). From RDAs to LEPs: A new localism? Case examples of West Midlands and Yorkshire. *Local Economy, 25*(7), 535–557.

BERR. (2008). *Simple support, better business: Business support in 2010*. London: Department for Business, Enterprise & Regulatory Reform.

BIS. (2015). 2010 to 2015 government policy: Local Enterprise Partnerships (LEPs) and enterprise zones. Retrieved from https://www.gov.uk/government/publications/2010-to-2015-government-policy-local-enterprise-partnerships-leps-and-enterprise-zones

Bolton, J. E. (1971). *Small firms: Report of the committee of inquiry on small firms*. London: HMSO. Cmnd. 4811.

Bridge, S. (2010). *Rethinking enterprise policy*. Basingstoke: Palgrave Macmillan.

Burrows, R., & Curran, J. (1989). Sociological research on service sector small businesses: Some conceptual consideration. *Work, Employment and Society, 3*(4), 527–539.

Capelleras, J. L., Mole, K. F., Greene, F. J., & Storey, D. J. (2008). Do more heavily regulated economies have poorer performing new ventures? Evidence from Britain and Spain. *Journal of International Business Studies, 39*(4), 688–704.

Culkin, N. (2016). Entrepreneurial universities in the region: The force awakens? *International Journal of Entrepreneurial Behavior & Research, 22*(1), 4–16.

Curran, J. (2000). What is small business policy in the UK for? Evaluation and assessing small business policies. *International Small Business Journal, 18*(3), 36–50.

Dennis, W. J., Jr. (2011). Entrepreneurship, small business and public policy levers. *Journal of Small Business Management, 49*(2), 149–162.

Devins, D. (1999). Research note: Supporting established micro businesses: Policy issues emerging from an evaluation. *International Small Business Journal, 18*(1), 86–86.

Devins, D., & Gold, J. (2002). Social constructionism: A theoretical framework to underpin support for the development of managers in SMEs? *Journal of Small Business and Enterprise Development, 9*(2), 111–119.

Edwards, P., Ram, M., & Black, J. (2004). Why does employment legislation not damage small firms? *Journal of Law and Society, 31*(2), 245–265.

Forte, E. (2011). *Intervention: The battle for better business*. Retrieved from http://www.Lulu.com

Gibb, A. A. (2000). SME policy, academic research and the growth of ignorance, mythical concepts, myths, assumptions, rituals and confusions. *International Small Business Journal, 18*(3), 13–35.

Gooderham, P. N., Tobiassen, A., Døving, E., & Nordhaug, O. (2004). Accountants as sources of business advice for small firms. *International Small Business Journal, 22*(1), 5–22.

Greene, F. J., Mole, K., & Storey, D. J. (2008). *Three decades of enterprise culture? Entrepreneurship, economic regeneration and public policy*. Basingstoke: Palgrave.

Harris, L. (2000). Employment regulation and owner-managers in small firms: Seeking support and guidance. *Journal of Small Business and Enterprise Development, 7*(4), 352–263.

Hart, M., & Blackburn, R. (2005). Labour regulation and SMEs: A challenge to competitiveness and employability? In S. Marlow, D. Patton, & M. Ram (Eds.), *Managing labour in small firms* (pp. 133–158). London: Routledge.

HM Government. (2011). One-in, one-out: Statement of new regulation. Retrieved from https://www.gov.uk/government/collections/one-in-two-out-statement-of-new-regulation

Hunt, R. A., & Kiefer, K. (2017). The entrepreneurship industry: Influences of the goods and services marketed to entrepreneurs. *Journal of Small Business Management, 55*(S1), 231–255.

Jarvis, R., & Rigby, M. (2012). The provision of human resources and employment advice to small and medium-sized enterprises: The role of small and medium-sized practices of accountants. *International Small Business Journal, 30*(8), 944–956.

Kitching, J. (2006). A burden on business? Reviewing the evidence base on regulation and small-business performance. *Environment and Planning C: Government and Policy, 24*(6), 799–814.

Kitching, J. (2016). Between vulnerable compliance and confident ignorance: Small employers, regulatory discovery practices and external support networks. *International Small Business Journal*, *34*(5), 601–617.

Kitching, J., Hart, M., & Wilson, N. (2015). Burden or benefit? Regulation as a dynamic influence on small business performance. *International Small Business Journal*, *33*(2), 130–147.

Kitching, J., Kašperová, E., & Collis, J. (2015). The contradictory consequences of regulation: The influence of filing abbreviated accounts on UK small company performance. *International Small Business Journal*, *33*(7), 671–688.

Luetkenhorst, W. (2004). Corporate social responsibility and the development agenda. *Intereconomics*, *39*(3), 157–166.

MacDonald, R., & Coffield, F. (1991). *Risky business? Youth and the enterprise culture*. Abingdon: Routledge.

MacKenzie, R., & Martínez Lucio, M. (2005). The realities of regulatory change beyond the fetish of deregulation. *Sociology*, *39*(3), 499–517.

Mallett, O., Richter, P., Whitehurst, F., & Sear, L. (2016). Reconceptualising anchor institutions: A new direction for regionally-focused small firm support. *39th Institute for Small Business and Entrepreneurship Conference*, Paris, October 27–28.

Mallett, O., & Wapshott, R. (2015a). Making sense of self-employment in late career: Understanding the identity work of olderpreneurs. *Work, Employment and Society*, *29*(2), 250–266.

Mallett, O., & Wapshott, R. (2015b). Entrepreneurship in a context of pending retirement. In N. Sappleton & F. Lourenco (Eds), *Entrepreneurship, self-employment and retirement*. (pp. 67–89) London: Palgrave Macmillan.

Mallett, O., Wapshott, R., & Vorley, T. (2018). How do regulations affect SMEs? A review of the qualitative evidence and a research agenda. *International Journal of Management Reviews*. Early View.

Marriott, N., & Marriott, P. (2000). Professional accountants and the development of a management accounting service for the small firm: Barriers and possibilities. *Management Accounting Research*, *11*(4), 475–492.

Mason, C. (2009). Public policy support for the informal venture capital market in Europe a critical review. *International Small Business Journal*, *27*(5), 536–556.

Mason, C., & Brown, R. (2013). Creating good public policy to support high-growth firms. *Small Business Economics*, *40*(2), 211–225.

Mason, C., & Brown, R. (2014). *Entrepreneurial ecosystems and growth oriented entrepreneurship*. Final Report to OECD, Paris.

Matthias, P. (1969). *The first industrial nation*. London: Methuen & Co. Ltd.

Mole, K. (2002). Business advisers' impact on SMEs: An agency theory approach. *International Small Business Journal*, *20*(2), 139–162.

Mole, K., Hart, M., Roper, S., & Saal, D. (2008). Differential gains from Business Link support and advice: A treatment effects approach. *Environment and Planning C*, *26*(2), 315–334.

Molina-Morales, F. X., & Martínez-Fernández, M. T. (2009). Too much love in the neighborhood can hurt: How an excess of intensity and trust in relationships may produce negative effects on firms. *Strategic Management Journal*, *30*(9), 1013–1023.

OECD (2005). *OECD SME and entrepreneurship outlook: 2005* (p. 17). Paris: OECD.

Powell, J. A., & Houghton, J. (2008). Action learning as a core process for SME business support. *Action Learning: Research and Practice*, *5*(2), 173–184.

Pugh, R., Hamilton, E., Jack, S., & Gibbons, A. (2016). A step into the unknown: Universities and the governance of regional economic development. *European Planning Studies*, *24*(7), 1357–1373.

Priest, S. J. (1999). Business Link services to small and medium-sized enterprises: Targeting, innovation, and charging. *Environment and Planning C*, *17*, 177–194.

Prochorskaite, A. (2014). University-led business support: A case study of a regional programme. *Industrial and Commercial Training*, *46*(5), 257–264.

Rainnie, A. (1985). Small firms, big problems: The political economy of small businesses. *Capital & Class*, *9*, 140–168.

Rainnie, A. (1989). *Industrial relations in small firms: Small isn't beautiful*. London: Routledge.

Rainnie, A. (1991). Small firms: Between the enterprise culture and new times. In R. Burrows (Ed.), *Deciphering the enterprise culture: Entrepreneurship, petty capitalism and the restructuring of Britain* (pp. 176–199). London: Routledge.

Ram, M., Jones, T., Edwards, P., Kiselinchev, A., Muchenje, L., & Woldesenbet, K. (2013). Engaging with super-diversity: New migrant businesses and the research–policy nexus. *International Small Business Journal, 31*(4), 337–356.

Ramsden, M., & Bennett, R. J. (2005). The benefits of external support to SMEs: "Hard" versus "soft" outcomes and satisfaction levels. *Journal of Small Business and Enterprise Development, 12*(2), 227–243.

Richard, D. (2008). *Small business and government: The Richard report.* Retrieved from http://www.conservatives.com/pdf/document-richardreport-2008.pdf

Sanderson, M. (1972). *The universities and British industry 1950–1970.* London: Routledge.

Scott, J. M., & Irwin, D. (2009). Discouraged advisees? The influence of gender, ethnicity, and education in the use of advice and finance by UK SMEs. *Environment and Planning C, 27*(2), 230–245.

Scott, M., Roberts, I., Holroyd, G., & Sawbridge, D. (1989). *Management and industrial relations in small firms.* Department of Employment Research Paper No. 70. London: HMSO.

Shane, S. (2009). Why encouraging more people to become entrepreneurs is bad public policy. *Small Business Economics, 33*(2), 141–149.

Smallbone, D., Baldock, R., & Burgess, S. (2002). Targeted support for high-growth start-ups: Some policy issues. *Environment and Planning C, 20*(2), 195–209.

Smallbone, D., Kitching, J., Blackburn, R., & Mosavi, S. (2015). *Anchor institutions and small firms in the UK.* UK Commission for Employment and Skills. Retrieved from https://www.gov.uk/government/uploads/system/uploads/attachment_data/file/414390/Anchor_institutions_and_small_firms.pdf

Storey, D. J. (1994). *Understanding the small business sector.* Abingdon: Routledge.

Storey, D. J. (2005). Entrepreneurship, small and medium sized enterprises and public policy. In Z. J. Acs, & D. B. Audretsch (Eds.), *International handbook of entrepreneurship research* (pp. 473–511). London: Springer.

Thorpe, R., & Rawlinson, R. (2014). Engaging with engagement: How UK business schools could meet the innovation challenge. *Journal of Management Development, 33*(5), 470–486.

Verduyn, K., & Essers, C. (2017). A critical reflection on female migrant entrepreneurship in the Netherlands. In C. Essers, P. Dey, D. Tedmanson, & K. Verduyn, (Eds.), *Critical perspectives on entrepreneurship: Challenging dominant discourses* (pp. 161–176). London: Routledge.

Wapshott, R., & Mallett, O. (2015). *Managing human resources in small and medium-sized enterprises.* London: Routledge.

Wapshott, R., & Mallett, O. (2018). Small and medium-sized enterprise policy: Designed to fail? *Environment and Planning C: Politics and Space, 36*(4), 750–772.

Wilson, T. (2012). *A review of business-university collaboration.* Retrieved from https://www.gov.uk/government/uploads/system/uploads/attachment_data/file/32383/12-610-wilson-review-business-university-collaboration.pdf

Wren, C., & Storey, D. J. (2002). Evaluating the effect of soft business support upon small firm performance. *Oxford Economic Papers, 54*(2), 334–365.

CHAPTER 7

THE ROLE OF MENTORING IN YOUTH ENTREPRENEURSHIP FINANCE: A GLOBAL PERSPECTIVE[1]

Robyn Owen, Julie Haddock-Millar,
Leandro Sepulveda, Chandana Sanyal,
Stephen Syrett, Neil Kaye and David Deakins

ABSTRACT

Introduction – General Principles

The chapter examines the role of volunteer business mentoring in potentially improving financing and financial management in under-served (i.e. schemes aim to assist deprived neighbourhoods and youth entrepreneurs) youth enterprises.

Youth entrepreneurship (commonly defined as entrepreneurs aged up to 35 years) is regarded by the OECD as under-represented, within entrepreneurship as a general social phenomenon, and young entrepreneurs as disadvantaged through being under-served. Indeed, young people with latent potential for entrepreneurship have been defined as a component of 'Missing Entrepreneurs' (OECD, 2013). This under-representation of nascent entrepreneurs within young people under 35 is partly theoretical. While examining entrepreneurship as a social phenomenon and taking a resource-based approach (Barney, 1991), young people are perceived at a particular disadvantage compared with older members of society. That is, however creative, they lack the experience and network resources of older members.

Theoretically, from a demand-side perspective, young people may have aspirations and the required skills for start-up entrepreneurship, but are

Creating Entrepreneurial Space: Talking Through Multi-voices, Reflections on Emerging Debates
Contemporary Issues in Entrepreneurship Research, Volume 9B, 115–135
ISSN: 2040-7246/doi:10.1108/S2040-72462019000009B007

disadvantaged from a supply-side perspective since financial institutions, such as the commercial banks, private equity investors and other suppliers of financial debt and equity, will see greater risk combined with a lack of track record and credibility (pertaining to information asymmetries and associated agency and signalling problems: Carpenter & Petersen, 2002; Hsu, 2004; Hughes, 2009; Mueller, Westhead, & Wright, 2014). This means that aspiring nascent youth entrepreneurs face greater challenges in obtaining mainstream and alternative sources of finance. Practically, unless such young entrepreneurs can call upon deep pockets of the 'bank of Mum and Dad' or family and friends, we can expect them to resort to pragmatic methods of stretching their resources, such as financial bootstrapping and bricolage (Mac an Bhaird, 2010; Mac an Bhaird & Lucey, 2015). Although these theoretical and practical issues have long existed for youth entrepreneurship, they have only been exacerbated in the post-2007 Global financial Crisis (GFC) financial and economic environment, despite the growth of alternative sources such as equity and debt sources of crowdfunding.

Prior Work – Unlocking Potential

There has been an evidence for some time that young people have a higher desire to enter entrepreneurship and self-employment as a career choice, in preference to other forms of employment (Greene, 2005). Younger people are also more positive about entrepreneurial opportunities. For example, a Youth Business International, Global Entrepreneurship Monitor (YBI/GEM) (2013) report indicated that in the European Union (EU), 'younger youth' were more positive in their attitudes to good business opportunities and in seeing good opportunities than older people. Theoretically, the issues of low experience and credibility can be mitigated by the role of advisors, consultants and/or volunteer business mentors. In corporations and large organisations, mentors are known to be valuable for early career staff (Clutterbuck, 2004; Haddock-Millar, 2017). By extension with young entrepreneurs, business mentors raise credibility, develop personal and professional competence, business potential and entrepreneurial learning. From a supply-side perspective, this reduces risk for financial institutions, potentially increasing the likelihood of receiving external finance and improving the likely returns and business outcomes of such financing.

Methodological Approach

In examining the role of business mentoring in youth entrepreneurship finance, the chapter poses three research-related questions (RQs):

(1) To what extent is the youth voluntary business mentoring (VBM) associated with access to external finance?
(2) Where access to external finance takes place, does the VBM improve the outcomes of the businesses?
(3) To what extent do VBMs make a difference to the performance of businesses receiving financial assistance?

The chapter draws on primary evidence from an online Qualtrics survey of 491 (largely) youth entrepreneur mentees drawn from eight countries in the YBI network. These were selected for their contrasting high (Sweden and Spain), middle (India, Argentina, Chile, Russia and Poland) and lower (Uganda) income economies, global coverage of four continents and operation of established entrepreneurship mentoring schemes. The study provides collective quantitative data on the current relationship between mentoring and the access and impact of external finance. It surveyed current or recently completed mentees during Autumn 2016 – the typical mentoring cycle being 12 months. Additionally, the chapter draws on further qualitative insight evidence from face-to-face interviews, with current mentor-mentee case study pairings from the eight countries.

Key Findings

In summary, the profile of surveyed mentees demonstrated even gender distribution, with three-fifths currently in mentoring relationships. At the time of commencing mentoring, nearly four-fifths were aged under 35, half being self-employed, one quarter employed, with the remainder equally distributed between education and unemployment. At commencement of mentoring, mentee businesses were typically in early stages, either pre-start (37%) or just started trading (34%), the main sectors represented being business services (16%), education and training (16%), retail and wholesale (12%) and creative industries (8%), with the median level of own business management —one to two years.

For one-third of mentees, mentoring was compulsory, due largely to receiving enterprise finance support, whilst for the remainder, more than a quarter stated that access to business finance assistance was either considerably or most important in their choice to go on the programme.

In terms of business performance, businesses receiving external finance (loans or grants through the programme) or mentoring for business finance performed significantly better than the rest of the sample: amongst those trading 47% increased sales turnover, compared to 32% unassisted (<0.05 level); 70% increased employment, compared to 42% (<0.05); 58% directly attributed improved performance to mentoring, compared to 46% (<0.1).

Contribution and Implications

The chapter provides both statistical and qualitative evidences supporting the premise that youth business mentoring can both improve access to external finance and lead to improved business performance. This provides useful guidance to youth business support, given that in some of the countries studied, external financing in the form of grants and soft micro loans for youth entrepreneurs are not available.

Keywords: Youths; businesses; start-ups; mentoring; support; microfinance

INTRODUCTION

The chapter examines the role of volunteer business mentoring (VBM) in potentially improving financing and financial management in under-served youth enterprises. Youth entrepreneurship may be viewed as under-served both in terms of the lag in supporting the need for employment through youth enterprise globally and the need to support youth employment in deprived lower-income economies. Indeed, in economies where self-employment provides a large share of employment (e.g. Chile) or is increasing, such as the UK (UK Parliament, 2015), and particularly where it is amongst youths (e.g. Spain and the Netherlands, Hatfield, 2015), facilitating youth enterprise development has profound economic implications. The VBM programmes, examined in this chapter, operate in low, middle and high-income countries, aiming to assist under-served youth entrepreneurs, including in deprived neighbourhoods.

Youth entrepreneurship (commonly defined as entrepreneurs aged up to 35 years) is regarded by the OECD as under-represented, within entrepreneurship as a general social phenomenon, and young entrepreneurs as being a group that is largely disadvantaged in relation to their older counterparts. Indeed, young people, with latent potential for entrepreneurship, have been defined as a component of 'Missing Entrepreneurs' (OECD, 2013). This under-representation of nascent entrepreneurs within young people under 35 is partly theoretical. Examining entrepreneurship as a social phenomenon and taking a resource-based approach (Barney, 1991), young people are perceived at a particular disadvantage compared to older members of society. That is, however creative, they lack the experience and network resources of older members to successfully access and utilise external finance required to start and develop their businesses.

More specifically, this chapter focusses on overcoming the demand failures of early-stage youth enterprise in seeking external finance, potentially resulting in underfunding and inability to effectively manage financial resources. Youth entrepreneurs face a number of 'barriers' to start up and grow, but two are the most commonly highlighted in the literature. First, they need to find and effectively signal themselves to appropriate forms of external finance (Mueller et al., 2014). For the vast majority of start-ups seeking external finance, it is typically small grants or soft loans (at relatively low interest) that are required – often, under £10,000, to facilitate cash-flow until regular trading income is achieved (Greater London Authority [GLA], 2013). Second, even when funding is secured, youth entrepreneurs often lack the financial management skills to effectively utilise the funds. For example, Baldock (1998) recognised that the failure of Urban Fund small business grants in London during the 1980s was largely due to the recipient entrepreneurs' poor financial and broader business management skills.

This suggests, *post finance*, a vital role for external management advice and information, which for potential higher growth businesses could be fulfilled by smart hands-on business angel and seed venture capital investors (Mason & Harrison, 2015). In the case of smaller-scale microfinance (seed grants and loans),[2] it is unlikely that the business will be able to afford to pay for advice, or that the funder will have the resources to offer the advice. A possible solution is therefore to develop the VBM services, which encourage experienced entrepreneurs and business managers to provide free advice and guidance.

In this chapter, we examine the twin premises that the VBM can potentially improve access to external micro finance and also lead to better business outcomes in terms of both hard sales turnover and employment growth measures and softer confidence and business skills measures. We proceed by underpinning the chapter with a theoretical discussion from which our research questions and methodology are derived. After outlining our methodological approach, we explore quantitative data from a survey of 491 (mainly) youth entrepreneur mentees drawn from eight countries from four continents served by the YBI volunteer youth business mentoring programme network. Contemporaneous qualitative case studies of mentor-mentee pairings from the YBI case study countries provide further explanatory insight to the findings and leads to the discussion and final conclusions for theory and practical policy development.

LITERATURE

There has been evidence for some time that young people have a higher desire to enter entrepreneurship and self-employment as a career choice, in preference to other forms of employment (Greene, 2005). Younger people are also more positive about entrepreneurial opportunities. A recent YBI/GEM (2013) report indicated that in the EU, 'younger youth' were more positive in their attitudes to good business opportunities and in seeing good opportunities than older people. This evidence is underpinned by a combination of socioeconomic 'pull and push factors', discussed below. These may be considered to have contributed to what Audretsch (2007) described as the rise of the 'Entrepreneurial Society', following the decline of the 'job for life' culture in post-industrial economies. In post-industrial UK, Parliamentary (2015) evidence points to a rise in the 'rate of self-employment' as a proportion of total employment (from 8% in 1975 to around 15% in 2014), driven mainly by people staying in self-employment rather than due to shorter-term economic cycles where higher levels of unemployment can push the unemployed into self-employment. This is due to a combination of 'pull and push factors'. Pull factors have included information technology facilitating home working and self-employment, including through the Gig economy (e.g. 'Uberisation' and Airbnb type promotional web and application channels), alongside the desire for SME growth through flexible tax efficient (or avoiding) labour networks and entrepreneurial lifestyle choices for home working and flexible working hours – particularly, amongst young mothers in a society which has increasingly seen young women seeking work. Push factors have included the out-sourcing of public sector and large corporate services.

Overall, the evidence on self-employment and micro business (businesses with up to 10 employees) growth is uneven over the last decade (Hatfield, 2015), both across Europe and globally. What is clearer is that in lower and developing income countries, such as Chile and India, the rates of self-employment remain high, particularly amongst youths and that within Europe, youth self-employment rates have increased sharply in, for example, Spain and the Netherlands, due to high youth unemployment levels and improved perceptions of self-employment (Hatfield, 2015). It is debatable as to whether this is leading to improved work opportunities and quality of living, or simply a drive to low wage, low production, economies (Lent, 2014; Toft, 2014). Since self-employment amongst youth entrepreneurs appears to have a sustainable and globally important role, what is perhaps more important is to establish how it can be supported and made more successful – and, therefore, more productive in contributing to sustainable economic growth.

From a theoretical perspective, youth entrepreneurs appear to be disadvantaged, as they may lack the experience, knowledge and networks that facilitate successful business start-up and sustainable development. This is particularly highlighted in resource-based theory (Barney, 1991) and associated business finance theories explained below, and was substantially supported by the Eurostat (2005) Factors of Business Success study across 15 European countries, which found that young and less educated entrepreneurs were particularly disadvantaged in accessing seed and early-stage external business finance.

Youth entrepreneurs seeking external finance face both demand-side and supply-side barriers. From a demand-side perspective, young people may have aspirations and the required skills for start-up entrepreneurship, but frequently lack investor readiness (Mason & Kwok, 2010), requiring financial and broader management skills to develop effective business plans and finance applications. They may also be disadvantaged from a supply-side perspective since financial institutions such as the commercial banks, private equity investors and other suppliers of financial debt and equity will see greater risk combined with a lack of track record and credibility, which gives rise to information asymmetries and associated agency and signalling problems (Carpenter & Petersen, 2002; Hsu, 2004; Hughes, 2009; Mueller et al., 2014). This means that aspiring nascent youth entrepreneurs face greater challenges in obtaining mainstream and alternative sources of finance. Practically, unless such young entrepreneurs can call upon deep pockets of the 'bank of Mum and Dad' or family and friends, they may be expected to resort to pragmatic methods of stretching their resources such as financial bootstrapping and bricolage (Mac an Bhaird, 2010; Mac an Bhaird & Lucey, 2015). Although these theoretical and practical issues have long existed for youth entrepreneurship, they have only been exacerbated, particularly in advanced economies, in the post-2007 GFC financial and economic environment, which has seen the withdrawal of mainstream bank debt finance and venture capitalists from seed start-up and early-stage business funding, despite the growth of alternative sources such as equity and debt sources of crowdfunding (Baldock & Mason, 2015; Cowling, Liu, & Ledger, 2012; Harrison & Baldock, 2015).

In the face of such an adversity, many governments (e.g. Chile, Italy, the Netherlands and Spain) have introduced financing instruments to provide microfinance seedcorn funding to assist start-ups (Wilson & Silver, 2013), but these have been less evident in Eastern Europe and few have specifically targeted youth enterprise (OECD, 2014). The UK (Business Innovation and Skills [BIS], 2012) serves as a prime example, establishing the national Start-up Loans company in 2012 to provide 'soft loans' (currently, 6% per annum repayable over five years) of up to £2,500 to youth entrepreneurs aged 18–24. This has subsequently been made available to all UK entrepreneurs aged over 18 with an early-stage business trading for less than two years (i.e. too young to receive either bank debt or government backed crowd funding lending, e.g., through Funding Circle or Zopa). Loans of up to £25,000 are operated through local providers experienced in delivering start-up finance and – learning from the failures of past schemes, such as the Urban Programme in the 1980s (Baldock, 1998), they require a mandatory minimum of 12 months free mentoring support to upskill and advise the young entrepreneurs. In the countries included in our YBI study, public interventions to assist youth entrepreneurship finance are less evident. The main exception is Argentina, where youth entrepreneurs are invited to compete for interest free loans. Each year, three successful applicants receive US $700, repayable over three years on condition that they accept 12 months of free mentoring guidance.

Theoretically, the issues of low experience and credibility can be mitigated by the role of advisors, consultants and/or 'volunteer business mentors' – the focus of this study. In corporations and large organisations, mentors are known to be valuable for early career staff (Clutterbuck, 2004; Haddock-Millar, 2017). By extension with young entrepreneurs, business mentors raise credibility, develop personal and professional competence, business potential and entrepreneurial learning. They may also perform a similar role to the so-called 'smart money hands-on' assistance provided by business angel investors who guide their portfolio businesses through early-stage development and financial managements (Baldock & Mason, 2015; Mason & Harrison, 2015; Whittam, Talbot, & Mac an Bhaird, 2015). From a supply-side perspective, this reduces risk for financial institutions, potentially increasing the likelihood of receiving external finance and improving the likely returns and business outcomes of such financing. Evidence from microfinance initiatives in the UK (see Whittam et al., 2015, on the operations of credit unions; GLA, 2013, in relation to London) and Belgium (OECD, 2014, case of 'Credal Microcredit Co-op') demonstrates that potentially high default rates amongst start-ups can be reduced by ongoing financial management and mentoring support.

> Strong leadership and strict administrative procedures are needed to launch effective microcredit programmes; targeted approaches in microcredit result in bringing excluded groups into mainstream economy; access to microcredit can reduce financial burdens, but not necessarily results in business development … support services such as financial education are effective in improving the general understanding of the borrowing process and can reduce over-indebtedness. OECD (2014, p. 15)

Reporting on lessons learned by the UK Fair Finance Microcredit Programme, guaranteed under the EU's 'Progress Microfinance Facility'.

YOUTH BUSINESS INTERNATIONAL
(YBI) PROGRAMME

At the time of the research, the YBI provided support for the voluntary mentoring of youth enterprises across 42 countries and four continents, working with 46 different member agencies to deliver business support and mentoring. The YBI global network is facilitated by a London-based Network Team, which co-ordinates and leads global activity and has responsibility for driving network growth and quality, including through the delivery of capacity development services to members – thus combining global experience with local delivery expertise. The aim is to encourage under-served youth enterprise start-up and development delivered by a consistent high-quality service that is continually learning and improving across the network and is inclusive to all types of youth entrepreneur. Members provide integrated support to under-served youth entrepreneurs, which typically include mentoring, business education and other business development services, combined in many cases with provision and/or facilitation of finance (generally loans). The YBI members adapt this support to the needs and opportunities in their local context, working in partnership with governments, businesses and multilateral and civil-society organisations.

A cornerstone of the service is the VBMs, who are attracted to the service through business networks or, in some cases, via partnership with large corporate sponsors, such as Accenture and JP Morgan, alongside local businesses. They therefore come from a wide range of backgrounds, quite often involving self-employment and business start-up experience, and include a wide range of managerial skills, such as finance, marketing and product/service development. They are typically mature, well-educated, experienced business people from a wide variety of social backgrounds and business sectoral activities, who share a common goal to help young in-experienced entrepreneurs through guidance and support.

Mentoring is often an essential part of the support package that the YBI members provide to young entrepreneurs. It is also a vital ingredient in the success of that support package, helping to ensure any finance is used effectively and complements the non-financial elements. Moreover, it is central to what makes the YBI model unique, distinguishing their approach from other microcredit-centred initiatives. The YBI network is sector leading, currently encompassing over 15,000 volunteer business mentors, who are dedicated to supporting young entrepreneurs. In 2015, the YBI network supported 18,949 young people to start or grow a business and provided practical skills-based training to more than 65,000 people.

Ultimately, since most VBM services are delivered one-to-one (an exception is Uganda, where entrepreneurial group mentoring is also held), the success of schemes may be largely down to the chemistry and meeting of minds between the mentor and mentee. Currently, within the YBI network, 29 member agencies offer VBM (including two in the UK) and seven countries have enterprise finance schemes. Amongst our case countries Russia, India and Argentina have enterprise finance schemes, which require the VBM assistance and, in India, this can continue formally beyond the YBI standard scheme duration of 12 months. Therefore, in the vast majority of cases, the use of VBMs is an optionally selected free service by the youth entrepreneur and is not accompanied by a specific finance scheme, although as we have discussed external enterprise finance can be an important element of business start-up and development. Whilst the VBM is demonstrably responsible for improved youth enterprise sustainability, for example, in Sweden recent research by the NyforetagarCentrum national agency offering the VBM indicated that 89% (circa 600 business start-ups are assisted annually) of VBM assisted businesses start-ups survive at least three years compared to 83% of their other assisted start-ups and 70% nationally.[3] There is a suggestion that, allied to better access to external finance, these businesses could perform even better. The chapter tests this proposition empirically as explained below.

METHODOLOGY

In examining the role of business mentoring in youth entrepreneurship finance, the chapter poses three distinct and research-related questions (RQs):

(1) To what extent is the youth VBM associated with access to external finance?
(2) Where access to external finance takes place, does the VBM improve the outcomes of the businesses?
(3) To what extent do VBMs make a difference to the performance of businesses receiving financial assistance?

The chapter utilises a mixed methods approach (Creswell, 2003) to collect primary evidence from complementary study approaches. It aims to triangulate evidence between the robust scale of a large quantitative survey and smaller-scale qualitative in-depth interviews with mentees and mentors to form insightful corroborative explanatory evidence, which filters out halo effects and negative bias. This included an online self-completion survey of mentee entrepreneurs to collect mainly quantitative data and case study evidence including in-depth face-to-face mentee-mentor interviews to gain qualitative insight into understanding the operation and value of the mentor process in relation to external finance.

The online Qualtrics survey collected 491 valid completed (largely[4]) youth mentee responses drawn from eight countries in the YBI network. These were selected for their contrasting high (Sweden and Spain), middle (India, Argentina, Chile, Russia and Poland) and lower (Uganda) income economies, global coverage of four continents and operation of established entrepreneurship mentoring schemes. The survey was pilot checked after the first 10 valid respondent cases in each country in order to ensure continuity of responses across the study and generated collective quantitative data on the relationship between mentoring and the access and impact of external finance. The survey was promoted by the lead VBM delivery organisation in each country amongst its current and recent alumni mentees and was held open for responses for one month. Therefore, it included data collected in Autumn 2016 from mentees in current or recently completed formal mentoring relationships within the eight VBM schemes. It should be noted that mentoring across the eight countries is typically delivered in the form of one-to-one mentor-mentee relationship pairings over a mentoring cycle of 12 months. Furthermore, our findings demonstrate that VBMs typically deliver their advice face-to-face on a monthly basis, supported by informal catch-ups by a variety of communication channels, such as telephone, email, Skype and social media.

Second, qualitative interview evidence is taken from the 64 mentor–mentee case study pairings undertaken as part of the eight countries research of the YBI VBM programmes. The Argentinian pairings are particularly relevant because they include recipients of the US$700 loan scheme that requires 12 months VBM support to assist the effective investment of the money in the business. Qualitative interviews were undertaken face-to-face in each of the eight countries with eight pairings of mentors and mentees separately to avoid response bias. Semistructured topic guides ensured the continuity of approach and exploration of the value of the mentoring process in managing the external funding received. Interviews were recorded and transcribed (in some cases, translated into English) and cross checked for accuracy with both the respondent mentors and mentees and also the local VBM programme managers. Case study analysis was undertaken on a case-by-case basis taking into account the comments of both mentor and mentees within each pairing (Eisenhardt, 1989).

FINDINGS

Survey Profile

Our findings are mainly derived from the YBI quantitative online mentee survey. Table 1 presents information on two groups: (i) group one is the combination of mentees indicating that they had received external finance or rated finance support as a high priority (within their top three reasons) for seeking mentoring help, representing 29% of those surveyed; and (ii) group two comprises the 16% of mentees surveyed that received external microfinance through the mentoring programme and were typically required to receive mentoring support for at least 12 months. Nearly two-thirds (64%) of the 80 recipients of programme funding were required to undertake mentoring support and this was largely compulsory in Russia (89%), but far more varied across the longer established widespread Indian network (where 54% of surveyed programme-funded participants were required to have mentoring support).

Table 1 demonstrates the variation of finance support received across the eight country case studies, indicating that it was significantly lower (at beyond 0.001 level) in Poland, Sweden and Spain, where there was little evidence of external finance being associated with the VBM provision. In contrast, we see far higher levels of finance mentoring support where external finance is more

Table 1. Distribution of Mentees by Country and Received
Finance or Financial Mentoring.

Country	(i) Finance Support (Row %)	(ii) Programme Finance Received (Row %)	$N =$
Uganda	70	13	16
Argentina	42	23	19
Chile	44	8	23
Poland	13*	0	32
India	49	42	66
Russia	43	42	84
Sweden	14*	2	110
Spain	19*	6	141
Total of survey	29	16	491

Source: YBI online survey of eight countries, Autumn 2016.
* Significant at >0.001 level.

readily associated with the programme, notably in Russia and India, and in Argentina, Chile and the fledgling Uganda network (although respondent numbers are small).

Taking a broader view across the YBI network countries examined, Table 2 contrasts the key characteristics of the mentee entrepreneurs and their enterprises in relation to whether they received finance support (including external finance). Overall, the data reveal very little difference between the characteristics of those receiving business finance support, which could include external finance, and relate to improving financial management practices, and their counterpart mentees surveyed. The only significant findings are that those receiving finance support were less likely to be female (39%; significant at beyond 0.05 level) and less likely to be older (only one-fifth were aged over 35, significant at >0.05 level).

What is most striking is that amongst the whole survey group, at the time of embarking on the mentoring process there is a very even gender split, which underlines a concern that surveyed women entrepreneurs appear less likely to require or receive finance support. Less than one in 10 consider themselves part of ethnic or minority groups, three-fifths are educated to at least degree level and just over half were already self-employed, with less than one in 10 being unemployed. The small proportion of those previously unemployed appears to support the argument that self-employment is largely a choice, even for youth entrepreneurs, despite the high levels of youth unemployment that exists in many of the case countries. Of course, it could be argued that self-employment was a necessity in order to avoid unemployment. However, unemployment was a more perceptible push factor amongst the over 30s; representing 17% compared to only 7% of younger mentees surveyed. Two-thirds were relatively inexperienced entrepreneurs with two or less years' experience of managing their own businesses, whilst a considerable spread of business activities is exhibited, with the main sectors represented being education, training and health (22%), business and

Table 2. Characteristics of Mentee Entrepreneurs/Enterprises
by Finance Support.

Mentee Characteristics	No Finance Support (Col %)	Finance Support (Col %)	Total (Col %)
Female	52	39*	49
Male	47	60	51
Ethnic minority (EM)	9	7	8
Degree+	60	58	60
Employed	27	25	26
Self employed	51	53	52
Unemployed	9	11	9
Education/training	8	6	8
Age up to 25	14	14	14
26 to 35	53	66	56
36+	33	20*	30
Managed own business – duration			
Not yet	12	11	12
<1 year	25	27	25
1 to 2 years	35	22	31
2–5 years	21	28	23
5+ years	7	13	9
Enterprise activity sector			
Primary/agriculture	3	3	3
Manufacturing/construction	6	6	6
Wholesale/retail/food/accommodation	12	13	12
Infocomms	7	9	7
Bus/professional services	19	11	16
Education/training/health	20	25	22
Personal services	4	7	5
Creative and tourism	12	6	10
Other	18	17	18

Source: YBI online survey of eight countries, Autumn 2016.
*Significant at >0.05 level.

professional services (16%), retail, wholesale, food and accommodation (12%) and tourism and creative industries (10%).

Relationship between VBM and External Finance (RQ1)

We now turn to our twin research questions in relation to: (i) the relationship between VBM and finance support and additionally an assessment of how it may be related to improving access to external microfinance for start-up and early-stage enterprise development; and (ii) whether it adds value to the overall performance of the enterprises supported. Our approach here is relatively straight-forward. Principally, we have a data set of mentees that can be segmented into the following groups: first, those that have received mentoring but did not seek or receive either external finance or business finance advice (which could include financial management advice); second, within our focus counterpart receiving finance support group ($n = 142$) over half (56%, 80 mentees) received programme finance and the majority of these (64%) were then required to receive at least 12 months mentoring assistance. Where mentoring was not a mandatory requirement, it can be stated that, in some of these cases, the received mentoring contributed to accessing finance. Whilst this question was not directly asked, we use the mentees' VBM satisfaction rating for the mentoring assistance received as a proxy for successfully obtaining external finance (Table 3).

Examining the group where finance received was not a mandatory VBM requirement (Table 3 [i]), we find that most (86%) were at least fairly satisfied and 17% felt that the VBM received was most beneficial to them. One in five within this group receiving programme funding viewed the VBM service as least beneficial to them, perhaps, because they felt that the service did not directly contribute to accessing the funds, or that they did not receive sufficient funds to meet their expectations.

This situation is exemplified in India where the process for application for bank loan with support from the VBM organisation worked well. However, several mentees suggested that they would benefit from further loans to expand their business. One specifically mentioned that 'bank loans are given mainly to cover raw material, machinery and infrastructure costs but not for marketing and advertising which has been a challenge'.

Turning to the remaining group, which primarily sought VBM to improve access to finance and financial management skills but did not receive programme funding (Table 3 [ii]), we find that satisfaction levels are less high, with 8% dissatisfied and almost one quarter finding VBM least beneficial for finance related support. The indication here is that dissatisfaction is related to inability to access external finance and that the higher proportion of 'don't knows' (12%) is reflective of uncertainty over accessing funding in the future.

Overall, the evidence suggests that VBM can assist in accessing programme funding (i.e. where programme funding is selectively available to those receiving VBM), but that where external funding may be more difficult to access VBM is

Table 3. Satisfaction with VBM Finance-related Support and Whether Most or Least Beneficial for Finance Support for (i) Programme Funded Recipients not Required to Receive VBM and (ii) Non-recipients of Programme Finance.

Satisfaction Rating	Programme Finance Not Compulsory VBM (Col %)	Assisted, Not Programme Financed (Col %)
Very dissatisfied	0	3
Dissatisfied	0	5
Neutral	10	11
Fairly satisfied	17	18
Very satisfied	48	35
Completely satisfied	21	16
d/k	4	12
Mentoring most beneficial	17	8
Mentoring least beneficial	21	24
Total number	29	62

Source: YBI online survey of eight countries, Autumn 2016.

still helpful, but less successful. Here, it is worth noting that YBI programme funding may be available and lead to mandatory requirement for VBM (e.g. in Russia and Argentina, albeit on a small selective scale), be available through linkages with lenders once VBM is in place and provides intellectual collateral to propositions (e.g. India), or not available at all (e.g. Poland).

Indeed, it should be noted that half (51%) of those using VBM support for finance advice (not programme funded) were very or completely satisfied with the service. Qualitative evidence from Sweden – drawn from programme manager, mentor and mentee interviews – where there is very limited availability of public microfinance suggests that VBMs face a very tough task to satisfy their mentees and that, however creative the advice provided in supporting bootstrapping activities such as cost savings, personal and buyer/supplier finance, these enterprises will be constrained and potentially held back from realising their full growth potential.

Problems associated with the lack of microfinance are evidenced from the Swedish mentee cases. Sweden has no national start-up microfinance programme and very few agencies in the VBM network offer access to microfinance. Several mentees mentioned that such 'finance would help with initial cash-flow, service and marketing development'. This view was also shared by the mentors and the national agency operating the VBM scheme, who would like to see a national scheme in place, which they believe would lead to faster growing and more sustainable businesses through VBM support. In Spain, similar views were also expressed about the lack of national support for existing SME early growth finance.

Impacts of VBM and Finance Support on Business Development (RQ2)

Turning to our second question in relation to the VBM assisting businesses to utilise external finance more effectively and develop, the evidence is a little clearer. Table 4 demonstrates that for our finance support group (the majority of whom received programme finance), there are no significant differences with the comparator non-finance VBM group.[5] Importantly, it can be seen that both groups contain similar proportions of enterprises by the stage of development at the outset of the VBM relationship with 37% in pre-start and 32–35% in early trading up to two years. Although the finance group contains a slightly higher proportion established enterprises, this is not significantly different. Furthermore, each group contains very similar proportions currently in mentoring relationship or completed and similar lengths of mentoring relationships (including where they have followed on) – with a median relationship length of nine months. The slightly longer timescales of mentoring relationships for finance group mentees largely relates to India, where the scheme formally operates beyond 12 months. In conclusion, the main significant difference (>0.1 level) is that a far higher proportion of mentee enterprises in the finance group have progressed to currently being established (71%, compared to 51%).

Further examination of the impacts of VBM in relation to mentee enterprise performance comparing between where the VBM was not related to finance (Table 5 [i]) to where either finance advice and support (Table 5 [ii] – group

Table 4. Mentoring Relationship and Business Stage Development.

Mentoring Relationship ($n = 485$)	Not Finance Support (Col %)	Finance Support (Col %)	Total (Col %)
Pre-mentoring	4	2	4
Current	59	58	59
Completed	32	35	32
Ended prematurely	6	5	5
Time in mentoring relationship (including where follow-on)			
Up to 3 months	20	19	20
3–6 months	16	18	16
6–9 months	15	14	14
9–12 months	31	24	29
12+ months	18	25	21
Business stage at start of mentoring			
Pre-start	37	37	37
Just started	35	32	35
Established	23	30	26
Business stage currently			
Pre-start	15	11	15
Just started	23	14	20
Established	51	71*	62

Source: YBI online survey of eight countries, Autumn 2016.
*Significant at >0.1 level.

includes where programme finance used) or the sub-group receiving programme finance (Table 5 [iii]) demonstrates a clear trend towards improved performance for the finance group, particularly for the programme funding recipients – both in terms of hard indicators, such as employment and job generation, and softer indicators, such as improved management skills and confidence.

Comparing the finance and non-finance VBM groups, sales turnover and job increases are significantly (>0.05 level) more likely to occur within the finance group. Furthermore, these significant differences are even more pronounced amongst the group receiving programme finance, with almost twice the proportion mentee enterprises increasing sales turnover (63%) and jobs (86%) since starting VBM compared to the non-finance group. Also, those receiving VBM finance assistance were significantly (>0.1 level) more likely to attribute this growth to the mentoring support received.

In terms of softer indicators, the abovementioned trends are similarly evident although the only significant improvement evidenced in the finance group relates to business planning (>0.1 level).

Qualitative Case Study Evidence
Drawing on the qualitative case study evidence there is clear instructive evidence from entrepreneur mentees interviewed from the Argentinian VBM scheme that have benefited considerably from receiving programme funding allied to 12 months VBM support. The following two cases are highly illustrative of this.

Table 5.   Mentee Business Development Indicators by (i) Non-finance,
(ii) Finance Support and (iii) Programme Finance Groups.

	Not Finance (Col %)	Finance Group (Col %)	Programme Finance (Col %)	Total ($n = 385$)
Sales turnover increase	32	47**	63	37
Jobs increase	42	70**	86	64
Range jobs increase	1–182	1–250	1–100	1–250
Median jobs increase	3	4	4	3
VBM attributed % of jobs increase	46	58*	57	48
Soft indicators (where perceived significant or complete improvement)				
Management skills	39	51	61	43
Financial management skills	36	38	44	37
Presentation/promotion	29	38	47	32
Networking	34	38	42	36
Confidence running business	51	57	63	53
Personal confidence	40	43	45	41
Self esteem	49	53	57	50
Decision making	49	53	53	50
Business Plan	32	40*	46	35

Source: YBI online survey of eight countries, Autumn 2016.
*Significant at >0.1 level; ** significant at >0.05 level; soft indicators are drawn from perceived significant or complete improvement responses from a Likert scale.

The first case relates to a lady who moved out of employment to start up her own children's party business in 2014. She successfully applied for a US$700 loan to assist start-up from Fundacion Impulsar, the organisation running the VBM programme, and was provided with a mentor for 12 months with experienced in business strategy and possessing a post-graduate business coaching qualification. The mentee explained that 'Taking the risk of going independent when other people depend on you is scary … my mentor guided and accompanied me in the process of investing the funds'. It was clear that the relationship really 'connected' and made fundamental differences to how the business plan was developed and funds were invested. 'I was questioned and challenged about marketing, pricing and costs and guided towards better investments'. This has resulted in reassessing marketing expenditure and switching from less successful magazine advertising to developing a highly successful promotional website for the business. The business now employs six people alongside several subcontractors undertaking catering and photography and is well established with a wide client base in Buenos Aires.

The second case relates to a rural business manufacturing and selling marmalade, which originally failed due to poor management decisions, mainly through failure to understand planning regulations, which prevented manufacturing taking place in the premises that were acquired. The male mentee decided to re-start the business and successfully secured a start-up loan alongside 12 months free mentoring in 2015. 'The loan and mentoring advice has been helpful in contributing towards the costs of designing product labelling to attract the tourist market, transforming the business'. The business is now on a stable footing and looking to scale-up. A sign of the successful bonding of these two mentoring relationship cases is that they have both continued informally since the formal 12 month's cycle has been completed.

DISCUSSION: THEORETICAL AND POLICY IMPLICATIONS FOR VBM AND MICROFINANCE

This extensive study of the VBM across eight country case studies in the YBI network has demonstrated that there is a close association between the VBM and access to external finance (RQ1) and the VBM can considerably enhance the performance of assisted businesses, most notably when external finance is accessed (RQ2). We also consider here the extent to which VBM has made a difference in the performance of the businesses where finance has been received (RQ3).

First, with regard to RQ1, the VBM is closely associated with access to microfinance, either through the direct requirement for programme finance to be supported by the VBM (i.e. in Argentina and Russia), or through the VBM leading to access to bank loans in the case of India. This evidence strongly supports the resource based view (Barney 1991; Mac an Bhaird, 2010) that start-ups and young entrepreneurs benefit from external assistance to overcome a series of shortcomings in relation to their lack of trading track record, collateral and the information asymmetries, which would otherwise prevent them from accessing finance. Having a VBM can help investment readiness (Mason & Kwok, 2010) in terms of developing business plans and financial forecasts, but can also boost their reputation as a legitimate recipient of external support and provide the lender with confidence that an experienced business manager will be guiding the investment decisions and business development, therefore, making the business far more likely to succeed and grow sustainably (Baldock, 1998).

Second, with regard to RQ2, there is very strong evidence from our study that those mentee enterprises receiving the VBM assisting accessing finance and financial management, particularly those receiving programme microfinance have performed significantly better than those that have not been associated with the VBM for financial assistance. Furthermore, with regard to RQ3, the findings here are strikingly consistent and send a clear message in terms of the value of the VBM when associated with external finance. They completely support the findings of Baldock (1998) and assertions of Clutterbuck (2004) and Greene (2005) that the VBM can add considerably to the performance of young enterprises by guiding them through strategic business planning for development, ensuring efficient and effective use of external finance in meeting practical and achievable objectives. Our quantitative evidence is backed up by case studies demonstrating the value of this guidance in improving business plans, improving services and products and developing appropriate marketing and pricing strategies. Furthermore, experienced VBMs are well networked and can help to find customers and develop mentee skills in a whole range of key business and personal areas such as raising confidence and self-esteem and improving marketing and presentational skills, as well as improving management and financial management skills. It appears that the development of these skills allied to accessing external microfinance can make a significant difference to the growth (in terms of sales turnover and job creation) and sustainability of the youth business through start-up and early growth phases. There is strong support, therefore, for the view that microfinance is most effectively used when there is ongoing support to overcome young entrepreneur management deficiencies, and that the VBMs can affectively provide guidance that is similar to the 'smart money hands-on management role' that business angel investors can perform for their portfolio firms (Baldock & Mason, 2015; Mason & Harrison, 2015; Whittam et al., 2015).

These findings have important policy ramifications. First, they demonstrate that the VBM can improve start-up and early growth stage business viability and position it better in terms of finding, applying and successfully accessing external microfinance. Indeed, some members refer to the crucial role that the VBM plays in providing additional 'intellectual collateral' to facilitate loans. This is important as it potentially speeds up the process of accessing appropriate finance, ensures that viable businesses are funded and reduces the likelihood of wasting the time of financiers and problems of adverse selection, making the whole process more efficient and ultimately more successful for all parties. Second, the outcome of the microfinance investment is considerably improved in terms of sustainability of start-up and young business, loan repayment and wider economic growth outcomes, if the VBM is employed for at least 12 months. A final point here is that the VBM is a free service to entrepreneurs, the cost of administering such a service is very low, relating to recruiting, training and retaining a network of suitable mentors. Providing post start-up support can be expensive, whereas operating a VBM service can considerably lower costs – a factor which may not be widely appreciated outside of the YBI network. It would appear that for a relatively small investment, the VBM can add considerable value to a start-up microfinance programme and this has been adopted by the UK's start-up Loans company scheme (GLA, 2013). For countries, such as Sweden, where there is no national start-up microfinance scheme, or Spain, where there is no SME early-stage business growth finance scheme, it would appear that there are strong arguments for doing so.

CONCLUSIONS

Given the continuing importance of self-employment, particularly for youth entrepreneurs across the globe, this chapter provides some important theoretical and policy messages. An important observation is that for the vast majority of youth entrepreneurs, self-employment is a choice (not a forced out of economic recession and high unemployment) and that it is likely to continue to be so. If this is the cases, it is probably wise to assist under-served youth business start-ups, including those from diverse cultural backgrounds and neighbourhoods, and to ensure that they have the best chance of success and can contribute effectively to the wider economy.

This chapter has demonstrated the value of the VBM both in terms of improving access to external microfinance, and in improving the performance of assisted youth enterprises. The study provides a global perspective and consistent evidence in terms of quantitative survey findings and also qualitative case interviews. The message for theory and policy would appear to be that the VBM has a crucial role to play in providing a cost-effective way of accessing and successfully utilising microfinance to grow sustainable youth enterprises that such businesses can be economically productive, providing a blueprint for other countries to follow.

The study has some limitations associated with cross-sectional research with relatively small numbers of respondents in some countries. However, it does provide a robust and clear evidence in support of the VBM in relation to improving access and use of microfinance and a framework for future longitudinal research.

ACKNOWLEDGMENTS

The researchers are grateful for funding received from the YBI through its partnership with Accenture and the OECD's programme for Local Economic and Employment Development (LEED).

NOTES

1. Paper for Finance Track at ISBE, Belfast 2017.
2. The EU defines microfinance/credit (e.g. grants, loans, subsidies and guarantees) as valued up to 25,000 Euros for microbusinesses with under 10 employees (OECD, 2014).
3. Almi (2015), Swedish national business support programme 2015 research.
4. The Swedish voluntary mentoring scheme is not exclusive to youth entrepreneurs and some entrepreneurs were marginally over the age of 35, at the time of starting their programmes.
5. Mann–Whitney two-tail U-test shows no statistical difference for the pre-mentoring characteristics between the two groups at 0.05 level, with p-value of 0.97606 (z-score $= -0.02887$; critical value $= 37$; U-value $= 71$).

REFERENCES

Almi. (2015). *Almi foretagspartner utvarderang av mentorprogram, 2015*. Sweden: Stockholm.
Audretsch, D. B. (2007). *The entrepreneurial society*. Oxford: Oxford University Press.
Baldock, R., & Mason, C., (2015). UK government equity schemes, post GFC: The roles of the Enterprise Capital Funds and Angel Co-investment Fund in the new UK finance escalator. *Venture Capital, 17*(1–2), 59–86.
Baldock, R. (1998). Ten years of the urban programme 1981–91: The impact and implications of its assistance to small businesses. *Urban Studies, 35*(11), 2063–2083.
Barney, J. (1991). Firm resources and sustained competitive advantage. *Journal of Management, 17*(1), 99–120.
BIS. (2012). Start-up loans for young entrepreneurs. Department for Business Innovation and Skills (BIS, now BEIS), posted May 28, 2012. Retrieved from https://www.gov.uk/government/news/start-up-loans-for-young-entrepreneurs

Carpenter, R. E., & Petersen, B. C. (2002). Capital market imperfections, high-tech investment, and new equity financing. *The Economic Journal, 112*(477): F54–F72. doi:10.1111/14680297.00683

Clutterbuck, D. (2004). *Everyone needs a mentor: Fostering talent in your organisation,*. London: Chartered Institute for Personnel and Development.

Cowling, M., Liu, W., & Ledger, A. (2012). Small business financing in the UK before and during the current financial crisis. *International Small Business Journal, 30*(7), 778–800.

Creswell, J. W. (2003). *Qualitative, quantitative and mixed methods approaches*. Thousand Oaks, CA: Sage.

Eisenhardt, K. M. (1989). Building theories from case study research. *Academy of Management Review, 14*(4), 532–550.

Eurostat. (2005). Factors of Business Success. Data retrieved 01/07/2018 https://ec.europa.eu/eurostat/web/structural-business-statistics/ad-hoc-data-collections/business-success?p_p_id=NavTreeportletprod_WAR_NavTreeportletprod_INSTANCE_yEOylYvlwNOW&p_p_lifecycle=0&p_p_state=normal&p_p_mode=view&p_p_col_id=column-2&p_p_col_pos=1&p_p_col_count=2

GLA. (2013). SME Finance in London. Report by SQW and CEEDR to the Greater London Authority.

Greene, F. J. (2005). *Evaluating youth entrepreneurship: The case of the Prince's Trust*. Working Paper, No. 8. Warwick Centre for SMEs, Warwick University.

Haddock-Millar, J. (2017). The mentoring cycle. In D. A. Clutterbuck, F. K. Kochan, L. Lunsford, N. Dominguez, & J. Haddock-Millar (Eds.), *The SAGE handbook of mentoring* (pp. 156–168). London: SAGE.

Harrison, R., & Baldock, R. (2015). Financing SME growth in the UK: Meeting the challenges after the global financial crisis. *Venture Capital, 17*(1–2), 1–6.

Hatfield, I. (2015). *Self-employment in Europe*. Report by the Institute for Public Policy Research (IPPR), London. Retrieved from http://www.ippr.org/files/publications/pdf/self-employment-Europe_Jan2015.pdf?noredirect=1. Accessed on January 2015.

Hsu, D. (2004). What do entrepreneurs pay for venture capital affiliation? *Journal of Finance, 59*(4), 1805–1844.

Hughes, A. (2009). Innovation and SMEs: Hunting the Snark: Some reflections on the UK experience of support for the small business sector. *Innovation, Management, Policy and Practice, 11*(1), 114–126. doi:10.5172/impp.453.11.1.114

Lent, A. (2014). *International data shows there's no need to panic about the rise in self-employment and micro businesses*. The Regional Studies Association, posted 13/04/2014. Retrieved from https://www.thersa.org/discover/publications-and-articles/rsa-blogs/2014/04/international-data-shows-theres-no-need-to-panic-about-the-rise-in-self-employment-and-micro-business. Accessed on April 5, 2017.

Mac an Bhaird, C. (2010). Firm financing: A resource based view. *Paper to the 33rd Institute of Small Business and Entrepreneurship conference*, November, London.

Mac an Bhaird, C., & Lynn, T. (2015). Seeding the cloud: Financial bootstrapping in the computer software sector. *Venture Capital, 17*(1–2), 151–170.

Mason, C., & Harrison, R. (2015). Business angel investment activity in the financial crisis: UK evidence and policy implications. *Environment and Planning C: Government and Policy, 33*, 43–60.

Mason, C. M., & Kwok, K. (2010). Investment readiness programmes and access to finance: a critical review of design issues, *Local Economy, 25*(4), 269–292.

Mueller, C., Westhead, P., & Wright, M. (2014). Formal venture capital acquisition: Can entrepreneurs compensate for the spatial proximity benefits of south east of England and 'star' golden triangle universities? *Environment and Planning A, 44*(2), 281–296.

OECD. (2013). The missing entrepreneurs: Policies for inclusive entrepreneurship in Europe. Paris: OECD Publishing.

OECD. (2014). Policy Brief on Access to Business start-up finance for Inclusive Entrepreneurship. Published by the European Commission, Luxembourg. Retrieved from http://www.oecd.org/cfe/leed/Finacing%20inclusive%20entrepreneurship%20policy%20brief%20EN.pdf

Toft, S. (2014). *More freelancers than public employees, is that really a good thing?* Posted 10/04/2014. Retrieved from https://flipchartfairytales.wordpress.com/2014/04/10/more-freelancers-than-public-employees-is-that-really-a-good-thing/. Accessed on April 5, 2017.

UK Parliament. (2015). The self-employment boom: Key issues for the 2015 parliament. Retrieved from https://www.parliament.uk/business/publications/research/key-issues-parliament-2015/work/self-employment/. Accessed on April 5, 2017.

Whittam, G., Talbot, S., & Mac an Bhaird, C. (2015). Can credit unions bridge the gap in lending to SMEs? *Venture Capital.*, *17*(1–2), 113–128.

Wilson, K., & Silva, F. (2013). *Policies for Seed and Early Stage Finance: Findings from the 2012 OECD Finance Questionnaire*, OECD Science, Technology and Industry Policy Papers No. 9. OECD Publishing, Paris.

YBI/GEM. (2013). *Generation entrepreneur? The state of global youth entrepreneurship: Understanding the entrepreneurial attitudes, aspirations and activities of young people.* London: Youth Business International, Global Entrepreneurship Monitor.

CHAPTER 8

REFLECTIONS ON TECHNIUM SWANSEA: AMBITION, LEARNING AND PATIENCE

Gareth Huw Davies, Sian Roderick, Michael D. Williams and Roderick Thomas

ABSTRACT

The Technium initiative started in 2001 with an initial Business and Innovation Centre established in the Swansea docklands area. Early success of this first Technium building led to the concept being rapidly proliferated into a pan-Wales network of primarily sector-focussed centres. Although the Welsh Government withdrew its support for the Technium network initiative in 2010, the individual centres continued under a range of ownerships and the historic initiative of continued interest, particularly with respect to regional policy.

A vibrant policy and practice debate subsequently emerged together with strident media comment. Lack of coherence between Technium Centres and weaknesses in monitoring systems meant this debate has been poorly informed. This case study helps address the evidence deficit within this debate by revisiting the initial Technium Swansea initiative and its subsequent development.

The case study provides an insight into what can realistically be expected of such initiatives in the short, medium and long terms, with realistic time-horizons for 'success' and the role of learning for knowledge-based development in similar initiatives and regions.

Keywords: Incubation; clusters; regional innovation systems; regional policy; innovation; Public Policy

Creating Entrepreneurial Space: Talking Through Multi-voices, Reflections on Emerging Debates
Contemporary Issues in Entrepreneurship Research, Volume 9B, 137–151
Copyright © 2019 by Emerald Publishing Limited
All rights of reproduction in any form reserved
ISSN: 2040-7246/doi:10.1108/S2040-72462019000009B008

INTRODUCTION

The Technium initiative was created as a pan-Wales business incubation and support network during the period 2000–2010, as part of the then recently devolved nation's efforts to support knowledge-based economic development. While the Technium Centres now operate independently, the initiative continues to feature in academic and policy debate as providing learning for the support of knowledge-based enterprise in the context of regional economic development. The debate, to date, has focussed predominantly on the fortunes of the 'network', which emerged, though without reference or detail relating to the initiative's initial stated ambitions.

This chapter uses the origins of the Technium initiative to explore implications for technology entrepreneurship support within regional economic development policy. The initiative's context also relates significantly to the role of universities and other agencies in supporting enterprise. The aim of this chapter is to revisit the original Technium ambition in order to identify learning from both its own progress and subsequent discourse.

The Technium initiative started in 2001 with an initial Business and Innovation Centre in the Swansea docklands area, since rebranded as the 'SA1 Waterfront'. The Centre became a flagship project in the emerging economic development policy of the then recently devolved Welsh Assembly Government and the longer-standing Welsh Development Agency (WDA). Early success of the first 'Technium' building led to the concept being rapidly proliferated into a pan-Wales network of primarily sector-focussed Centres (WEFO, 2007).

Growing interest in knowledge-based economic development, particularly in the context of recently devolved UK nations (Cooke, 2004; Huggins & Kitagawa, 2012) made the programme of significant interest, due mainly to its scale, nature and ambition. A vibrant policy debate subsequently emerged around the effectiveness of this concentrated capital investment (Abbey, Davies, & Mainwaring, 2008; Cooke, 2004; Cooke & Clifton, 2005), together with what could be viewed as sensational media comment.

This chapter works to address a widely accepted evidence deficit, revisiting the initial SA1 site to examine Technium Swansea (including its Technium 2 grow-on phase) and the subsequent development of companies observed during a 2007 benchmark study. The chapter undertakes this review within the initial and current contexts, with a particular regard to the Centre's role within the sub-Regional Innovation System (RIS) described by Abbey et al. (2008).

ECONOMIC AND DEVOLVED GOVERNMENT POLICY CONTEXT

South-west Wales was the crucible of the first Industrial Revolution, providing coal and steel that powered an empire. However, the massive contraction of these industries, which started with the Great Depression, saw accelerated decline in the 1970s and 1980s (Morgan, 2001). This led to a regional development strategy delivered by the WDA, attracting significant inward investment and employment, primarily in branch plant manufacturing for multinational enterprises (Heidenreich et al., 1998). However, weak embeddedness (Phelps, Mackinnon, Stone, & Braidford, 2003) and emergence of lower-cost destinations (Chen, 1996) saw investments and employment starting to drift elsewhere. Continued contraction of heavy industries, coupled with erosion of existing, and intense competition for new inward-investment manufacturing opportunities shifted economic policy towards the development of indigenous and inward-investing knowledge-based enterprise, as called for by leading observers (Cooke & Clifton, 2005).

Devolution brought to Wales responsibility for its own economic policy, which led to a number of key strategies (WAG, 2004b, 2005, 2010; WG, 2013), with the focus on innovation to develop technology clusters (WAG, 2003; WG, 2014) and the role of the regional science base, which consisted primarily of university research output (WAG, 2009). This policy context had led to a vibrant research and policy debate (Abbey et al., 2008; Salvador & Harding, 2006), including comparison with other devolved nations within the UK (Cooke & Clifton, 2005), and specifically the role of universities in economic development (Huggins & Kitagawa, 2012).

During the period prior to comparatively low regional Business Expenditure on Research & Development (Rogers, 2006) to support innovation brought attention to the role of universities, during a period of particular interest from national (Lambert, 2003) and regional (WAG, 2004a) governments. Universities are intensely studied as drivers of innovation and regional development (Audretsch & Lehmann, 2005), including their role of creating mass within peripheral regions (Siegel, Wright, & Lockett, 2007), though the mechanism by which this may occur remains subject to continued debate (Casper & Karamanos, 2003; Huggins & Kitagawa, 2012; Power & Malmberg, 2008).

In this context, the Technium network became a significant part of this policy agenda (WAG, 2003, 2004b), with this now historic initiative being of continued interest, particularly with respect to regional policy (Cooke, 2013; Huggins & Kitagawa, 2012; Morgan, 2013).

THEORETICAL CONTEXT

The Technium initiative relates to a broad theoretical context involving regional development, urban regeneration, knowledge-based enterprise and University–Industry interaction. At its core, a primary stated ambition was cluster development, with the aim of providing high-value enterprise and employment within a RIS.

Cluster theory, particularly since the concept was pioneered by Porter (1998), has attracted significant interest of policy makers (BEIS, 2017; DTI, 2001; EU, 2010) with the the attraction of potential for sustained high-value employment (McKinsey, 2014), greater productivity and firm growth (Delgado, Porter, & Stern, 2010; Porter, 2000), and increased levels of innovation (Baptista & Swann, 1998).

There has been a longstanding debate regarding government ability to 'pro-gramme' cluster development (Chiaroni & Chiesa, 2006; Menzel & Fornahl, 2009; Porter, 2000), while the effectiveness of programmed cluster development is chal-lenged (Brakman & van Marrewijk, 2013; Swords, 2013), with efforts required to provide a deeper understanding of the concept (Ketels, 2013). Embedded in much of this discussion is the role of universities as sources of knowledge and skills, particularly with regard to knowledge-based technology-focussed sectors (Cooke, 2001; McKinsey, 2014; Porter, 2000).

The cluster concept aligns with the Innovation Systems concept introduced by Lundvall (1992) and Nelson (1993), and developed at a regional level (RIS) by researchers, including specifically in the context of Wales (Cooke, 2001; Heidenreich et al., 1998), and sub-regionally with discussion of the role of Technium (Abbey et al., 2008; Cooke, 2001) framed with five key linked concepts of *Region, Innovation, Network, Learning* and *Interaction*, which are useful in considering the role of Technium along with the 'programmed' cluster requirements identified by Su and Hung (2009) of: *a strong science and industry base; finance supporting mechanisms; entrepreneurship; social capital;* and *networking*.

More recently, this regional economic development context has evolved to include smart specialisation (Foray, 2014; Foray, David, & Hall, 2009), including specifically with regard to Wales (Morgan, 2013; Pugh, 2014) and Technium itself (Morgan, 2013).

TECHNIUMS 1 AND 2: TECHNIUM SWANSEA

Technium Swansea was originally proposed as an independent Business Innovation Centre (BIC) in south-west Wales. The initial European Regional Development Fund (ERDF) 'Objective 2'-supported initiative involved a capital funding project running from September 1999 to December 2001. The project proposal (SIHE, 1999) presented a central objective that it 'supports the crea-tion of a diversified industrial base and the successful exploitation of innovation'. This was positioned as a response to the 1998 RTP Action Plan (WDA, 1996) statements that 'Incubator facilities are a proven success in Wales and need to be developed further' and for 'new forms of Higher Education/Business Interface to support wealth creation'. The initial project proposal also cited a report from con-sultants DTZ on 'Economic Strategy for Swansea' calling for flagship schemes, which 'centre on physical building' and 'brings together a number of firms which are succeeding through knowledge-driven strategies'.

The Technium 1 facility provided 1,400s.m. lettable space, which was then followed by 2,600s.m. of space in the Technium 2, subsequently combining to become Technium Swansea. Technium 2, per the project application, had the pri-mary objective 'to help satisfy the demand created by the successful Technium I project' (WDA, 2001). The project described anticipated 'longer-term tenancies' stating that 'typically, a knowledge driven business would take five years to evolve', and that supported companies would 'eventually' be located in private sector facilities. The application also introduced the concept of an 'emerging Technium network'. Evidence of demand for the project is presented as the growth of companies within the fully occupied Technium 1 together with the continued absence of suitable private sector facilities.

The Key Performance Indicators (KPIs) for the two projects also reflected a mission broader than solely relating to start-up and incubation of new firms. As shown in the summaries below (Tables 1 and 2), drawn as excerpts from the original project proposals, these KPIs included activity relating to engagement with existing enterprises and supporting safeguarding of jobs in the wider region.

Technium 2 is explicitly defined in its ERDF funding application as an expansion of the first facility, though in parallel, by 2002 the ambition to realise a 'network' of sector-specific centres across Wales had been developed (Clement & Davies, 2002). This rollout of further Centres followed, supported primarily by the ERDF and the Welsh Government investment (WEFO, 2007). The transition to the following (2007–2013 Convergence) EU Structural Funds Programme saw

Table 1.   Technium 1: ERDF Project Indicators Excerpt (SIHE, 1999).

Technium 1: Project Cost: £3,154,140	Grant: £1,558,320
ERDF Monitoring Indicator	Amount
Jobs created directly within Technium 1	6
New companies created within Technium 1	15
New products processes adopted by assisted SMEs	30
Number of existing SMEs contacted	600
New products and processes developed by assisted SMEs	60
R&D centres created	1
Jobs created within expanding SMEs and new companies in the period of the project	60
New productive linkages between SMEs and technology providers	90
Percentage increase in turnover in assisted SMEs	15%

Table 2.   Technium 2: ERDF Project Indicators Excerpt (WDA, 2001).

Technium 2: Project Cost: £6,436,977	Grant: £3,288,257
ERDF Monitoring Indicator	Amount
Firms provided with advice on innovation and Research & Technology Development	300
Collaborative projects between firms and research institutions	50
Projects transferring environmental technology to the business sector	1
Creation of one innovation centre	1
Floor space constructed in innovation centre	39,000 sq.ft.
New firms created including those from academic institutions	50
Increase in turnover of supported firms	£50 m
Gross new firms created	50
Gross jobs safeguarded	500
Gross jobs created in high technology sectors	150
New patents / trademarks registered	15
R&D expenditure	£10 m

the request for further investment (WG, 2009), though the Welsh Government withdrew its support for the Technium network in 2010 (WG, 2011). Individual centres continued under a range of ownerships, including Techniums 1 & 2, which were sold by the Welsh Government to the University of Wales Trinity Saint David, which continues to operate them as an integrated BIC.

APPROACH

Recognising the study's ambition to explore how the Technium concept developed in terms of policy and practice, together with the inherent complexity presented earlier, a case study approach has been adopted. The aim of reviewing the initiative against its evolving context and accompanying discourse lends itself to this approach.

Drawing upon principles of Yin (2017), the retrospective nature of the study involves no control over events, while the unstructured existing literature makes for valuable though disparate inputs. Adopting this case study approach, this Chapter investigates the Technium 1 & 2 Centres by reviewing their progress against their original objectives, using the case study approach below adapted from Stake (1995), and applied by Huxtable-Thomas, Hannon, and Thomas (2015) to examine an European Social Fund activity, itself a retrospective review of a complex case in a similar context. This approach supports the inclusion of multiple contexts and aligns with the continued development of the research, including through an ongoing longitudinal study (Fig. 1).

As introduced in prior sections, the Technium case exists in the contexts of RISs, Cluster Development, Local Regeneration and the Welsh Government

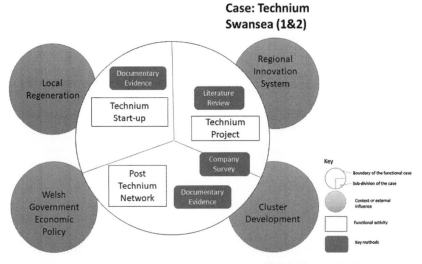

Fig. 1.   Case Approach. Adapted from Huxtable-Thomas et al. (2015).

Economic Policy. It is approached in this chapter applying mixed methods (Creswell & Clark, 2007) involving:

* Review of the original Techniums 1 & 2 project proposals provided by the project sponsors.
* A survey of Technium firms, undertaken in 2007, using data collection subsequently used in later studies of other knowledge-based development initiatives (RLP, 2013).
* Review of current occupancy and recent notable throughput, drawn from Companies House, landlord and other public records.

The aforementioned framework also supports the integration of further data and methods to build upon findings from within this chapter and elsewhere. This incorporates insight from quantitative work such as that of DTZ (2010) and Murphy, Huggins, and Thompson (2015), along with qualitative work including that from Cooke (2004) and Pugh (2017). This approach has been adopted to also support continued development of the longitudinal study of Technium Swansea, as well as providing a basis for planned examination of the cases of other Technium centres.

EXISTING DISCUSSION OF TECHNIUM

Technium has been a cause célèbre for academics and political pundits, though debated with limited data apart from headline figures, with the notable exception of the work of Murphy et al. (2015) and the facts contained within a report by DTZ (2009) as the part of an evaluation undertaken for the Welsh Government. Commentary from observers spanned from 2003, when the UK Government was calling for its continued support (Lambert, 2003), through to the Welsh Government was withdrawing its support for the wider network in 2010 (WG, 2011), and beyond (Cooke, 2013).

Lack of coherence between Technium Centres and weaknesses in monitoring systems, as noted in the DTZ (2009) evaluation, has contributed to this debate being poorly informed. This echoed observation highlighting that limited, and often erroneously quoted, figures were misinforming the debate (Abbey et al., 2008). Indeed, lack of clarity even within the Welsh (Assembly) Government, during the early stages (2003), was highlighted by Cooke (2004).

Much debate has focussed on the network, or simply the aggregate, of Technium Centres (Cooke, 2004) without consideration at the level of the individual centre. The discussion of Huggins and Kitagawa (2012) and the insight of Murphy et al. (2015) recognise that the set of Centres is heterogeneous, and noting much Technium success is associated with a small number of Centres. This is also reflected more recently by Cooke (2013), in his discussion of the positive and negative aspects of path interdependence, demonstrated respectively by the initial Technium 1, and the subsequent 'network' Centres.

A lack of management control/coherence (DTZ, 2009; Morgan, 2013) and an apparent focus on property development rather than operating as a knowledge/ innovation initiative (Cooke, 2004) and (Gibson, 2007) are central criticisms of Technium. These are accompanied by a charge of overcapacity in sectors/regions (Cooke, 2004) and weak academic links in some Centres (Huggins & Kitagawa, 2012) (Cooke, 2013). Further, it is regarded by some as there having been a missed opportunity to learn from the first Technium, prior to the rollout of the network (Cooke, 2013; Morgan, 2013), or establish a rationale for further intervention as firmly as for the first Centre (DTZ, 2009). It is suggested that this may be at least partly attributable to haste in exploiting the ERDF funding window, which was open at the time (Cooke, 2013).

Positive contributions of Technium noted in the literature focus on its early stages, including initial performance in job creation and strong links with academia (Abbey et al., 2008; Huggins & Kitagawa, 2012), underscoring the importance of looking back to its origins.

An interesting more recent discussion is provided by Morgan (2013), presenting a comparison between more focussed sector-specific smart specialisation interventions and the state-orchestrated rather diverse foci of the Technium network. Ironically, the highly successful 'SPECIFIC' solar energy initiative, offered by Morgan as an example of good practice, has been based in the former Technium Sustainable Technologies centre, undertaking precisely the form of innovation desired by the original Technium vision.

However, perhaps the most notable aspects of the existing academic debate are the notable gaps, including any granularity, apart from work by Murphy et al. (2015), and sparse consideration of the years since the withdrawal of the Welsh Government support. Individual Technium Centres continue to operate with local management arrangements with new branding, and the lessons learned from the process appear to have informed subsequent incubation and acceleration activities across the region (Morgan, 2013; SU, 2017).

SURVEY RESULTS AND DOCUMENTARY EVIDENCE

An initial baseline for a survey of Technium Swansea is provided by the initial Technium 1 project summary, cited in the DTZ (2010) report. The project phase ended in September 2001 reporting creation of 54 jobs (90% of 60 job target). A later survey of Technium Swansea firms was undertaken by Swansea University in June 2007, after the Technium 2 project phase had concluded in March 2006. This presented an 82% response rate (nine of 11 companies) from tenants. The respondents reported a combined employment of growth of 116.5 FTE during the supported period, which aligns with the 110 (73% of 150 target) noted in the 2006 progress report (DTZ, 2010) and which would (or at least should, according to the ERDF targets in Table 2) have also included wider sector employment created. Five of the respondent firms were founded prior to Technium, with a combined employment of 25.5 FTE during their first year, though collectively added 44FTE in the period to 2007 (i.e. 48% of new employment).

While the DTZ (2009) evaluation refers to a lack of data relating to the nature of jobs created, notably in terms of graduate opportunities, the 2007 survey presents that 77% of employees are graduates, predominantly in science and engineering roles. The same percentage was observed in the proportion of graduates coming from Welsh universities. The proportion of employees with postgraduate qualifications was lower at 43%, and 24% of employees were female. All respondent companies stated that these higher-level skills were 'fundamental' to their activities. The survey also presents that five of nine companies involved founders from universities, with the majority (seven of nine) being in the age range 25–55 years. The remaining two companies were founded by a young inward-investor and local graduates.

Almost all respondents (eight of nine) reported collaborations with Further Education/Higher Education institutions in Wales, predominantly in Knowledge Transfer Partnerships and student placements. Institutions involved included Gorseinon College, Cardiff University, Swansea Institute of Higher Education, and Swansea University. Collaboration with other Technium firms was reported by three respondents, though all reported collaborations with other Welsh/UK firms.

The survey data, essentially a 2007 census, together with ERDF project monitoring information, provide useful summaries at key points. This is of help primarily for reviewing Technium as a project (i.e. time and scope bound) but is limited in providing insight for any intended longer-term effect. Consideration beyond the walls and timescales of the ERDF-supported project is therefore required to investigate for the desired greater longer-term benefits, as noted by DTZ (2009).

Follow-up of the 2007 cohort shows that four subsequently 'graduating' companies relocated into the privately financed Ethos building adjacent to Technium 1. This 4,000s.m. development now houses a diverse range of knowledge-based enterprise from software development through to advanced medical devices manufacturing services.

Of the 2007 cohort, all companies are still trading according to Companies House filings, with six companies having progressed to premises elsewhere in the region and the remaining three remaining in Technium but having grown to occupy more space (units). Those located elsewhere have remained in the Swansea area.

The current (2017) occupancy of Techniums 1 & 2 includes 14 new tenants since the 2007 cohort. Notably, this includes an inward-investing operation of financial services company OSTC, which alone employs 40 staff. Other companies include construction and digital/media technologies, reflecting strengths within the University of Wales Trinity Saint David.

The 2007 cohort has continued to develop both in-situ and further afield, while further companies have progressed through Technium Swansea since the survey. The survey data do not include a number of companies, which entered and graduated from Technium without monitoring of their progress. For example, two Technium firms (one of which graduated prior to the survey) now manufacture products in partnership with a local subcontract manufacturing firm, supporting over 100 manufacturing jobs. However, this has only been shown through a review of other initiatives (Davies, Roderick, & Williams, 2017).

DISCUSSION

The strong job creation of Techniums 1 & 2 during their project phases supports earlier observation that much Technium network success was focussed within certain sites (Huggins & Kitagawa, 2012), while the diversity of founders and throughput of firms into the region suggests a level of success against original objectives at a Centre level.

This sits in the context of the wider Welsh university sector during this period as already making a positive contribution to knowledge-based enterprise (Huggins & Cooke, 1997; Huggins, Jones, & Upton, 2008; WAG, 2004a), though with well-noted capacity challenges for Higher Education (HE) to support such a development, particularly in forming sufficient spin-outs to support the desired economic transformation (Brooksbank & Thomas, 2001; Cooke, 2004).

Focus on activity solely within the Centres, particularly from the spin-out activity, during their initial project phase does however miss their wider purpose in both time and region. For example, research into the regional Life Sciences & Health sector shows later meaningful recent job creation resulting from linkages between both former and current Technium firms, other regional firms and research organisations (Davies et al., 2017). This echoes the observation in the DTZ (2009) report stating that the evaluation of such initiatives should give focus to performance in the subsequent growth of incubated firms, which is where and when the most significant benefits should be expected.

The aforementioned points draw attention to the fact that the Technium 1 project is heading towards two decades from its initiation, the time horizon point at which the evaluation of such initiatives is deemed appropriate by the primary funders (EU, 2002, 2014). Much commentary on Technium arrived when Centres were in early stages of operation (Cooke, 2004), and even before the original 'typical' five years (SIHE, 1999) of company evolution described in the plans of the first Centre. Abbey et al. (2008) and Huggins and Kitagawa (2012) recognise the long-term nature of the initiatives, echoing the original stated purpose and ambitions. The continued activity of the Technium 1 & 2 Centres, and discussion thereof, two ERDF Programmes (14 years) later suggests that they are indeed part of established infrastructure rather than simply an historic project.

The structural and cultural changes sought by the initial project and related policies, and the observation by DTZ (2009) that Technium was a long-term, and infrastructure, initiative is not reflected in the evidence or most of the discussion previously produced. This disconnect between purpose and measurement challenges whether the targets attached to projects set *pro rata* against the proportion of programme funding (CRG, 2003), were appropriate measures, both in nature and scale. Clearly, a capital investment opportunity existed through the then ERDF programme, and seizing upon this is identified as a potential driver of the 'hasty' rollout (Cooke, 2013).

Thus, Technium Swansea remains full with continued throughput of knowledge-based enterprise into the region suggests a level of success in its long-term aim of 'developing a culture which encourages and values innovation' (SIHE, 1999). However, it is of note that this occupancy rate is above the 85% best practice referenced by DTZ (2009), which may create operational/capacity issues for the activity.

The SA1 Swansea docklands regeneration is still a work in progress; however, the trend over the period since the establishment of Technium Swansea has been of continuing inward-investment, including significant employment sites for insurance company Admiral and PRA Healthcare, along with recent announcement of an expanding private hospital. Continued investment by private enterprise, and the mixed development underway led by the University of Wales Trinity Saint David provides a foundation for the proposed next phase of SA1 development (SU, 2017).

The long-term nature of the endeavour, and its existence within an evolving region/economy accompanied by continuous technological change emphasises the need for proper consideration within such context. The follow-up of a number of Technium companies and noting of local regeneration activity underscores this need for context to be properly considered, recognising low initial levels of entrepreneurship (GEM, 2000), weak Business Expenditure on R&D (Rogers, 2006) and limited, though (since Technium 1) rapidly growing, in scale and quality, regional universities (Brooksbank & Thomas, 2001; SU, 2017).

Work such as that of Murphy et al. (2015) provides a deeper understanding of the innovation activity within Technium, while the additional data and context, introduced in this chapter, show that there is more to the Technium than headlines suggest.

Importantly, the *Learning* concept within RIS described by Cooke (2001) now appears to be more prominent within recent initiatives, such as the Institute of Life Science at Swansea University, which co-locates science and business, with space for other essential innovation services such as finance, legal advice and accountancy, as suggested by Cooke (2004). This learning shows that the 'experimental' approach within Technium, has at least informed more recent efforts, with a greater emphasis on smart specialisations, as called for by Morgan (2013). This deeper exploration of the initial Technium activity also sets the scene for a more insightful longitudinal study, including the review of these initiatives involving both smart specialisation and diversity of enterprise and innovation.

CONCLUSION AND POLICY IMPLICATIONS

In short, to paraphrase the Welsh poet Dylan Thomas (1954), this chapter does not posit that Technium are 'wholly bad or good', but contributes to addressing the evidence deficit that has featured in prior debate of the initiative. In this respect, it has highlighted the need to objectively consider with greater care and detail the role such an activity can play within a region to support enterprise and innovation. Performance during the Technium Swansea project period broadly in line with its ambitions, together with the throughput of incubated companies, presents positively for the original initiative. Gibson (2007) noted a need for 'evolution' in commercialisation, which echoes with the call for learning from other observers (Cooke 2004; Heidenreich & Braczyk, 2004; Huggins & Kitagawa, 2012). This suggests that the strategic ambition of developing knowledge-based enterprise requires more adaptive and informed policy and practice, though recognising how timescales and context need critical consideration.

This chapter has provided a further perspective for developing appropriate expectations of such initiatives in the short, medium and long terms, with realistic time-horizons for 'success'. Indeed, even the guidance of the key funding partner, the EU Commission, suggests costs and benefits should be considered over a time horizon of 15–30 years (EU, 2002, 2014). This reflects the development of absorptive capacity and cycles of enterprise and innovation within supported firms, along with the evolution timescale of the initiative which supports them. In doing so, it identifies a need for rational objective debate – with an approach to appraisal, evaluation and discourse that recognises such initiatives' inherent complexity, and their role as limited components situated within a RIS.

The findings from observers (Abbey et al., 2008; Cooke, 2013; Huggins & Kitagawa, 2012; Morgan, 2013) are all valuable; however, such an insight is limited without continuous and more effective monitoring to inform such work. This is an important component in development and delivery of interventions (HMTreasury, 2003) with monitoring from prior activities playing a critical role in the cycle of setting out long-term objectives, determining relevant KPIs/monitoring arrangements, – and supporting governance and management that transcends political, funding and media cycles.

Techniums 1 & 2 have highlighted the path dependency issues described by Cooke (2013), along with the long-term nature of such infrastructure development. It is therefore important that policy makers both recognise and embrace this in formulation, delivery and oversight of future initiatives such as the Swansea Bay City Region City Deal (SU, 2017).

REFERENCES

Abbey, J., Davies, G., & Mainwaring, L. (2008). Vorsprung durch Technium: Towards a system of Innovation in South-west Wales. *Regional Studies*, *42*(2), 281–293.

Audretsch, D. B., & Lehmann, E. E. (2005). Does the knowledge spillover theory of entrepreneurship hold for regions? *Research Policy*, *34*(8), 1191–1202. http://dx.doi.org/10.1016/j.respol.2005.03.012

Baptista, R., & Swann, P. (1998). Do firms in clusters innovate more? *Research Policy*, *27*(5), 525–540.

BEIS. (2017). *Building our Industrial Strategy: Green Paper*. HM Government. Retrieved from https://beisgovuk.citizenspace.com/strategy/industrial-strategy/supporting_documents/building-ourindustrialstrategygreenpaper.pdf, accessed 18th April 2018

Brakman, S., & van Marrewijk, C. (2013). Reflections on cluster policies. *Cambridge Journal of Regions, Economy and Society*, *6*(2), 217–231. doi:10.1093/cjres/rst001

Brooksbank, D., & Thomas, B. (2001). An assessment of higher education spin-off enterprises in Wales. *Industry and Higher Education*, *15*(6), 415–420.

Casper, S., & Karamanos, A. (2003). Commercializing science in Europe: the Cambridge biotechnology cluster. *European Planning Studies*, *11*(7), 805–822.

Chen, C.-H. (1996). Regional determinants of foreign direct investment in mainland China. *Journal of Economic Studies, 23*(2), 18–30.

Chiaroni, D., & Chiesa, V. (2006). Forms of creation of industrial clusters in biotechnology. *Technovation, 26*(9), 1064–1076. http://dx.doi.org/10.1016/j.technovation.2005.09.015

Clement, M., & Davies, S. (2002). *Technium concept.* Paper presented at the Education and Training in Optics and Photonics 2001.

Cooke, P. (2001). Regional Innovation systems, clusters, and the knowledge economy. *Industrial and Corporate Change, 10*(4), 945–974. doi:10.1093/icc/10.4.945

Cooke, P. (2004). The regional innovation system in Wales. *Regional Innovation Systems. The Role of Governances in a Globalized World.* London: Routledge.

Cooke, P. (2013). *Re-framing regional development: Evolution, innovation and transition*: New York, NY: Routledge.

Cooke, P., & Clifton, N. (2005). Visionary, precautionary and constrained 'varieties of devolution' in the economic governance of the devolved UK territories. *Regional Studies, 39*(4), 437–451.

Cooke, P. N., Heidenreich, M., & Braczyk, H.-J. (2004). *Regional innovation systems: The role of governance in a globalized world.* Psychology Press.

Creswell, J. W., & Clark, V. L. P. (2007). Designing and conducting mixed methods research. London: Sage publications.

CRG. (2003). *Mid-term evaluation of the objective 1 programme for West Wales and the valleys: Final report.* Retrieved from http://e4g.org.uk/wp-content/blogs.dir/112/files/2013/07/MidTerm-Evaluation-Obj1-WWales-and-the-Valleys.pdf, Accessed 14th April 2018

Davies, G., Roderick, S., & Williams, M. (2017). *A sub-regional innovation ecosystem? Life sciences & health in the Swansea Bay City Region.* Paper presented at the 12th European Conference on Innovation and Entrpreneurship, Paris.

Delgado, M., Porter, M. E., & Stern, S. (2010). Clusters and entrepreneurship. *Journal of Economic Geography, 10*(4), 495–518. doi:10.1093/jeg/lbq010

DTI. (2001). *Business clusters in the UK: A first assessment.* Report for the Department of Trade and Industry by a consortium led by Trends Business Research, London.

DTZ. (2009). *Evaluation of the Technium Programme, final report to the Welsh Assembly Government, Stage 1: Scoping and review.* Retrieved from https://gov.wales/docs/caecd/research/101119techniumstage1en.pdf, Accessed 14th April 2018

DTZ. (2010). *Technium case studies: Appendix 1 to Evaluation of the Technium Programme Stage 1: Final report.* Retrieved from http://gov.wales/docs/caecd/research/101119techniumcasestudyen.pdf

EU. (2002). *Guide to cost-benefit analysis of investment projects.* DG Regional Policy, European Commission, Brussels.

EU. (2010). *Clusters and clustering policy: A guide for regional and local policy makers.* INNO Germany AG. Retrieved from https://cor.europa.eu/en/engage/studies/Documents/Clusters-and-Clustering-policy.pdf, Accessed 18th April 2018

EU. (2014). *Guide to cost-benefit analysis of investment projects, economic appraisal tool for cohesion policy 2014–2020.* Retrieved from https://ec.europa.eu/inea/sites/inea/files/cba_guide_cohesion_policy.pdf, Accessed 18th April 2018

Foray, D. (2014). *Smart specialisation: Opportunities and challenges for regional innovation policy* (Vol. 79). New York, NY: Routledge.

Foray, D., David, P. A., & Hall, B. (2009). Smart specialisation: The concept. *Knowledge Economists Policy Brief, 9*(85), 100.

GEM. (2000). *Global entrepreneurship monitor: 2000 Wales executive report.* Retrieved from http://www.esbri.se/gem-rapport.pdf Accessed 14th April 2018

Gibson, S. (2007). *Commercialisation in Wales: A report by the Independent Task and Finish Group.* Retrieved from http://www.assembly.wales/commercialisation_in_wales_-_gibson_review.pdf

Heidenreich, M. E., Clapson, M., Fine, B., Hall, T., Karan, P., Stapleton, K. E., ..., Tucker, B. (1998). Braczyk, Hans-Joachim, Cooke, Philip. *Urban Studies, 35*(8), 1411–1412.

HMTreasury. (2003). *The green book Appraisal and evaluation in central government: Treasury guidance (0115601074).* Norwich: TSO.

Huggins, R., & Cooke, P. (1997). The economic impact of Cardiff University: Innovation, learning and job generation. *GeoJournal, 41*(4), 325–337.

Huggins, R., Jones, M., & Upton, S. (2008). Universities as drivers of knowledge-based regional development: A triple helix analysis of Wales. *International Journal of Innovation and Regional Development, 1*(1), 24–47.

Huggins, R., & Kitagawa, F. (2012). Regional policy and university knowledge transfer: Perspectives from devolved regions in the UK. *Regional Studies, 46*(6), 817–832. doi:10.1080/00343404.2011.583913

Huxtable-Thomas, L., Hannon, P., & Thomas, S. (2015). Using a mixed method 'Petri-Dish' diagram to determine complex impacts of leadership development in extant entrepreneurs. Paper presented at the 14th European Conference on Research Methodology for Business Management Studies.

Ketels, C. (2013). Recent research on competitiveness and clusters: What are the implications for regional policy? *Cambridge Journal of Regions, Economy and Society, 6*(2), 269–284. doi:10.1093/cjres/rst008

Lambert, R. (2003). *Lambert review of business-university collaboration: Final Report.* London: HMSO.

Lundvall, B.-Å. (1992). *National systems of innovation: Towards a theory of innovation and interactive learning.* London: Pinter.

McKinsey. (2014). *Industrial revolutions: Captruing the growth potential.* Centre for Cities. Retrieved from https://www.centreforcities.org/wp-content/uploads/2014/07/FINAL_Centre-for-cities-report2014.pdf, Accessed 14th April 2018

Menzel, M. P., & Fornahl, D. (2009). Cluster life cycles–dimensions and rationales of cluster evolution. *Industrial and corporate change, 19*(1), 205–238.

Morgan, K. (2001). The new territorial politics: Rivalry and justice in post-devolution Britain. *Regional Studies, 35*(4), 343–348.

Morgan, K. (2013). The regional state in the era of Smart Specialisation. *Ekonomiaz, 83*(02), 103–126.

Murphy, L., Huggins, R., & Thompson, P. (2015). Social capital and innovation: A comparative analysis of regional policies. *Environment and Planning C: Government and Policy, 34*(6), 1025–1057. doi:10.1177/0263774X15597448

Nelson, R. R. (1993). *National innovation systems: A comparative analysis*: Oxford: Oxford University Press.

Phelps, N. A., Mackinnon, D., Stone, I., & Braidford, P. (2003). Embedding the multinationals? Institutions and the development of overseas manufacturing affiliates in Wales and North East England. *Regional Studies, 37*(1), 27–40.

Porter, M. E. (1998). *Clusters and the new economics of competition* (Vol. 76). Boston, MA: Harvard Business Review.

Porter, M. E. (2000). Location, competition, and economic development: Local clusters in a global economy. *Economic Development Quarterly, 14*(1), 15–34.

Power, D., & Malmberg, A. (2008). The contribution of universities to innovation and economic development: In what sense a regional problem? *Cambridge Journal of Regions, Economy and Society, 1*(2), 233–245.

Pugh, R. (2017). Universities and economic development in lagging regions: 'Triple helix'policy in Wales. *Regional Studies, 51*(7), 982–993.

Pugh, R. E. (2014). 'Old wine in new bottles'? Smart Specialisation in Wales. *Regional Studies, Regional Science, 1*(1), 152–157. doi:10.1080/21681376.2014.944209

RLP. (2013). *Life science skills for life, Regional Learning and Skills Partnership.* Retrieved from http://www.rlp.org.uk/about-us/publications/, Accessed 14th April 2018.

Rogers, M. (2006). R&D and productivity in the UK: Evidence from firm-level data in the 1990s, Discussion Paper, University of Oxford, ISSN 1471–0498

Salvador, E., & Harding, R. (2006). Innovation policy at the regional level: The case of Wales. *International Journal of Foresight and Innovation Policy, 2*(3), 304–326.

Siegel, D. S., Wright, M., & Lockett, A. (2007). The rise of entrepreneurial activity at universities: Organizational and societal implications. *Industrial and Corporate Change, 16*(4), 489–504.

SIHE. (1999). Creation of a business and innovation centre for the South West Wales Area: Project summary sheet. Welsh European Programme Executive Ltd. Provided by Project Sponsor, Reviewed 14th April 2018.

Stake, R. E. (1995). *The art of case study research.* New York, NY: Sage.

SU. (2017). *Internet coast: Phase 1: City deal proposal impact appraisal.* Project Document, Swansea University, Wales, UK.

Su, Y.-S., & Hung, L.-C. (2009). Spontaneous vs. policy-driven: The origin and evolution of the biotechnology cluster. *Technological Forecasting and Social Change, 76*(5), 608–619.

Swords, J. (2013). Michael Porter's cluster theory as a local and regional development tool: The rise and fall of cluster policy in the UK. *Local Economy*, *28*(4), 369–383. doi:10.1177/0269094213475855

Thomas, D. (1954). *Under milk wood*. New York, NY: New Directions Publishing.

WAG. (2003). *Wales for innovation*. Cardiff: Welsh Assembly Government.

WAG. (2004a). *Knowledge economy nexus: Role of higher education in Wales*. Cardiff: Welsh Assembly Government.

WAG. (2004b). *A winning Wales; The national economic development strategy of the Welsh Assembly Government*. Cardiff: Welsh Assembly Government.

WAG. (2005). *Wales: A vibrant economy: The Welsh Assembly Government's strategic framework for economic development consultation document*. Cardiff: Welsh Assembly Government.

WAG. (2009). *Science for Wales: A strategic agenda for science and innovation in Wales*. Cardiff: Welsh Assembly Government.

WAG. (2010). *Economic renewal: A new direction*. Cardiff: Crown Copyright.

WDA. (1996). *Wales regional technology plan: An innovation and technology strategy for Wales*. Cardiff: Welsh Development Agency.

WDA. (2001). Technium II, A business and innovation centre for the South West Wales Region, Grant Application. Cardiff: Welsh Development Agency.

WEFO. (2007). Approved projects, 2000–2006 West Wales & Valleys Operational Programme. In W. G. Welsh European Funding Office (Ed.). Retrieved from https://gov.wales/funding/eu-funds/previous/searchprojects1/?lang=en, Accessed 14th April 2018.

WG. (2009). Technium Pan-Wales. Retrieved from http://gov.wales/funding/eu-funds/previous/search projects1/80312?lang=en

WG. (2011). Written statement: Technium Update [Press release]. Retrieved from http://gov.wales/about/cabinet/cabinetstatements/previous-administration/2011/techniumupdate/?lang=en

WG. (2013). *Sectors delivery plan*. Department for Business, Economy and Transport, Cardiff: Welsh Government.

WG. (2014). *Innovation Wales*, Welsh Government. Retrieved from https://gov.wales/topics/science-and-technology/innovation/innovation-wales-strategy/?lang=en, Accessed 14th April 2018.

Yin, R. K. (2017). *Case study research and applications: Design and methods*. New York, NY: Sage Publications.

CHAPTER 9

ENTREPRENEURSHIP IN THE OPEN SPACE: A NEW DYNAMIC FOR CREATING VALUE?

David Rae

ABSTRACT

Entrepreneurship as a socially engaged and responsible movement is increasingly conceptualised as creating multiple sources of value: social, environmental, technological, cultural as well as financial, all contributing to wider economic performance. There is a rapid growth in the availability and expectation of 'Open' tools and resources, including innovation; data; research access; source code; educational and learning materials; and government. There is an increasing interest in their potential for value creation, requiring research attention and clarity of what 'Open' means in this context.

This chapter explores the following three dimensions of the 'Open Space' of freely available resources for entrepreneurship:

(1) What is 'Open' in the context of entrepreneurship?
(2) Why is Open Entrepreneurship (OE) important for conceptualisation, education and practice?
(3) Can OE provide significant new opportunities for innovation, value creation and learning, and if so, how can these be realised?

The chapter defines 'OE' as a unifying approach for value creation through a conceptual model combining 'Open' tools and resources. Open resources for digital and data-led entrepreneurship offer conditions for new, pervasive and

Creating Entrepreneurial Space: Talking Through Multi-voices, Reflections on Emerging Debates
Contemporary Issues in Entrepreneurship Research, Volume 9B, 153–172
Copyright © 2019 by Emerald Publishing Limited
ISSN: 2040-7246/doi:10.1108/S2040-72462019000009B009

*distributed forms of value-creating entrepreneurial activity. These can cre-
ate learning environments with rich access to data and resources, innovative
connections and opportunities for co-creating value in multiple forms. This
learning-centred approach builds on the concept of entrepreneurship as an educational philosophy of value creation for others. Without this, there are risks
that entrepreneurial education, and the capabilities of micro-business owners
and managers, may lag the development of an Open digital economy, rather
than creating new forms of OE.*

Keywords: Open innovation; open data; entrepreneurship; enterprise education;
value creation; open resources

INTRODUCTION

Does the global movement towards the availability and use of freely available
'Open' resources represent a challenge or opportunity for entrepreneurs? There
is an international Open movement for scientific and public resource sharing
(Royal Society, 2012), as well as wider societal expectations of openness, transparency and democratic access. Open resources offer a continuously growing
free reserve of information, tools and opportunities, which can be used for scientific, public and entrepreneurial development (OECD, 2004; 2015a, 2015b;
Ramjoué, 2015).

Major public organisations have proposed that the availability of Open
resources, especially Open data, have the potential to energise scientific enterprise; and create major sources of new value through business and social innovations (Ramjoué, 2015; Royal Society, 2012; World Bank, 2014). The increasing
free availability and access to Open resources internationally offers potential for
entrepreneurs and educators to learn, innovate and create value more quickly
than before. Social innovation and enterprise offer scope for researching social
issues and problems using Open data, and developing solutions and applications using Open source and other resources. But, is this promise being fulfilled
by entrepreneurs and social innovators to translate Open resources into value
creation, and realise the full benefits?

Entrepreneurship is a major driver for value creation (Mishra & Zachary,
2014), has a diverse intellectual heritage and can be defined in different ways.
The classical free-enterprise model which viewed entrepreneurial value creation simply as the pursuit of profit from risky ventures has been questioned for
its limited ability to deliver necessary wider social and economic outcomes in
a changing context (Baumol, Litan, & Schramm, 2007; Mazzucato, 2013). The
growth in recent decades of social enterprise and innovation has brought a wider
understanding of entrepreneurship as creating multiple sources of value: social,
environmental, technological, cultural as well as financial, which all contribute
to wider economic performance (Royal Society, 2012). At European levels, an
accepted definition of entrepreneurship is acting on opportunities and ideas to
transform them into value for others (Bacigalupo, Kampylis, Punie, & Van den

Brande, 2016; Lackéus, 2018, p. 53). This socially engaged and responsible approach is congruent with the need to expand the scope and aims of entrepreneurship globally as a means of meeting the united nations sustainable Development goals (UN, 2015), which address poverty, health, education, economic growth and environmental concerns.

Recent years have seen massive growth in the availability of openly available, shared tools and resources. The Open definition used in this paper is:

Open data and content can be freely used, modified, and shared by anyone for any purpose.

(Open definition 2.1 2005)

The 'Open' movement offers citizens the right to access and use freely available data and other resources, accompanied by increasing expectations that governmental and public resources should be open and accountable. The 'Open' concept prefixes an ever-growing list of categories, including: innovation; data; research and access; source code; educational and learning materials; government; and recently contracting. An array of organisations, networks and collaborations have created rights, standards, protocols and searchable databases of Open resources. However, whilst resources constantly increase, they are also transient, and a growing challenge for practitioners remains 'how to find what is most useful?' in relation to a problem, opportunity or innovation.

The Open movement changes the dynamics and economics of how information-based societies work, as presaged by Benkler (2006). 'Open' can provide essential resources for more connected, inclusive and transparent societies. The interactions between Open resources and entrepreneurship are emergent and bring problematic questions, such as who owns the value created, and what economic model governs value creation from freely available resources? Can entrepreneurship which creates private profit from public resources be described as 'open'? Where current value streams which depend on proprietary resources are threatened by open access to free resources, how serious is the value lost?

There also remain questions relating to the ownership of resources created from personal data; over the proprietary platforms used to extract value from these; and over the intellectual property within the data sets and platforms. Events such as the exposure of how 'FaceBook' collected, used and made available vast quantities of personal data in ways which were improper, not anticipated by users and in some ways illegal, have contributed to this. They bring calls to regulate and control such organisations and offer systemic alternatives such as the 'Hub of All Things' (HAT). Pollock (2018) addressed this in 'The Open Revolution' by calling for shared and open, rather than closed and proprietary data ownership:

We need an Open world...where all digital information is open, free for everyone to use, build on and share; and where innovators and creators are recognized and rewarded. (p. 18)

This tension between open or closed access and ownership lies at the heart of the history and future of the Internet and the digital economy. Duopolies between open and proprietary access are likely to continue and grow, although there are signs that greater freedom and open access is expected (Shadbolt & Hampson, 2018).

There is increasing interest and evidence of the potential for value creation through using Open resources and methods at the levels of small and corporate businesses (Open Data Institute [ODI], 2015, 2016). The combination of the Open movement; Open data; digital and data-led entrepreneurship; 'Internet of Things' and other, connected, changes increasingly offers conditions for new, pervasive forms of value-creating digital entrepreneurial activity. The intensive innovation and connectivity in some 'Smart Cities' already demonstrate this, both in the United Kingdom (UK), and internationally.

Given the significance and value of the digital, knowledge economy and the growth of Open resources and means of working, this chapter explores the idea of entrepreneurship as an Open process which can connect other forms of Open activity for new forms of value creation.

Such combinations of 'Open' tools, resources and social movements already generate conditions which can make entrepreneurship open to all more feasible; but depend crucially on increasing widespread human capability and learning to use them. There is evidence of the limitations of digital literacy and related skills, so learning to use Open resources effectively is an essential dimension (Atenas & Havemann, 2015; Open Data for Development [OD4D], 2015). However, the Open movement also offers increasing potential to create learning environments, which afford people-rich access to data and resources, innovative connections, and opportunities for co-creating value in multiple forms. Learning is a major dimension, since without a significant uplift in the access, rate and levels of learning to use and apply Open resources for entrepreneurship, it will underperform. Hence, a learning-centred approach is required, building on the notion of entrepreneurship as an educational philosophy of value creation for others (Lackéus, 2016).

As the category of Open Innovation (OI) is well established, its relationship with Open entrepreneurship (OE) requires exploration, including the self-defined limitations in the scope of OI (Chesbrough & Bogers, 2014; Eftekhari & Bogers, 2015), which focussed its main contributions on knowledge flows in the corporate sector. Potentially, could a human-learning rather than information-centred OE offer a wider, connective and inclusive scope, and address vital global social and policy expectations and outcomes?

CHAPTER PURPOSE AND STRUCTURE

The chapter maps the relevant strands of the Open movement and their connections with the proposed conceptualisation for OE. It explores the following three related questions:

(1) What is 'Open' in the context of entrepreneurship?
(2) Why is the idea of 'Open' entrepreneurship important for conceptualisation, education and practice?
(3) Can OE provide significant new opportunities for innovation, value creation and learning, and if so, how can these be realised?

Firstly, the approach is explained, before an overview of the categories of Open resources and relevant prior work. This leads to a proposed rationale, definition and conceptualisation for OE, based on the connections between Open resources and processes. This is discussed and proposed actions for development are outlined. A reflection on the third question provides the conclusions.

THE RESEARCH APPROACH

The study tracked the evolution and development of Open data and related resources over a 3-year period from 2015 to 2018. It followed research and developments in public policy, academic, business, data science and innovation in the UK, the EU and North America. This informed an understanding of the evolving dynamics of Open data and shaped several project proposals, including the Lincolnshire Open Research & Innovation Centre. This continuing investigation is different in nature from a single research study although it has included consultations, surveys and interviews with business owners and other stakeholders at various points.

In 2015, a provisional set of principles based on using Open Data for Community Economic Development was used with researchers, development organisations, students and small businesses to raise awareness and motivation, and subsequently explored with many groups to develop the concept in this paper (Rae, Sorrie, & Syms, 2017). A result of this ongoing work was research by a PhD student team in 2018 to create an initial data set of Open Knowledge resources for use by students, researchers and innovators, led by the Centre for Enterprise & Innovation at De Montfort University in the UK. These are being made publicly available via the portal www.open-ent.com.

CATEGORIES OF OPEN RESOURCES AND PROCESSES

The different strands of Open resources are mapped to suggest how they can contribute to an OE framework. The categories and types of Open resources continually increase as the use of the prefix spreads, recent examples being Open Banking and Open Contracting. This proliferation raises the question: 'what does Open mean in this situation?'. Not everything which purports to be 'open' conforms to the Open definition (2005). The term 'openwashing' refers to activities and processes being presented as 'open' when access, re-use or freedom to use is restricted.

This profusion of Open types of resources represents dynamism and growth, but makes the analysis complex. They include, in the established categories: Open source software code; Open research with access to research results and publications and data collected by research, public and other agencies; OI and Open collaboration as inclusive, permeable and public processes; Open educational and learning materials as publicly available courseware; and ultimately the

Open resources & processes available for value creation

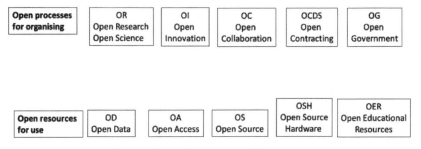

Fig. 1. Open Resources and Processes.

accountability and transparency of Open Government by access to the data and processes by which decisions are made. These provide an ever-growing collection of digitally available assets with enormous potential for value creation, limited by a lack of popular understanding of their existence, value and applications.

The evolution of each of these types of resources has been achieved by their own communities of developers and users, often working independently with quite limited 'bridging across' into other Open spaces to exchange perspectives and methods. Pollock (2018) tellingly observed that:

> We need a broad-based Open movement with a common language and goals – both are currently lacking. (p. 115)

Each main category of Open resources and processes is illustrated in Fig. 1, with its abbreviation used within the chapter. A distinction is made in relation to the Open categories, that they include both freely available resources, as well as processes for organising and using the resources for the various forms of activities, including value creation. Hence, Open Data (OD), Open Access (OA), Open Source (OS), Open Source Hardware (OSH), and Open Educational Resources (OER) mainly constitute resource bases available for use. Open Research (OR), Open Innovation (OI), Open Collaboration (OC) and Open Government (OG) can be viewed largely as organising processes, which draw on Open and a range of other, closed resources processes. As Ing (2018) demonstrated, innovation and value creation often take place by using private (non-open) sources combined with open. As multiple connections could be shown between any of these categories, for clarity none are indicated.

OPENNESS IN ENTREPRENEURSHIP AND INNOVATION

It is necessary to explore the relationship between entrepreneurship and the well-established concept of OI. The interface between OI and entrepreneurship research remained unexplored until recently, yet many topics studied in relation to OI also fall within the ambit of entrepreneurship research, including business models, venture management, opportunities, human variables and innovation within networks of Small-medium sized Enterprises (SMEs) (Burcharth, Knudsen, & Søndergaard, 2014, Hossain, 2015, Lee, Park, Yoon, & Park, 2009; Popa, Sota-Acosta, & Martinez-Conesa, 2017).

Debates over the definition, scope and boundaries of OI (Hossain, 2015) led to its revision by Chesbrough and Bogers (2014, p. 27), as shown below. This emphasised the role of intra- and inter-organisational knowledge flows in an innovation process, but omitted reference to human, social policy or environmental factors. This distinction assists in understanding the distinctions between entrepreneurship and innovation necessary in the Open context.

> open innovation is a distributed innovation process based on purposively managed knowledge flows across organizational boundaries, using pecuniary and non-pecuniary mechanisms in line with each organization's business model. These flows of knowledge may involve knowledge inflows to the focal organization (leveraging external knowledge sources through internal processes), knowledge outflows from a focal organization (leveraging internal knowledge through external commercialization processes) or both (coupling external knowledge sources and commercialization. (Chesbrough & Bogers, 2014, p. 27)

The debate on the scope of OI also related to the role of social innovation, and a reluctance to accept OI outside a commercial for-profit model. Chesbrough and Bogers (2014, p. 19) proposed the term 'open collaborative innovation' to refer to innovation for low-cost or free production of 'public, non-rivalrous non-excludable goods'. Other researchers challenged these boundaries. Tracey and Stott (2017) framed a research agenda for social innovation across processes of social entrepreneurship, social intrapreneurship, and social extrapreneurship, developing a typology which connects these differing forms of entrepreneurial action through the use of innovation to achieve social change, and introducing the concept of 'extrapreneur' to innovate across organisational boundaries. They also highlighted the challenges and opportunities for innovation in addressing the global challenges of social, environmental and economic issues, which are neglected by pure for-profit-driven innovation. This is an important contribution in conceptualising OE.

West and Bogers (2014, p. 816) proposed a framework for OI research which proposed a range of research studies, but omitted entrepreneurship from this analysis, contributing to a sense of the disconnect between OI and entrepreneurship research. However, a small study by Eftekhari and Bogers (2015) explored the application of OI principles to new venture creation, developing a framework showing that new venture survival is influenced by ecosystem collaboration; user involvement; open environment; and that this relationship is moderated by the entrepreneur's open mindset:

> an open mindset fosters the entrepreneur's opportunity recognition and commercialization, thus positively influencing the likelihood of new venture survival. (Eftekhari & Bogers, 2015, p. 500)

This observed the importance of the entrepreneurs' way of thinking and mindset in relation to openness variables and culture, addressing human cognitive and behavioural aspects of entrepreneurship, which tended not to be included within

OI research. A major recent study by Bogers et al. (2017) surveyed established perspectives and emerging themes in OI. It commented that, whilst established perspectives deliver unique insights into the understanding of specific distributed innovation processes, there are only limited connections across them, and observed that:

> At the organisational level of analysis, OI is associated with entrepreneurial opportunities, processes and outcomes. (Bogers et al., 2017, p. 15)

OI now takes an interest in identifying how its approaches can lead to varied types of entrepreneurial opportunities, processes and outcomes and organisational-level issues overlapping or connecting OI and entrepreneurship. (Bogers et al., 2017, p. 15). Bogers, Chesborough, and Moedas (2018, p. 5) recently observed extensions of current research on OI into domains such as SMEs, high- and low-tech industries, and even 'not-for-profit organizations' and public policy, which had not previously been of interest to OI research. Ing's contribution to OI literature on Open Innovation Learning (2018) charts the development of 'open source with private source' IT development in the context of IBM and the OS industry, illustrating the ways in which inter-organisational learning enabled sustained innovation and value creation to occur. It offers valuable insights into the prevailing corporate managerial mindsets and motivations for OI.

There are multiple connections and synergies as well as overlaps between entrepreneurship and innovation, apparent in prior seminal works dating back to Drucker (1985) and even Schumpeter (1948). As the OI concept is self-limited to 'the distributed innovation process based on purposively managed knowledge flows across organizational boundaries' which results in knowledge sharing and innovation, there should be an interdependent relationship with entrepreneurship which contributes the essential human and social agency of learning, creating and acting on opportunities through organisational means, which is only partially addressed, in limited ways, through OI. This will be considered in defining OE.

VALUE CREATION FROM OPEN RESOURCES AND PROCESSES

It is proposed that Open resources are latent, constantly changing and increasingly available for value creation. People and organisations use the social and informational processes of OI and OC to engage with these and other inputs to create forms of new value. OG is perhaps distinct, in that the aims of creating transparency and accountability in government are not be principally concerned with value creation. However, transparency in public affairs is an important contributor to OE and a stimulant for other forms of openness.

Benkler (2003, 2006) discussed the development of the 'networked information economy' and creative commons peer production, based on freely produced and shared digital materials. He proposed that a digitally networked social environment, with free social exchange and sharing, enhances both the productivity of ideas and the values of autonomy, democracy and social justice in ways that market mechanisms do not. He also identified new opportunities for open tools, platforms for exchange and collaboration through social production, which challenged accepted industrial and economic structures. Benkler's contributions presaged the economy of freely shared digital resources.

There are recent perspectives on entrepreneurial ecosystems and digital platforms as economic environments and processes for innovation, opportunity exploitation and value creation (Autio, Nambisan, Thomas, & Wright, 2018; Srinivasan & Venkatraman 2018; Spigel & Harrison, 2018). These are framed in the perspective of regional innovation systems, yet have surprisingly little to say on the use of Open processes and resources. These may be simply 'taken for granted' in environments where there are high levels of connectivity, entrepreneurial intensity, and free access to financial and informational resources. However, such factors are far from universal.

The concept of place is increasingly significant in entrepreneurial ecosystems, especially in the city. The global 'Smart Cities' movement indicates potentially important aspects of OE. For example, Bristol is branded as an 'Open Programmable City', combining software, hardware and telecom networks with 'Internet of Things', using the OpenFlow standard and Network Function Virtualisation http://www.bristolisopen.com/. This type of city-wide ecosystem project connects with the prospect of enabling rapidly growing cities, such as many in China and India, to move directly to Open systems to manage their operations, rather than migrating through intermediate technologies (Anthopoulos, 2017). Singapore has expanded the concept to become a 'Smart Nation', developing a technological OE model through using networks, data and info-comm technologies to improve living standards, economic opportunities and community cohesion https://www.smartnation.sg/. This aims for value creation as a primary driver for smart city design and implementation, together with improving the quality of residents' lives, such as through digital inclusion and automation of routine work. Even in crisis-challenged cities, Open data contributes to entrepreneurial city transformation, such as the regeneration of Detroit, USA. The Detroit Future City strategic framework demonstrates a city-wide and data-driven entrepreneurial approach: detroitfuturecity.com.

Value creation from Open resources is not new. The open source movement is the foundation for a well-established and continually innovating industry. Based on shared source code, the applications and services developed are used worldwide by organisations and citizens, directly and indirectly creating huge financial and wider value. Open source developers earn revenues from bespoke development, selling additional services and extensions, which complement OS applications, and dual-licensing applications. Apache Software Foundation, the Linux Foundation and Mozilla Foundation exemplify highly influential and successful open-source based organisations (Ing, 2018; von Hippel, 2005). The OS example of a highly innovative and entrepreneurial industry, based on translating freely shared code into non-commercial and commercial applications, demonstrates that such a value-creation model already exists. The Microsoft acquisition of GitHub for $7.5 billion in 2018 signalled the growing scope for co-creating value through connecting Open and proprietary networks and resources.

This partly resolves a tension within the concept of OE, that value creation is based, in part or entirely, on the use and combination of proprietary with open, freely available resources. It is a normal expectation of using open resources that the results are then shared with the community. A problem with entrepreneurial activity may be that, whilst some forms of value can be shared freely, for commercial reasons it is necessary for the entrepreneurial venture to capture a proportion of the value created. Whilst this may not be ideal for altruists, it is essential in a competitive, capitalist economy, and should provide for intellectual property rights and confidentiality of information to be protected for commercial purposes. However, the mutuality of the Open movement, in sharing the results of OE for wider use, should also be respected, as has been achieved within the OS community.

In a digital economy, where all information exists as, or can be reduced to, digital code, this essentially means that the code of open resources is shared freely, whilst access to protected code is restricted. Trade secrets such as the formula for Coca-Cola, the content of patents, registered trademarks and confidential data such as personal and customer records can all be protected, as now, under the category of 'restricted code'.

EVIDENCE OF VALUE CREATION

The connections between using Open resources and innovation are increasingly attractive to the Open movement, but until recently value creation was unproven, with limited evidence of wider impact. There is now increasing recognition of the economic and wider social value of Open data applications from innovation. Whilst precise measurement of the impacts is challenging, partly due to the absence of a robust economic theory covering the value of freely available network resources (e.g. Economides 1996), there is a growing number of studies which demonstrate the value created and economic impacts of OD. The ODI published a study showing corporate value created through OD with examples from Arup, Thomson Reuters and Syngenta (ODI, 2016).

Transport for London (TfL) commissioned an evaluation of the impact of their open data sets, which they encouraged a community of innovators to use in creating a range of applications. This proposed a 'virtuous circle' from OD being used by businesses and innovators to create Apps and other commercial and free offers; user benefits from access to these; and data use revealing new insights (Deloitte, 2017). This estimated the gross value-added from the data annually at £12–15 million, with 500 jobs created directly and 230 indirectly, and many network benefits arising including journey time saved, valued at £69–89 million. This could be replicated in other major cities with complex transport and data infrastructures.

The EU has undertaken studies which showed the value created and the economic benefits of OD (Berends, 2017). The EU Data Portal research is probably the most thorough work undertaken to date on the economic value and benefits of OD as well as the costs of providing it through OD portals (Walker & Simperl, 2018).

The report on the European data economy (2017) showed its growth in economic scale and impact, with its market size projected to increase in value for the period 2016–2020 to €325 billion, supporting 100,000 jobs by 2020 (Carrara et al., 2017).

The Open Data Incubator Network Europe business incubation project to develop Open data-oriented businesses ran from 2014 to 2016 and was evaluated by the IDC (2017). This demonstrated that the 57 participating firms' subsequent activities were projected to:

> result in an estimated 110 €M of cumulative revenues in the period 2016-2020, plus 784 jobs created. Average revenues per company by 2020 should be around €1M, corresponding to €55,000 per employee. (IDC, 2017, p. 6)

Collectively, these studies demonstrate that Open resources and processes can result in entrepreneurial value creation. A major project is being undertaken by the OD4D to review the capacity of open data to address social and economic challenges over a 10-year period of progress, development, and to assess its impact (http://www.stateofopendata.od4d.net/).

OE FOR INCLUSIVE DEVELOPMENT

The idea of Open enterprise and entrepreneurship emerged in a few studies, such as Eftekhari and Bogers (2015) and ODI (2015, 2016), but was not otherwise developed. Why is OE needed, adding to the extant Open categories? It may actually name an activity which already exists, as outlined in the aforementioned examples and evidence.

In addition to the accepted Open Definition (2005) of free access and re-use, there is an increasingly pervasive view that entrepreneurship, as an activity, should be universally open to all, arguing that it is a fundamental human right for individuals and groups be empowered to act entrepreneurially (Aerni, 2015). For example, United Nations Strategic Development Goal (UN SDG) 8, which promotes inclusive and sustainable economic growth, employment and decent work for all, undertakes to 'promote development-oriented policies that support productive activities, decent job creation, entrepreneurship, creativity and innovation, and encourage the formalization and growth of micro-, small- and medium-sized enterprises' (http://www.un.org/sustainabledevelopment/economic-growth/0). Entrepreneurship at a mass level will be essential to create the 30 million jobs annually projected to be required.

Whilst entrepreneurship was not explicitly protected by the 1948 Universal Declaration of Human Rights, Articles 22 and 23 protecting the economic, social, cultural and rights to work presage this (UN, 1948). However, studies by Vinod (2005), Aerni (2015), the World Bank (2008) and UNDP all support the connection between human and economic rights and entrepreneurship. UNDP attest that:

> the rights that allow someone to start a business or become self-employed are 'essential for the livelihoods of the poor', as micro-entrepreneurship and self-employment are often the only option for the poor to generate money. (http://mcnair.bakerinstitute.org/blog/entrepreneurship-human-rights)

Aerni (2015) proposed, making the case for entrepreneurship as a human right, that in developing countries, innovators with low incomes can produce low-tech innovations, but still require IP protection through utility models, and that 'an enabling environment for the creation of ideas and their commercial use is vital for economic development' (Aerni, 2015, p. 40). The availability of Open resources for innovation which can result in proprietary innovation acts as a growing stimulus for this.

The World Bank study (2008) underlines the contribution of entrepreneurship to economic and social inclusion as well as a means of poverty reduction. From a developed world perspective, it is unarguable that everyone should have the right to entrepreneurship. However, globally, there are many groups within societies who are constrained, discriminated or prevented from entrepreneurship, on the grounds of gender, status, caste, ethnicity, belief, ability, location and other categories. If entrepreneurship is open to all, irrespective of sectionality, the economic and social benefits effects of entrepreneurship will be greatly amplified.

DEFINING OE

OE is proposed as translating and applying Open resources into innovations, processes and models, which create multiple forms of value, not only financial, but also economic in the widest sense, as well as social, cultural and environmental. The innovation process may draw on OI, but the vital collective human and social agency of relating this to available resources, creating and acting on opportunities, and organising to enact value creation, is entrepreneurial. This agency, together with opportunity identification, organisation, leadership and associated learning, cognition and decision-making, is central to entrepreneurship, and hence within the scope of OE.

The definition of OE also includes the role of entrepreneurship in economic and social inclusion at a global level, as signalled by major international organisations, including the Global Entrepreneurship Monitor (GEM, 2018) studies, the UN Sustainable Development Goals (UN, 2015), UNCTAD (2013) and World Bank (2008). In turn, OE may provide a working framework for entrepreneurial policies and practices to provide access, capability and uptake of open resources for entrepreneurship.

The definition is intentionally inclusive, based on an increasingly accepted European conception of entrepreneurship as 'creating shared value for others' (Bacilapugo et al., 2016; Lackéus, 2016, 2018). This definition follows, and is intended for discussion with communities of entrepreneurs, researchers, experts and policy-makers.

OE: Proposed Definition:

OE is activity which creates multiple forms of value (such as economic, social, cultural and environmental) for entrepreneurs and others: investors, co-workers, customers, the community at large.

The entrepreneurial person or organisation is able to access, freely* and fairly, the resources, means and opportunities for entrepreneurial activities of value creation.

OE is open to all members of society; inclusivity regardless of culture, gender, age, ability, or section. OE is a means of personal, economic and social development locally and globally.

The Principles of OE are to operate with:

Equity: free* and fair access wherever possible; transparency of process and outcome

Ethicality and legality are to be respected and exercised

Mutuality: sharing of investment and outcome

*'free/freely' means with unlimited access; this may not be cost-free in every case.

OE connects with and is enabled by all other forms of the Open [O] movement

OE recognises that the results of entrepreneurial activities, based on access to open resources, may subsequently be subject to assertion of intellectual property rights and protection of confidentiality of information, for commercial purposes.

This definition forms the basis of a conceptual model introduced in Fig. 2. OE arises through using and combining Open resources and processes. It is an entrepreneurial process which provides for free and fair access to entrepreneurial resources, means and opportunities; in other words, it is open to all. This enables new market entrants, and the creation of new value opportunities through their making new connections and generating innovations.

OE as an entrepreneurial process requires explanation. OE should provide for free-and-fair access to the resources, means and opportunities for entrepreneurial activities of value creation. A convenient and inclusive way of identifying these

Value creation through Open Entrepreneurship

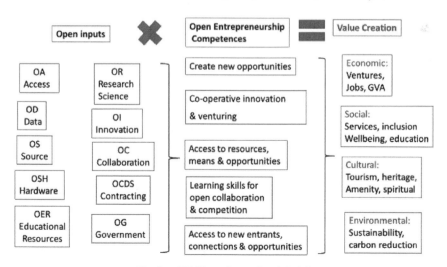

Fig. 2. OE Transformation Model.

'resources, means and opportunities' is through the GEM entrepreneurial framework, which identifies 12 dimensions of a national entrepreneurial economy, available for international comparison. These include:

- Entrepreneurial finance.
- Government policy support, relevance; taxation and bureaucracy; entrepreneurship programmes.
- Entrepreneurship education at school stage, post school and training.
- Research and development transfer.
- Commercial and legal infrastructure.
- Internal market dynamics.
- Internal market dynamics or entry regulation.
- Physical infrastructure.
- Cultural and social norms (GEM, 2018, p. 18).

These framework conditions provide internationally recognised, annually assessed and comparable indicators, at a macro (global, national and in some cases regional/provincial levels), for access to the resources and means for entrepreneurship.

Every individual experiences these at a personal, micro-level, which may not reflect a general national picture. It is the openness of information and knowledge about entrepreneurial resources, inclusion in communities of practice, and access to opportunities, which is essential. The Internet has done much to provide this access, but free web access is not universal, especially in developing and non-democratic countries. Also, the quality, reliability and currency of sources vary widely, and digital skills are required to filter these. Whilst there has been significant progress on entrepreneurship education worldwide, many students and entrepreneurs are simply not aware of essential freely available resources.

Ideally, OE would operate in conditions which enable both free and open collaboration and competition. Realistically, this may be transitional and imperfect in many instances. Co-creation, innovation and co-production can arise through collaboration. Equity of access to entrepreneurial opportunities is a necessary feature of openness. Whilst from a Kirznerian perspective, alertness to opportunities is a necessary characteristic, the role of the state as market-maker and purchaser is also an important one in signalling openness and equity in market access.

Practices such as open competition, tendering and contracting for public contracts and services through OC are essential for transparency and fairness, both to stimulate competition and reduce the scope for collusion, cronyism or corruption. These present major disadvantages to the development of an open, competitive economy in many countries, as evidenced by the Corruption Perceptions Index https://www.transparency.org/. Singapore is an example: by making public procurement opportunities and contract awards available as open data sets and being amongst the top six least corrupt nations.

OE is visualised as an input/output model which follows from Fig. 1. It can be expressed in an accessible way as 'being able to find what you need, to do what you want', through accessing chosen Open inputs and processes (from Fig. 1) and transforming these through OE competences to generate multiple forms of value creation. It both draws on, and contributes to, a range of Open and non-open inputs and processes, transforming these into innovative forms, which result in new value creation. OE as a process enables the discovery of resources with latent value, such as data sets of public land, buildings, disused and surplus assets. It enables new combinations, such as travel Apps from TfL data and OS code. Networking, collaboration and co-creation occurs both remotely and locally, enabling larger-scale projects to be addressed.

OE includes entrepreneurial competences and processes of organising for opportunity creation and discovery, collaboration, innovation, venturing and enactment, which have become mainstream in entrepreneurship studies. There is also an essential learning dimension which enables transition from prior modes of entrepreneurship, which can be informed from the entrepreneurial learning literature and reflect current entrepreneurial competences (Bacilagupo et al., 2016). Recent advances in theorising OI Learning may also offer useful insights (Ing, 2018). OE can be conceptualised as a process of learning to work within and through an environment of open, closed (private or proprietary) and liminal networks and resources.

OE generates a range of economic and wider social and environmental benefits (value creation) and impact. The literature on Social Innovation (Murray, Caulier-Grice, & Mulgan, 2010) and open collaborative innovation shows that the forms of value creation are much wider than purely financial and economic, and can be quantified through evaluation, though further advances in this field are required.

Fig. 2 proposes conceptually how OE transforms Open inputs into outputs of value creation with economic, social, cultural and environmental impact.

In relation to economic impact, economics has yet to provide a robust theory for the valuing of freely available resources, though there is research on economics of networks (e.g. Economides, 1996). Given that valuing the benefits created by freely available resources is a real-world problem of increasing significance, further work is required to address this gap. However, if open resources are seen as an unlimited digital and *global public good* (GPG; Kaul, 2013) then users are in economic terms 'beneficial free-riders' (Pasour, 1981). The GPG concept defines open resources ideally; whilst, OE itself could become a GPG.

Making open resources available as a GPG incurs costs, which in the case of OD has been researched (Walker & Simperl, 2018) and includes costs of standardising, maintaining and hosting data sets through data portals, for example. These increasing costs are generally met by public organisations. The direct and indirect costs, as well as value creation, can also be represented as an economic model.

DISCUSSION OF THE QUESTIONS RAISED

The chapter set out to explore three questions, which are considered in this final section.

(1) What is 'Open' in the context of entrepreneurship?

There has been rather slow exploration of the contribution of Open data and resources to entrepreneurship. The meaning of Open in relation to entrepreneurship should simply be consistent with the Open definition (2005) of freedom to use, modify and share the resources in question. 'Open' must mean the universal freedom to access and use entrepreneurial knowledge resources.

In comparison, the domain of OI has burgeoned and spilled over into areas in which entrepreneurship research has traditionally been active, such as small firm strategy and behaviour. Yet, how 'open' is this domain in reality? There was apparent reluctance and delay by entrepreneurship theorists and researchers to engage seriously with the Open world and connect this with entrepreneurship, although some recent contributions have finally moved in this direction (e.g. Autio et al., 2017). Also, whilst corporate and smaller organisations espousing OI are keen to use publicly available resources, they are much less inclined to make their own knowledge resources and the results of their innovation open to others.

(2) Why is the idea of 'Open' entrepreneurship important for conceptualisation, education and practice?

The world of free and Open resources is part of the everyday reality for many, yet still far from universal. To those with such access, it provides a resource of great potential value which should neither be ignored not taken for granted. Those without or unaware of such access are significantly disadvantaged. Possibly, the question has moved from 'can entrepreneurship be Open?' to 'how can entrepreneurship not be Open?'. This matter is more important than simply one for researchers, because it is essential to advance knowledge and practice in this area for broader economic and social goals of world development and inclusion. The assertion that OE creates multiple forms of value for a range of stakeholders is uncontroversial from a European perspective; there may be discussion on this from other world regions.

It may also be argued that the idea of OE is unnecessary; that it is covered satisfactorily by other concepts such as OI; or that entrepreneurship is already 'open' so it is a tautology. This is why a debate is needed. There is a gap in theory, because the Open movement requires a category for entrepreneurship; and the changing environment for global development requires means and frameworks, which can make entrepreneurship as universally accessible as possible. Also, by being 'open' in the accepted sense, it cannot simply be appropriated or 'owned' by a single new project or organisation.

(3) Can OE provide significant new opportunities for value creation, and if so, how can these be realised?

This proposed definition of OE invites differing and dissenting views and contributions to the debate. The conceptualisation of OE in the OE transformation model (Fig. 2) is ambitious, building on a high-level mapping of Open resources and processes (Fig. 1), which represents what essentially exists. The OE processes are based on existing entrepreneurial behaviours and principles, centring on opportunity, enactment, resourcing, learning and market access. More research is needed to understand how entrepreneurial processes and behaviours are used in working with Open resources.

Whilst the proposed results of value creation are at a relatively generic level, there is increasing evidence, albeit from a small base of studies, that multiple forms of value creation can be generated from entrepreneurial activity using Open resources. Economic impact is still more readily demonstrated than social, cultural and environmental. However, the essential alignment between OE and the UN SDGs, for example, means that the evaluation of wider forms of value creation from entrepreneurship is increasingly necessary (Baumol et al., 2007).

There has been a lag between the provision of some types of Open resources and their utilisation for entrepreneurial purposes. The Open Source movement has demonstrated a high level of entrepreneurial productivity from shared code over a long period. Translating public data sets into value creation may be ten years behind; yet, the data revolution, enabled by OS and increasingly by OpenAI, is already changing that. There are gaps in data literacy and skills, even at graduate, teaching and professional levels (UK Digital Strategy, 2017) and learning to make effective use of data for decision making and enhancement in many fields is a competitive issue which DigComp (Ferrari, 2013) is addressing at a European level.

So, the question about OE is less whether it can generate value creation, but how? Again, greater understanding is required of the entrepreneurial processes through which different forms of value are created, and the types of open and other resources, which are used. Learning seems to be an essential enabler for OE value creation; hence, understanding optimal forms and means of learning for Open value creation is necessary. We do not yet have a satisfactory and effective learning model for OE, although this chapter may contribute to developing one. The conceptions of learning for OI (e.g. Ing, 2018) may inform this, but there is more work to do.

Many people already use Open resources and processes for learning, innovation and value creation. The proposed model of OE simply develops this at a more general level and provides a name. However, the levels of awareness, capability and adoption of Open resources for entrepreneurship lag their availability and there is great scope for increasing these globally, and for significantly increasing entrepreneurial outcomes by doing so. Hence, one of the major challenges is of learning. Learning to adopt, use and innovate with Open resources, and specifically data, needs to become a mainstream aspect of entrepreneurship, which will act to raise expectations, increase resources and multiply outcomes.

In conclusion, this chapter offers two contributions. First, it proposes the concept of OE as a way of expressing how entrepreneurship can be used to create multiple forms of value from Open processes and resources through an open system. Second, it proposes a conceptual model for this approach. Both propositions are there to be explored, debated, tested and enhanced, or alternatively discarded if not required.

There is value to be gained in engaging business, academic research and educational, and wider Open and policy communities to explore emerging perspectives on OE. There are risks that entrepreneurial education, not least in the UK, and the working practices of 'traditional' small business owners and managers, may lag the development of an Open digital economy, rather than appreciating and seizing opportunities to create new forms of value through OE. At a global level, there is the prospect of being able to use such approaches to develop inclusive approaches, which enable 'entrepreneurship for all' in addressing the multiple challenges of economic, social, ecological and other issues, which are articulated by the UN SDG, for example. Are we ready to address this challenge?

REFERENCES

Aerni, P. (2015). *Entrepreneurial rights as human rights: Why economic rights must include the human right to science and the freedom to grow through innovation.* Cambridge: Banson.

Anthopoulos, L. (2017). *Understanding SmartCities: A tool for smart government or an industrial trick?* Berlin, Germany: Springer.

Atenas, J., & Havemann, L. (Eds.). (2015). *Open data as open educational resources: Case studies of emerging practice.* London: Open Knowledge, Open Education Working Group. http://dx.doi.org/10.6084/m9.figshare.1590031

Autio, E., Nambisan, S., Thomas, L., & Wright, M. (2018). Digital affordances, spatial affordances, and the genesis of entrepreneurial ecosystems. *Strategic Entrepreneurship Journal, 12,* 72–95.

Bacigalupo, M., Kampylis, P., Punie, Y., & Van den Brande, G. (2016). *EntreComp: The entrepreneurship competence framework.* Luxembourg: Publication Office of the European Union EUR 27939 EN. doi:10.2791/593884

Baumol, W. J., Litan, R. E., & Schramm, C. J. (2007). *Good capitalism, bad capitalism, and the economics of growth and prosperity.* New Haven, CT: Yale University Press.

Benkler, Y. (2003). Freedom in the commons: Towards a political economy of information. *Duke Law Journal, 52,* 1245–1276. Retrieved from https://scholarship.law.duke.edu/dlj/vol52/iss6/3

Benkler, Y. (2006). *The wealth of networks: How social production transforms markets and freedom.* New Haven, CT: Yale University Press.

Berends, J., Carrara, W., & Radu, C. (2017). *Analytical report 9: The economic benefits of open data.* Brussels, Belgium: EU Data portal.

Bogers, M., Chesborough, H., & Moedas, C. (2018). Open innovation: Research, practices, and policies. *California Management Review, 60*(2), 5–16.

Bogers, M., Zobel, A.-K., Afuah, A., Almirall, E., Brunswicker, S., Dahlander, L., … et al. (2017). The open innovation research landscape: Established perspectives and emerging themes across different levels of analysis. *Industry and Innovation, 24*(1), 8–40.

Burcharth, A. L. D., Knudsen, M. P., & Søndergaard, H. A. (2014). Neither invented nor shared here: The impact and management of attitudes for the adoption of open innovation practices. *Technovation, 34*(3), 149–161.

Carrara, W., San Chan, W., Fischer, S., van Steenbergen, E., & EU Report on the European Data Economy. (2017). *Creating value through open data: Study on the impact of re-use of public data resources.* Brussels, Belgium: European Data Portal.

Chesbrough, H., & Bogers, M. (2014). Explicating open innovation: Clarifying an emerging paradigm for understanding innovation. In H. Chesbrough, W. Vanhaverbeke, & J. West (Eds.), *New frontiers in open innovation* (pp. 3–28). Oxford: Oxford University Press.

Deloitte. (2017). *Assessing the value of TfL's open data and digital partnerships.* London: Deloitte.

Drucker, P. (1985). *Innovation and entrepreneurship.* London: Heinemann.

Economides, N. (1996). The economics of networks. *International Journal of Industrial Organization, 14,* 673–699.

Eftekhari, N., & Bogers, M. (2015). Open for entrepreneurship: How open innovation can foster new venture creation. *Creativity and Innovation Management, 24,* 574–584.

Ferrari, A. (2013). *DIGCOMP: A framework for developing and understanding digital competence in Europe.* European Commission EUR 26035 EN. doi:10.2788/52966

Global Entrepreneurship Monitor (GEM). (2018). *Global report 2017/2018.* Global Entrepreneurship Research Association (GERA, London).

Hossain, M. (2015). A review of literature on open innovation in small and medium-sized enterprises. *Journal of Global Entrepreneurship Research, 5*(6), 1–12.

IDC. (2017). Impact assessment of ODINE programme. Open Data Incubator Network Europe (ODINE). IDC, Framingham, MA.

Ing, D. (2018). *Open innovation learning: Theory building on open sourcing while private sourcing.* Toronto, Canada: Coevolving Innovations.

Kaul, I. (2013). *Global public goods: A concept for framing the post-2015 agenda?* Bonn, Germany: German Development Institute.

Lackéus, M., (2016). Value creation as educational practice – Towards a new educational philosophy grounded in entrepreneurship? Thesis for Doctorate in Engineering, Chalmers University of Technology, Gothenburg, Sweden.

Lackéus, M. (2018). "What is Value?" – A framework for analyzing and facilitating entrepreneurial value creation. *Uniped, 41*, 10–28.

Lee, S., Park, G., Yoon, B., & Park, J. (2009). Open innovation in SMEs—An intermediated network model. *Research Policy, 39*(2), 290–300.

Mazzucato, M. (2013). *The entrepreneurial state: Debunking public vs. private sector myths.* New York, NY: Anthem Press.

Mishra, C. S., & Zachary, R. (2014). The entrepreneurial value creation theory in the theory of entrepreneurship: Creating and sustaining entrepreneurial value (pp. 253–292). London: Palgrave MacMillan.

Murray, R., Caulier-Grice, J., & Mulgan, G. (2010). *The open book of social innovation.* London: NESTA.

OECD. (2004). Declaration on open access to publicly funded data. Paris, France: OECD.

OECD. (2015a). Data-driven innovation for growth and well-being. Paris, France: OECD.

OECD. (2015b). Open government data – OECD. Retrieved from http://www.oecd.org/gov/public-innovation/open-government-data.htm. Accessed on July 27, 2015.

Open Data Barometer. (2015). Retrieved from http://opendatabarometer.org/3rdEdition/report/#executive_summary

Open Data for Development Annual Report. (2015). Building an inclusive data revolution. Open Data for Development Network. Retrieved from http://www.stateofopendata.od4d.net/

Open Data Institute. (2015). Open data means business: UK innovation across sectors and regions. London. Retrieved from http://theodi.org/open-data-means-business-uk-innovation-sectors-regions. Accessed on November 24, 2015.

Open Data Institute. (2016). Open enterprise: How three big businesses create value with open innovation. London. Retrieved from http://theodi.org/open-enterprisebig-business

Open Data Institute. Retrieved from http://opendatainstitute.org/. Accessed on March 18, 2015.

Pasour, E. (1981). The free rider as a basis for government intervention. *The Journal of Libertarian Studies, 5*(4), 453–464.

Pollock, R. (2018). The open revolution: Rewriting the rules of the information age. Retrieved from https://openrevolution.net/. Accessed on June 23, 2018.

Popa, S., Sota-Acosta, P., & Martinez-Conesa, I. (2017). Antecedents, moderators, and outcomes of innovation climate and open innovation: An empirical study in SMEs. *Technological Forecasting & Social Change, 118*(2017), 134–142.

Rae, D., Sorrie, R., & Syms, L. (2017). How can open data inform community economic development? Open Access paper. Retrieved from www.academia.edu/32324047/How_can_Open_Data_inform_community_economic_development

Ramjoué, C. (2015). Towards open science: The vision of the European Commission. *Information Services & Use, 35*(2015), 167–170. doi:10.3233/ISU-150777

Schumpeter, J. (1934). *The theory of economic development.* MA: Harvard University Press.

Shadbolt, N., & Hampson, R. (2018). *The digital ape: How to live (in peace) with smart machines.* London: Scribe.

Spigel, B., & Harrison, R. (2018). Toward a process theory of entrepreneurial ecosystems. *Strategic Entrepreneurship Journal, 12*, 151–168.

Srinivasan, A., & Venkatraman, N. (2018). Entrepreneurship in digital platforms: A network-centric view. *Strategic Entrepreneurship Journal, 12*, 54–71.

State of Open Data, OD4D. Retrieved from http://www.stateofopendata.od4d.net/. Accessed on June 23, 2018.

The Royal Society. (2012). *Science as an open enterprise.* The Royal Society Science Policy Centre report 02/12. Retrieved from https://royalsociety.org/~/media/policy/projects/sape/2012-06-20-saoe.pdf

Tracey, P., & Stott, N. (2017). Social innovation: A window on alternative ways of organizing and inno-
    vating. *Innovation: Organization & Management,19*(1), 51–60.
UK Digital Strategy. (2017). Retrieved from https://www.gov.uk/government/publications/uk-digital-
    strategy/uk-digital-strategy. Accessed on June 23, 2018.
United Nations. (1948). *Universal declaration of human rights.* New York, NY: United Nations.
UNCTAD. (2013). The least developed countries report 2013: Growth with employment for inclu-
    sive and sustainable development. *United Nations conference on trade and development,*
    Geneva, Switzerland. (October 10, 2014). Retrieved from http://unctad.org/en/pages/
    PublicationWebflyer.aspx?publicationid. Accessed on May 30, 2014.
Vinod, H. D. (2005, July 9). Common ground in promotion of entrepreneurship and human rights.
    Conference on entrepreneurship and human rights, Fordham University, Lincoln Center Campus,
    New York, August 1–3, 2005. Retrieved from https://ssrn.com/abstract=767484 or http://
    dx.doi.org/10.2139/ssrn.767484
von Hippel, E. (2006). *Democratizing innovation.* Cambridge, MA: MIT Press. Retrieved from https://
    mitpress.mit.edu/index.php?q=books/democratizing-innovation. Accessed on May 30, 2014.
Walker, J., & Simperl, E. (2018). *Analytical report 10: Open data and entrepreneurship, European
    data portal.* Brussels. Retrieved from https://www.europeandataportal.eu/sites/default/files/
    analytical_report_10_open_data_and_entrepreneurship.pdf. Accessed June 23, 2018.
West, J., Bogers, M. (2014). Leveraging External Sources of Innovation: A Review of Research on
    Open Innovation. *The Journal of Product Innovation Management, 31*(4), 814–831.
World Bank. (2008). *Human rights and economics: Tensions and positive relationships.* Prepared for the
    Nordic Trust Fund/World Bank by GHK Consulting.
World Bank. (2014). *Open data for economic growth.* Washington, DC: World Bank. Retrieved from
    https://openknowledge.worldbank.org/handle/10986/19997

CHAPTER 10

RESEARCHING ENTREPRENEURSHIP: CONFLICTUAL RELATIONSHIPS IN A TEAM-BASED PROJECT

Oswald Jones

ABSTRACT

Teamwork has become increasingly prevalent both in undertaking research projects and in preparing papers for publication. While there are some reflections on the process of teamworking in the organisational studies literature, there is little published work in the area of entrepreneurship. Most existing studies distinguish between problems associated with task-based conflict and relationship-based conflict. In this chapter, the author provides an ethnographic account of a team involved with preparing a proposal and, subsequently, undertaking a small firm research project. The Evolution of Business Knowledge (EBK) was a major Economic and Social Research Council (ESRC) initiative which funded 13 distinct projects. During the nine-month period of preparing and refining the research proposal, the team worked together extremely effectively. There were periods of intense knowledge sharing, which enabled the team to develop an impressive and successful bid to study the 'EBK in 90 small firms'. A major dispute between team members, during the early stages of the fieldwork, led to a period of both task-based and relationship-based conflicts, which threatened to undermine the project. As a result of my first-hand experiences with the EBK project, the author suggests that accounts such as this will

Creating Entrepreneurial Space: Talking Through Multi-voices, Reflections on Emerging Debates
Contemporary Issues in Entrepreneurship Research, Volume 9B, 173–196
ISSN: 2040-7246/doi:10.1108/S2040-72462019000009B010

help those who find themselves operating in dysfunctional teams make sense of
the underlying tensions associated with 'academic knowledge creation'.

Keywords: Academic knowledge; ethnography; conflict; researching; small
firms; teamwork

INTRODUCTION

There are many publications which discuss the research methods associated with
studying entrepreneurs and small firms. For example, Davidsson (2016) provides
an extensive guide to what he describes as the conceptualisation and design of
entrepreneurial research. He argues that in the 12 years since the first edition
(Davidsson, 2004) of his book 'entrepreneurship research has undergone a tre-
mendous explosion' with much greater emphasis on both theory and method
(Davidsson, 2016, p. v). In their earlier book, Curran and Blackburn (2001)
focus on small firms rather that the individual entrepreneur and draw attention
to renewed interest in smaller enterprises. Although, as pointed out by Jones,
Macpherson, and Thorpe (2010), one of the weaknesses of research on small
firms/SMEs is the focus on the entrepreneur without acknowledging the importance of other actors including employees (Stewart & Hoell, 2016), 'the house-
hold' (Jayawarna, Rouse, & Macpherson, 2014) and various social networks
(Lee, 2017; McKeever, Anderson, & Jack, 2014). In an extensive literature review,
Blackburn and Kovalainen (2009, p. 131) identify the following three main weaknesses in entrepreneurship and small business research:

(1) Diverse agendas and mixed stakeholder demands.
(2) Methodological under-developments.
(3) Failing to engage with mainstream literatures and disciplines.

However, Busenitz, Plummer, Klotz, Shahzad, and Rhoads (2014) were much
more positive about the state of entrepreneurship research, based on their analysis
of published work in seven[1] leading business and management journals between
1985 and 2009. They claimed that there were significant increases in the volume
of entrepreneurship research published in the leading journals as well as a rise in
the number of citations. Busenitz et al. (2014, p. 15) go on to state: 'Interest from
both micro and macro areas of organizational studies has resulted in scholars
from these fields increasingly integrating entrepreneurship-related'. This positive
view is echoed by Jones and Macpherson (2014), who agree the situation has
changed with the growing importance of entrepreneurship and small firm journals in the UK (*Entrepreneurship & Regional Development* and *International Small
Business Journal*) and the US (*Entrepreneurship: Theory and Practice, Journal of
Business Venturing, Journal of Small Business Management* and *Small Business
Economics*), which are all rated 3* or 4 according the Academic Journal Guide
(Chartered Association of Business Schools). The authors also point out that
there is an increasing evidence of entrepreneurship-related research appearing

in mainstream business and management journals. For example, current articles include: *British Journal of Management* (Jayawarna, Jones and Macpherson, 2018; Marlow, Greene, & Coad, 2018), *Journal of Management Studies* (Griffin-EL & Olabisi, 2018), *Organization Studies* (Munro, 2018), *Academy of Management Journal* (Kanze & Higgins, 2018), *Academy of Management Review* (Wry & York, 2018), *Administrative Science Quarterly* (Kacperczyk & Younkin, 2017) and *Organizational Science* (Bird & Zellweger, 2018).

Other authors discuss the philosophical underpinning of research related to entrepreneurship (Lee & Jones, 2016; Lindgren & Packendorff, 2009; Ramoglou, 2013; Ramoglou & Tsang, 2016) as well as the importance of 'engaged scholarship' amongst the small business community (Whitehurst & Richter, 2018). However, there is very little published research examining the problems associated with undertaking team-based research projects to study entrepreneurs and their businesses. The paper by Whitehurst and Richter (2018) does identify tensions between team members involved in a project designed to identify how universities engage with smaller firms. Given the pressures for larger research projects, which are increasingly team-based, it is surprising that there are not more reflective accounts of the problems associated with such activities (Jarzabowski, Bednarek and Cabantous, 2015). Therefore, in this chapter, I analyse the process of academic research on entrepreneurship by drawing on data associated with a major ESRC-funded project. This narrative provides an account of the inter-subjective world (Berger & Luckmann, 1966) associated with a research project that brought together a group of individuals with varying preferences, interests, expectations and identities (Spiller et al., 2015).

At the start of the project, five of the six team members were employed in a new University Business School, based in a large northern city. The team members were involved in preparing and writing a bid associated with an ESRC initiative known as the evolution of business knowledge (EBK) (Scarbrough, 2008). Ultimately, 13 bids were successful in obtaining ESRC funding, but only one focussed on small firms. Two team members were senior academics and their roles included 'managing' the project to ensure deadlines were met as well as providing academic leadership. Another two of the six team members were eventually employed as senior research fellows (SRF) on the project and were responsible for data collection and analysis. The other two team members (one of whom was employed in a different institution) worked on the project alongside their duties as senior lecturers (SLs) with the usual administrative and teaching responsibilities. These two academics carried out some fieldwork, assisted with the analysis and provided specific areas of intellectual expertise.

This ethnographic account illustrates the conflictual relationships associated with a team of small business researchers (Czarniawska-Joerges, 1995; Hammersley, 1992). The data originate from three sources. First, my experience as a team member for the three-year project as well as time preparing the research proposal and later working on conference papers and journal articles. Secondly, I draw on documents related to management of the project to confirm key dates – such as the employment of new team member. Thirdly, all team members were interviewed by one of the SRF1, during the course of the project.

These interviews were 'inspired' by an article that also used a series of inter-views to analyse 'learning' amongst a small group of business school academics (Oswick, Anthony, Keenoy, & Mangham, 2000). It was also an attempt to explore the extent of shared understanding and interpretation of the conceptual frame-work which underpinned the fieldwork and the data analysis. Our intention, at the time, was to open 'the black-box' of academic work by providing an in-depth account of the activities associated with a major research project. According to Alvesson and Skoldberg (2000, p. 5), reflections on the relationship between the process of knowledge production and context calls for attention to elements, such as social, linguistic, theoretical, historical and political factors.

The chapter begins with a brief review of the literature associated with con-flict amongst team members. This is followed by an examination of literature dealing with the production of knowledge in academic research teams. The research approach based on an ethnographic account (Van Maanen, 1988, 2011) is discussed and this is followed by a presentation of the data. I then critically examine the data by drawing on ideas related to conflict in teams (DeChurch, Mesmer-Magnus, & Doty, 2013) and modes of academic knowledge production (Mauthner & Edwards, 2010).

TEAM-BASED CONFLICT

The paper by Oswick et al. (2000, p. 888) is based on '90 hours of tape-recorded dialogue between a group of organisational stakeholders'. These five stakeholders, all academics in the Graduate Business School of a 'leading British University', were asked to recall their views about the appointment of a new member of staff by the incoming Director. It is claimed by the authors that 'Dialogical scripting has the potential to aid the creation of deeper and richer polyphonic understand-ings of organisations and the process of organisational learning' (Oswick et al., 2000, p. 900). Although the paper does hint at tensions and conflict between team members and their new director, this is not their primary focus. A more recent paper did carry out a longitudinal study of conflict, conflict management and team effectiveness (Tekleab, Quigley, & Tesluk, 2009). As the authors point out, much of the work on conflict in teams draws on Tuckman's (1965) stage model. Individual differences and clashes in teams become most overt during 'storm-ing', when members try to clarify their roles, establish relationships with the team leader and form coalitions (Tuckman & Jensen, 1977). Essentially, the argument is that overcoming such felt and assumed differences leads to greater team cohe-sion and ultimately more effective performance (Chang, Bordia, & Duck, 2003). Also, as pointed out by Wright, Barker, Cordery, and Malt (2003), the level of intragroup conflict directly influences collective beliefs related to effectiveness. This is based on the assumptions that conflicting views and interests can be a constructive tool, thus underplaying the depth and extent of members' negative feelings and emotions and their implications for team performance.

In an extensive literature review, De Dreu and Weingart (2003) distinguished between task-based conflict and relationship-based conflict (see Maltarich,

Kukenberger, Reilly, & Mathieu, 2018). Task conflict concerns 'disagreement amongst group members about the content of the tasks being performed'. Relationship conflict refers to 'interpersonal incompatibility amongst members, which typically includes tension, animosity and annoyance among members' (Jehn, 1995, p. 258). The resolution of task-related conflict appears to have a positive impact on cohesion and effectiveness. However, if task conflict develops into relationship conflict, there is likely to be a negative impact on team performance (Edmonson & Smith, 2006). According to Tekleab et al. (2009, p. 175) team members who 'become mired in relationship conflict typically exhibit declines in satisfaction, liking other team members, and intentions to stay' (see Peterson & Behfar, 2003). Based on their longitudinal study of 53 teams (undergraduate students), Tekleab et al. (2009) conclude that conflict management has a direct positive effect on team cohesion and moderates the relationship between task and relationship conflict. Lira, Ripolli, Peiro, and Orengo (2008) also used an experimental design to examine intragroup conflict based on 176 participants, who were sub-divided into 44 groups. Task conflict appeared to have no significant direct effects on group potency. Lira et al.'s (2008) findings confirmed that relationship conflict did have an impact on group potency and this was more negative amongst those groups who communicated using IT than those who communicated face-to-face. In other words, 'the relationship between intragroup conflict and group potency is contingent on the communication medium' (Lira et al., 2008, p. 112). In a more recent study, Tekleab, Karaca, Quigley, and Tsang (2016) claim that cross-functional teams are widely used in many organisations and the links with performance are more complex because homogeneous team members have similar attitudes and adhere to similar behavioural norms. Results from the study based on 132 four-member teams of undergraduate students involved in a business simulation game indicated that 'behavioural integration' helped decrease the negative effects of functional diversity. Behavioural integration concerns activities designed to encourage harmonious relationships between team members, which promote knowledge sharing and team learning (Tekleab et al., 2016, p. 3505).

A study of 84 teams based in 38 organisations from the public sector, banks retail and the food industry examined the links between conflict, learning and team performance (van Woerkom & van Engen, 2009). The study confirmed that task conflict and relationship conflict had a negative impact on team performance. While relationship conflict had a negative impact on team learning, task conflict did not influence learning. This is particularly significant because team information processing (one of three measure of learning) was the most important influence on team performance. The authors also note that, unlike previous studies, they did not find any evidence of a positive link between task conflict and team performance (van Woerkom & van Engen, 2009, p. 398). The results of a study by Prewett, Brown, Goswami, and Christiansen (2018) confirm that 'conscientiousness' and 'emotional stability' amongst team members are valuable predictors of performance and contribute to the development of team norms. Some argue that multiplex relationships within teams have a strong influence on the links between conflict and team performance. According to Hood, Cruz, and

Bachrach (2017), multiplex relationships are those in which two or more team members have friendship ties as well as task-based ties. The results of their study indicated that while conflict can have a positive impact on team performance, the presence of multiplex relationships makes that outcome less likely. As the authors state, 'Members focused on the quality of their personal relationships may be less able to leverage conflict as a means to enhance team performance' (Hood et al., 2017, p. 82). Another study based on students engaged in a business simulation game examined conflict management approaches at the various stages of the team life-cycle. Maltarich et al. (2018, p. 8) distinguish between *competitive* (individual and team goals are mutually exclusive) and *cooperative* (individual and team goals are congruent) conflict management approaches. Counterintuitively, the results indicated that the adoption of cooperative approaches to conflict management had a negative effect on team performance. The authors explain this outcome in the following manner: 'Members of less cooperative teams view their goals as less complimentary, so relationship conflict is more consistent with the team's approach and expectations, and therefore may be less disruptive' (Maltarich et al., 2018, p. 25).

Bennett and Kidwell's (2001) study of 'self-organising' academic teams has direct implications for the present work. The research is based on a questionnaire survey of teams of authors who had published in the *Academy of Management Journal* or the *Academy of Management Review,* between 1993 and 1995. The survey included papers with between two and five co-authors and responses were only included if at least two co-authors responded, which gave a final sample size of 165. The study was designed to measure the extent to which 'withholding effort', 'not conforming to group norms' and 'the degree of affiliation' influenced the attitudes of group members. *H1*, effort levels will decrease as group size increases, was not supported. *H2*, greater effort by co-authors if there is conformity to group norms, was supported. *H3*, the degree of liking lessens the likelihood of effort decrement, was not supported (Bennett & Kidwell, 2001, p. 735). The authors concluded that findings related to *H3* were particularly important: if group members liked each other this mitigated adverse actions towards group members who withheld effort (Bennett & Kidwell, 2001, p. 739).

This brief summary of literature dealing with group behaviour suggests that 'micropolitics' are present in the day-to-day activities of most participants in team-based projects (Witt, Hilton, & Hochwarter, 2001). Micropolitics draws attention to the way individuals pursue their own career interests by attempting to obtain political influence and power (Burns, 1961; Knights & Murray, 1994; Narayanan & Fahey, 1982). For example, Jones and Stevens (1999) describe how micropolitical activity was detrimental to the outcomes of a new product development project. Blau (1954) found that the relationship between co-operation and competition between groups was influenced by the extent to which individual group members were competitive. More recently, Mauthner and Edwards (2010, p. 491) argue that

the normative divisions of labour is 'political' as well as 'intellectual' – in that [they] reflect and reinforce the differential status, value and worth of research tasks as well as high and low status people.

While Wu, Loch, and Ahmad (2011, p.3) note that status differences represent differentiated expertise and, hence, result in group organisation generating predictable patterns of interactions. Accordingly, they hypothesise that if and when status is salient in a team, individual members will increase their effort while reducing the extent of their collaboration.

ACADEMIC MODES OF KNOWLEDGE PRODUCTION

There is a growing trend for funders such as the ESRC, Leverhulme Trust, Royal Society and RCUK (Research Councils United Kingdom) to prefer projects based on large, multidisciplinary teams (Spiller et al., 2015). According to Mauthner and Doucet (2008, p. 972), this trend has occurred as a result of factors such as: 'changes in funding mechanisms, career incentives, government rewards for increased productivity, the maturation of disciplines, increased complexity and scale of research, and ease of travel and information technology'. In the UK, this trend can also be attributed to Research Assessment Exercise/Research Excellence Framework (RAE/REF) pressures for research output in the form of papers published in leading journals. The popularity of large research teams is based on the 'big science' approach associated with the natural sciences. It appears to be 'taken for granted' that the benefits of large teams are directly transferrable to the social sciences. There is, as Mauthner and Doucet (2008, p. 972) point out, 'little discussion about the relationship between collaborative research, as a mode of production (Stanley, 1990, p. 4), and the knowledge that it produces'. Although there is some evidence of reflexivity at an individual level (Callaway, 1992), there has been little empirical research, which examines the scientific practices of research teams and the associated knowledge claims (Park & Zafran, 2018). Mauthner and Doucet (2008, p. 973) suggest that drawing on Bourdieu's 'epistemic reflexivity' is appropriate for examining the nature of team-based research and practices associated with hierarchies of knowledge production.

One of the key features identified by Mauthner and Doucet (2008) is the rationale which underpins the division of labour in collaborative research. In academia, particular research activities are allocated to different team members. Mauthner and Edwards (2010, p. 491) argue that

> different types of researcher ... are responsible for different types of labour ... and carry out different types of tasks ... are becoming normative in Britain and elsewhere .... The division of labour we find ourselves forced into undermine our commitment to shared –not necessarily equal – involvement in theoretical and empirical research tasks ... and on our belief that this enhances the professional and scientific and epistemological integrity of our scholarship.

Divisions of labour and knowledge depend on the nature of the particular project and its duration (Bell, 1974). Team-based research by definition brings together individuals with different research expertise and experiences who also have different strengths and weaknesses. At one level (foundational), it is entirely logical that combining the knowledge and experience of the team is beneficial to the project as a whole. Those operating within a post-foundational epistemology reject such an objectified view of knowledge.

> If knowledge is produced through located, embodied and specific subjectivities, contexts and relations, 'putting knowledge together' entails reflexive research practices that recognise and articulate such contexts and specificities, and use them as sources of knowledge in their own right. (Mauthner & Doucet, 2008, p. 976)

Jarzabowski et al. (2015, p. 7) discuss an ethnographic study of 25 global organisations and state that team organisation involved 'overlapping relations of labour' to ensure that there were multiple modes of knowledge-sharing. A number of activities were instigated to develop a shared understanding of the global phenomena: emotional sharing, empirical reflections sharing, thematic sharing, analytic output sharing and codified sharing. Interestingly, the authors state that conflict was not 'a central part of our experience' because the sole grant holder's decision making and her leadership 'were not contentious for other team members' (Jarzabowski et al., 2015, p. 26). In contrast, Spiller et al. (2015, p. 559) acknowledge that, in their experience as six researchers, working on a multidisciplinary project 'presented some uncomfortable and sometimes painful moments for the team'. Whitehurst and Richter (2018) report on a funded project examining the way in which universities engage with the small business community. The authors point to tensions between team members associated with the problems of providing funders with practical outcomes while maintaining scholarly concern for theorising. Fragmentation of the team 'gave rise to tensions and stresses for the team members because of the balance in the first iteration was towards "doing" at the expense of "knowing" ' (Whitehurst & Richter, 2018, p. 393).

All knowledge is context-related (Mauthner, 2015) and filtered through researchers' 'affective learning' and their 'cultural repertoires' (Jakimow & Yumasdaleni, 2016, p. 172). Increasingly, even qualitative research has become decontextualised as a result of division of labour in research teams and greater use of technologies such as *NVivo* for data analysis. For example, Robins and Eisen (2017, p. 770) acknowledge that separating data collection from data analysis can create problems:

> What was lost by this division of labor were the moderators' and note takers' first-person experiences in the field, observations and impressions that can be important to fully understanding a given social or cultural phenomenon.

Such a decontextualisation is more likely in team research when data collection and data analysis are often undertaken by different people. 'Contract researchers' are usually responsible for the fieldwork and may also take on responsibility for initial (NVivo) coding of the data. Erickson and Stull (1998) suggest that data interpretation and its 'moulding' into conceptual knowledge is generally undertaken by senior members of the research team. Consequently, contextual data collected during fieldwork are unlikely to be incorporated into the final analysis. It is also probable that in most cases, the names of those who carried out the fieldwork will not appear on any published outputs from the project. As a consequence of these team processes, data objectified as text take precedence over subjective knowledge acquired during the process of data collection (Mauthner & Doucet, 2008).

Some writers suggest that fieldwork is regarded as a low-status activity which can be carried by those with little research experience. For example, McKenna (1991) argues that the division of academic labour is constituted as mental versus manual work. A process described by Reay (2000, p. 19) as the creation of 'academic hierarchies of knowledge'. Ritzer (1998) goes as far as claiming that teams of 'specialised' researchers are engaged in activities, which bear strong similarities assembly-line work. For those operating with a commitment to a post-foundational epistemology, such an approach to research is at odds with the need for a reflexive social science (Mathner & Doucet, 2008). My intention in this chapter is to provide personal reflections on the interactions between a small team of researchers while undertaking a major ESRC grant associated with small firms. The research highlights how the power struggles, attempts to assert identity and emotions shaped the task and interpersonal relationships of team members and influenced the project outcomes and deliverables.

RESEARCH METHODS

This research project was based on 90 small firms (less than 50 employees) located in the Northwest of England (Appendix). The study was designed to develop an understanding of how entrepreneurs learn from 'critical incidents' such as financial crises, losing a key staff member staff or acquiring new customers (Cope & Watts, 2000). Of particular interest was the way in which such critical incidents led to the acquisition of new knowledge and the development of learning processes within smaller firms (Jones & Macpherson, 2014). The entrepreneurs were engaged in open-ended, in-depth interviews, lasting between 60 and 90 minutes. The approach was based on a number of key questions (focus), follow-ups (more depth) and probes (clarifications) to allow the interviewer to respond flexibly by following emerging themes during the course of the interviews (Rubin & Rubin, 2005). As stated in the original proposal, it was intended that researchers would collect observational data (Newth, 2018) as well as financial data available in company reports (Jones, Ghobadian, Antcliffe, & O'Regan, 2013). Observational data were planned to include a wide range of factors, which influence entrepreneurs managing smaller firms: the type of motor vehicles belonging to the entrepreneur, dress codes within the business (employees and owners), architectural aspects of the organisation as well as the nature of interactions between entrepreneurs and their staff (Clarke, 2011). The intention was to use this observational data to provide deeper insights into the nature of knowledge and learning within smaller firms than could be obtained by simply interviewing individual entrepreneurs. This objective proved to be impossible for a number of reasons, which will be set out in the following sections.

The EBK project began with five members: PI (principal investigator), CI (co-investigator/author), SRF1, SL1 and SL2. A further SRF2 joined six months after the team was formed. Interviews carried out with individual team members by SRF1 after the project had been operating for 12 months. Initially, our objective was to record the team members' attitudes and motivations, when relationships were still harmonious and everyone was cooperating effectively. We discussed writing a joint paper with the working title of 'we know more than we know we know', which indicated the powerful knowledge creation processes that we experienced while preparing the research bid. This is what Denzin (1989, p. 34) calls 'epiphanies, or moments of revelation', which are significant events that mark people's lives and have the potential for creating transformational experiences. As indicated in the introduction, this strong *espirit de corps* was replaced by interpersonal conflict and fragmented cooperation.

The ethnographic narrative (Van Maanen, 1988, 2011), which underpins this analysis of conflict in a small business research project, is based on notes I made when relationships between team members began to deteriorate during the project (Symon, Buehring, Johnson, & Cassell, 2008). It is supplemented by institutional records, which were kept during related to the recruitment of new team members during the course of the project. At the same time, I acknowledge that this is primarily a personal account and other team members would have very different views on what created discord during the project and how that discord was managed (Gabriel, 1991).

THE EVOLUTION OF BUSINESS KNOWLEDGE

At the time we became aware of the ESRC-EBK initiative, the CI was responsible for the *Centre for Enterprise* (*CfE*) in which staff were engaged on a number of ESF and ERDF projects (Jones, Macpherson, & Woollard, 2008). Both SRF1 and SRF2 were at that time employed on a major ERDF project and SRF1 was delegated to spend time preparing the ESRC bid. Later, when the outline proposal had been accepted, SRF2 was also invited to join the EBK team. The idea to bid for funding under the EBK project emerged as a result of my discussions with the colleague who eventually became PI. The core of the team comprised the PI, the CI (author), one member of the *CfE* (SRF1) and SL1 who had been working closely with *CfE* staff on an ESF project (in addition to his other duties). A colleague (SL2) of the CI, who worked at a nearby institution, was also invited to join the team as the process of formulating a research proposal began. Preparation of the bid was the highpoint of the project as the team worked together enthusiastically. In fact, it was at this stage that we first discussed writing a paper about our experiences of working on the project. The team certainly attributed our success in obtaining ESRC funding to the ways in which different areas of expertise were combined into a coherent research proposal. The following comment from SL1 summarises the excitement of those early meetings:

> As I recall that first session, it was somewhat chaotic with a free-flowing discussion ranging around the topic and considering the nature of the bid, and the areas to which we felt we could contribute. Ideas were floated, tested and revised in discussion. They seemed to develop in a very haphazard way with some comments triggering another's thought processes. My own contribution is very hard to recall, but I do remember considering ideas around 'pools of knowledge', which sparked off SL2's discussion on industry recipes, and Spender's work with which, at that time, I was not familiar. This process of exploring ideas seemed to provide triggers for

discussion that developed into themes that were made into a limited structure of topics that we would need to consider further. These ranged across a number of themes, but looking back (and rationalizing post hoc), it was clear that we provided ideas around areas with which we were familiar, and the structure that emerged at the end of the session was clearly related to our areas of comfort – the knowledge domains with which we were more familiar.

In the early stages, a considerable amount of was time spent discussing the research methods which, while based on interviews, were also intended to have other elements which would help capture the processual elements and assist with data analysis. The PI who had previous experience of using diaries as a research tool suggested this approach would provide unique insight into how entrepreneurs engaged in sense-making activities when confronted with critical incidents. The PI also suggested use of *Decision Explorer* (DE) as a means of analysing interview data. There was some scepticism about its value because of the perception that DE was associated with psychological approaches based on 'cognitive mapping'. As a result of some investigation of the literature and PI's idea of using DE, the team agreed that it should be adopted as a means of constructing 'composite maps' of management teams. Although at this stage, we did not make this very clear in the proposal that created some later problems because the ESRC reviewer(s) misinterpreted our intentions. At the same time, the team began to develop a theoretical framework that would guide the research. SL2 suggested that Spender's (1989) concept of 'industry recipe' would provide a useful way of examining firms of different sizes based in different sectors (Appendix). In other words, the research would provide the opportunity to examine whether similar 'recipes' were adopted according to firm size or sector. Each of the five team members agreed to provide material (5/6 pages) related to their particular areas of knowledge.

> To get some structure to our thoughts we were each tasked with developing some themes that had emerged from our discussions. CI on social capital, SL2 on recipes, PI I think was 'manager as practical author'. I ended up with the task of researching and writing on networks. I do remember considering this to be very daunting since I had to work almost from scratch as I had only a limited knowledge on the subject and a short timescale to complete the task. The idea here was to circulate our writings so that we could discuss them at the next meeting. (SL1)

SL1 and SRF1 then took responsibility for combining this material into a coherent document that provided the basis for subsequent discussions. Meanwhile, the outline research proposal was submitted and we received notification at that it had been shortlisted with full proposals required within three months (January 2002). There did not appear to be any other bids, which focussed on small firms. Consequently, we believed that if our proposal were competent it would have a good chance of being funded. Also, there was a strong belief amongst team members that the basic idea was sound and that the full proposal should follow the original version quite closely. At this stage, SRF2 was asked to join the team because of his expertise in the use of language and rhetoric, which were emerging as key elements in our approach to the research questions. The outline proposal was passed to SRF2 and he was then invited to attend our first meeting to discuss the full proposal.

The pre-award period was focused on explanation – bringing thought to the domain of one another, and then from ourselves as a group to the ESRC – emphasis placed upon telling a clear, integrated and original theoretical and methodological story. The first two meetings I attended were opportunities to explain our ideas to one another (all the time, assuming the research questions retained sense). Subsequent meetings were to clarify drafts of the research proposal document. During this period I saw myself as a kind of central repository of ideas and comments regarding the six plus two page proposal description document – pulling ideas into a coherent story. Others may have seen this role differently – it was not really agreed that this was a defined role – it panned out that way – I suggest this may have been because I came into the process at a later juncture, and was without 'baggage' and so in a position to assess/sift/describe the various ideas without the weight of sensitivities. (SRF2)

One idea that gradually emerged at this time was the need for the proposal to have a strong 'Mode 2' element (Gibbons et al., 1994). I (CI) prepared a summary of the Mode 2 literature and together with the PI began to contact individuals/institutions, who could contribute to the project from a policy perspective. We eventually set out a plan for Mode 2 engagement based on seven 'conferences' over the three years of the project. The general feeling was that we had prepared enough material for the outline proposal and the major task concerned integrating this material as well as improving the research methods. Although there was agreement about the general thrust of the proposal, there was considerable debate related to specific elements of the research. Most of this debate centred on interpretations of language, particularly the concept of *recipe* (Sharifi & Zhang, 2009; Spender, 1989). At the same time, these sessions were creative in terms of linking the various elements of the proposal together. Hence, adoption of the phrase 'we know more than we know we know' because ideas or suggestions would spark links with other work.

A significant change, at the time we were finalising the proposal, was a response to SL1's suggestion that the sample should be broadened beyond service and manufacturing sectors. As a consequence, we added a 'knowledge-based sector', which was sub-divided into 'bespoke advice' and 'formulaic advice' (Appendix). Perhaps, the most ambitious element of the proposal was our decision to interview each entrepreneur (owner-manager) on three occasions at six monthly intervals (3×90 firms $= 270$ interviews). We also decided to move away from the distinction of firms based on size to capture a more dynamic element and eventually we agreed on the following categorisation: start-up, stable and innovatory.

In the latter stages, each of the team members took responsibility for specific elements of the proposal. SL2 wrote the abstract, SRF1 concentrated on breakdown of costs/equipment and also did the majority of work on the electronic submission. I wrote the non-technical summary, user engagement and communication plans. PI dealt with the section on collaboration and co-funding, and SRF2 wrote the section related to 'contribution to overall programme'. We heard immediately before Christmas (2002) that we had been successful subject to a number of factors, which required further clarification. In particular, the referees expressed concern about the 'ambitious' nature of the research method as well as expressing concern about the use of 'cognitive maps'. I used the Christmas break to prepare a document which explained and justified the use of DE. The revised document was acceptable to the ESRC and our award was confirmed. For a little while after confirmation of the award, the team continued to work well together (SRF2):

> The post-award period has been focused on understanding methodology – bringing others' thoughts on methodological approach into our own domains. We have assumed (for the while) the grant award has validated the research approach and, accepting this, we are now focused upon the issues of method. It may be that this is allowing us to bond as a group – it is a relatively non-contentious area – allowing us not only to create sense by communication (making bridges between our respective domains), but also by absorption (we are beginning to see where we share worldviews). For example, by building up the interview structure and questions we invest in the pro-forma as a symbol of interaction. If we can do it for this, then we have demonstrated that we can absorb one another's perspectives on epistemological/ontological grounds. We do not want to absorb too much – value in conflict?

However, soon after receiving confirmation that the bid had been successful (March 2003) but, before the project actually started in September 2003, there was a major disagreement that threatened the future of the project. Essentially, this dispute concerned 'ownership' of EBK as the PI accepted a job at another business school and planned to transfer the project to his new institution. Eventually, the dispute was resolved with the project remaining at the original institution with a transfer of some funding to the PI's new institution. Nevertheless, ongoing conflict associated with this issue had a seriously destabilising effect on the project. Essentially, the team fragmented into two distinct groups: the PI and SRF2 and C1 and SL2. SRF1 was 'loosely' linked to the second group but largely isolated from the other team members. SL1 spanned the two groups and maintained a friendly working relationship with all the team members (Fig. 1).

This disagreement led to period of inertia which was particularly detrimental to progress with the fieldwork. In addition, neither of the core research staff (SRF1 and SRF2) were particularly motivated to engage with entrepreneurs. SRF1 lacked the appropriate interviewing skills and allowed his own

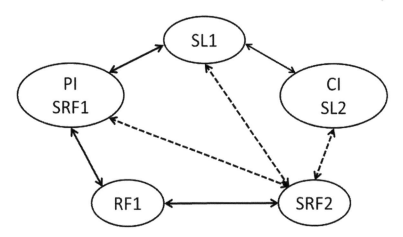

Fig. 1. Team Relationships at Start of Fieldwork.

monologues dominate the exchanges; gradually, he was diverted to other activities. SRF2 was primarily interested in the 'knowledge' work associated with the operationalisation of activity theory (AT) and the associated analyses. Consequently, in September 2004, an additional research fellow (RF1) was recruited to identify appropriate firms and carry out interviews. RF1 was highly skilled in negotiating access to owner-managed firms and extremely proficient in undertaking the interviews. Her interviews were done with consummate professionalism and she carried out approximately 80% of all the fieldwork. As discussed below, there were some negative aspects associated with RF1 carrying out bulk of the interviews.

RF1 had not been involved in the earlier conceptualisation and was not encouraged to have any greater involvement other than interviewing and transcribing, which meant there was a lack of 'epistemic reflexivity'. RF1 also seemed bemused by tensions within the group and the disharmony and hostility, which permeated most team meetings. She did, however, establish a reasonable working relationship with SRF1, who remained largely isolated from the other team members. Following the PI's decision to take up another appointment, the team never regained a coherent sense of purpose. Fragmentation and distrust were accentuated when SRF2 left at the end of 2005 to take up a post at the same institution as the PI. This created a number of major problems for the project as he had been the driving force behind the operationalisation of AT (Engeström, 2001), carried out all the data coding and most of the NVivo analysis. After leaving, SRF2 made no further contribution to the project. Another RF2 was recruited internally for the final 12 months of the grant. However, she had limited interest in either the conceptual approach (Engeström, 1987) or the topic of managing small firms. Consequently, other than continuing the data-coding as interviews were processed, she had very little direct impact on the project. The outcome of these changes in personnel meant that it was very difficult to maintain consistency or high levels of inter-rater reliability in the data-coding (Sanders & Cuneo, 2010).

After moving to his new post, SRF2 had no further engagement with the EBK project and there was a realignment of relationships amongst the group (Fig. 2). SRF1 and RF1 began to work more closely together but the newly recruited RF2 (NVivo coding) remained isolated from other team members. SL1 continued to act as a bridge between the PI and CI. Gradually, the team negotiated a reasonable (and tense) working relationship because the remaining members had a vested interest in the project's successful. As the team members were dispersed geographically, as well as emotionally and intellectually, the strong sense of a common purpose, so evident in the early stages, was never recaptured. For example, RF1 did not make any contribution beyond carrying out the majority of interviews with owner-managers and was never included on any publications. While the fieldwork was very important, she was not encouraged to make an intellectual contribution to the project. At the same time, SRF1 became increasingly isolated as a result of his apparent lack of motivation to engage fully with either the fieldwork or the data analyses. Ultimately, the project did achieve all objectives in terms of Mode 2 engagement and, in terms of academic outputs,

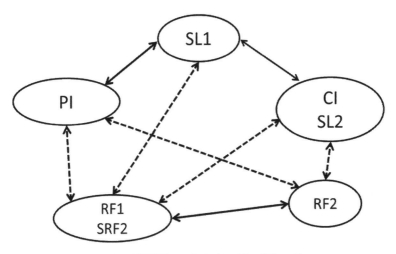

Fig. 2. EBK Team Relationships (Time 2).

including publications, events at major conferences such as the British Academy of Management and the Academy of Management. In addition, this project was the only one of 13 in the EBK initiative, which received an 'outstanding' grade from the ESRC assessors.

DISCUSSION: CONFLICT, KNOWLEDGE PRODUCTION AND THE EBK TEAM

As discussed in the introduction, there are a wide range of publications dealing with research related to entrepreneurship and smaller firms (Blackburn & Kovalainen, 2009; Busenitz et al., 2014; Davidsson, 2016; Jones & Macpherson, 2014; Whitehurst & Richter, 2018), as well as publications discussing the philosophical underpinnings of research related to entrepreneurship (Lee & Jones, 2016; Lindgren & Packendorff, 2009; Ramoglou, 2013; Ramoglou & Tsang, 2016). While there is published material which examines the various aspects of team-based research including reflexivity (Park & Zafran, 2018), emotions (Jakimow & Yumasdaleni, 2016), conflict (De Drue & Weingart, 2003; Hood et al., 2017; Lira et al., 2008; Maltarich et al., 2018), team learning (Tekleab et al., 2016), methodological and epistemological issues (Jarzabowski et al., 2015; Mauthner & Doucet, 2008), none of this focusses on teams engaged in the study of entrepreneurs and entrepreneurship. Therefore, a better understanding of the tensions and conflict associated with team-based studies of entrepreneurship/small business are important for future development of the field.

The EBK team did not follow the trajectory of group relationships described by Tuckman (1965), perhaps because most members were well-known to each other before the project was initiated. In terms of 'performativity', the group was most effective at the very early stages of brainstorming and writing the proposal.

In fact, there were strong friendship ties amongst most team members prior to the project (Hood et al., 2017). Towards the end of the project as relationships were gradually re-established, the group began to perform at quite a high level. Part of the reason for this was no doubt that, in the later stages, there was less need to work together as a group and many activities could be undertaken in relative isolation with most communication taking place *via* email. Writing the final report, for example, did not necessitate the kind of intellectual and emotional engagement, which was so evident during the 'brainstorming' phase of the project.

There were considerable amounts of relational conflict between myself and the PI, which, for at least 12 months, threatened to destabilise the entire project. There were also substantial amounts of task conflict (De Dreu & Weingart, 2003) within the group, related to responsibilities for carrying out the fieldwork. For very different reasons, neither of the two senior research fellows (SRF1 and SRF2), who were employed full-time on the project, were committed to the fieldwork. As described earlier, this was eventually rectified by taking on an additional researcher (RF1), who carried out most of the interviews without being conceptually or contextually embedded in the project. While this resolved the immediate problem of completing the fieldwork, it certainly did not help with the team's ambitions to go beyond conventional 'in-depth' interviews as a means of data collection. The original intention was to incorporate a range of data collection techniques in addition to interviews with the entrepreneurs. These included using *DE* to construct 'composite maps' of activities within the firms, diaries to obtain longitudinal data on 'critical incidents' and the collection of contextual data such as 'dress codes', interactions between owner-managers and their employees as well as status symbols including cars and office furnishing (Clark, 2011). While there was some attempt to encourage a small group of owner-managers to keep regular diaries, this activity did not make any real contribution to the project. This failure can certainly be attributed, in part, to the academic division of labour within the team (Mauthner & Doucet, 2010). While RF1 was excellent at negotiating access and conducting interviews, she was not an experienced researcher and was not encouraged to engage in data analysis or in preparing papers for publication.

The team had eventually agreed to adopt 'AT' (Engeström, 1991) as the intellectual basis of the research. AT places a great emphasis on the cultural and historical context in which social activities take place. Hence, it is necessary to identify the way in which community norms are negotiated, the artefacts that define those norms as well as the divisions of labour and tools (including language) associated with the activity system (Blackler, 1995; Engeström 1987; Engeström & Blackler, 2000). Tensions in a system result in reflection and negotiation with others in the community about how to solve problems creating a cycle of expansive learning (Engeström, 1991, 2001). Team members realised from the outset that adopting an AT approach required a range of sophisticated data collection techniques. While AT was regularly discussed at meeting attended by RF1, there was never any attempt to encourage her to engage with the intellectual ideas, which underpinned the project. Ultimately, AT was used in an extremely pragmatic fashion to structure the interview schedule and frame the data analysis. Gradually, we realised that our initial target of 270 interviews was impractical given the time lost during the early stage of the project. We, therefore, took a pragmatic decision to try and do at least two interviews in our sample of 90 small firms.

Our original ambition was to do research that really was different both in terms of scale and scope was certainly not achieved. Ultimately, the fieldwork was regarded as a 'low-status activity' (McKenna, 1991; Reay, 2000; Ritzer, 1998) as neither of the SRFs engaged with the data collection. RF1, who did most of the interviews, had no engagement with either analysis or interpretation of the data. In addition, a great deal of project time was devoted to using NVivo to code and categorise the interviews. SRF2 did most of this work during the early phases of the fieldwork as he had been primarily responsible for the 'operational-isation' of AT in the form of an 'interview schedule'. When SRF2 left the project, it created a number of major problems because he was the only one who really understood the coding system (Sanders & Cuneo, 2010). SRF1 was 'replaced' by RF2 (a recent graduate from the institution's doctoral programme), who was employed for a year to undertake the remainder of the coding. RF2 had very little intellectual engagement with project and had no desire to extend the work when her one-year contract was completed.

Despite many problems, the project was judged to be a 'success' and it achieved many of the original goals associated with a 'Mode 2' engagement and a respectable amount of publications. However, most outputs from the project appeared in 3* journals[2] with few publications in 4-rated journals. Nor was the project successful in terms of the team's original ambitions for EBK. For example, public claims for the uniqueness of 'EBK' always stressed the value of our sample (at least two interviews in 90 small firms representing a wide range of sectors and sizes). This 'rhetoric' has been used in many attempts to set a policy agenda and successfully obtain two ESRC 'follow-on' grants. Part of the motivation for this engagement has been prompted by a genuine desire to positively influence the political debate about the role of academics in supporting entrepreneurship and the small firm community (Trehan, Higgins, & Jones, 2018; Whitehurst & Richter, 2018). Much of this debate has been stimulated by a desire to rebut the influence of those such as Storey (2011) in the UK and Shane (2009) in the US, who argue for a 'free market' approach to the support of entrepreneurs and SMEs. At the same time, there has also been a strong micropolitical dimension as the project has been used to enhance the careers of a number of the participants (including my own of course). Also, as indicated already, many of these interviews were carried out in a cursory and mechanistic fashion with no attempt to capture any contextual data. Consequently, most of the published outputs from the project are based on a small number of companies, which were known to me and other members of the team (primarily SL1) from previous research projects. More than 12 years after the project was completed, there are still discussions about how we could achieve our original aim of analysing the whole dataset.

CONCLUSIONS

Writing this chapter was a cathartic activity to resolve some of the longstanding frustrations associated with my participation in the project. I have used the EBK as a touchstone in my career because of its status as one of the few major ESRC-funded studies of small firms. I certainly regarded our successful proposal as a major achievement for the team as it was the outcome of period in which our working relationships were extremely intensive and productive. I have also continued to promote the fact that our project was the only one of 13 associated with the EBK, which obtained an outstanding grade from ESRC assessors. At the same time, my frustration remains that, as a team, we did not achieve what we set out to do in our original objectives. There were four key failures: first, the majority of interviews were not informed by the theoretical underpinnings of the research proposal. This was certainly not the fault of RF1, who did her best to collect the data in a professional manner. Rather, it was a collective failure of the team in not encouraging the researcher to engage with AT (Blackler, 1995; Engeström, 1987) and recipes (Spender, 1989). Divisions of labour amongst team members meant that the data collection was entirely detached from the interpretation and moulding of conceptual ideas, which formed the basis of published work (Erickson & Stull, 1998; Mauthner & Doucet, 2008; Mauthner & Edwards, 2010).

Secondly, the related problem was that we did not collect contextual data associated with each of the small firms and relied entirely on interviews with individual entrepreneurs (Clark, 2011). Partly, this was a result of time pressures caused by delays associated with the team-based conflict described above. It was also result of RF1's isolation from the theories, which informed the writing of the research proposal. Thirdly, although all of the interviews were transcribed and coded the team members have never attempted to write-up the results of the project as a whole. Consequently, the majority of publications from the project were based on a very small subset of the total sample of 90 firms. Fourthly, as indicated earlier, none of the research outputs appeared in leading entrepreneurship journals (*Entrepreneurship: Theory and Practice*; *Journal of Business Venturing*) or other top-rated journals.

In this chapter, I have discussed the internal conflicts that weakened the EBK team's ability to function as an effective unit. I acknowledge that this is a subjective account and no doubt the other five participants would provide different narratives of the EBK project. While not all team members would agree with the source of the conflict, there is no doubt that once the project began it was plagued by task and relational conflict, which were major contributory factors in terms of the failure to meet our more ambitious goals. This is my own personal story, which does not consider the views of other team members about the way in which the EBK project evolved. However, since completing my PhD, I have been committed to the importance of researchers providing realistic accounts of what 'doing' research is really like in practice (Jones, 1995). Therefore, however flawed this account, it is a genuine attempt to reveal some of the darker elements associated with knowledge-based teamwork in academia. In their introduction to a recent special issue, Linstead, Maréchal, and Griffin, (2014) suggest that there are a wide range of approaches to studying the dark side of organisation life. According to the authors, early studies concentrated on *abnormal* or *deviant* behaviours, while later work focusses on 'the ambiguous, motivated behaviours that contribute to human and organizational processes that can simultaneously become functional or dysfunctional depending on the nature of motivation' (Linstead et al., 2014, p. 167). I am certainly not suggesting that there was any behaviour that could be termed abnormal or deviant within the EBK team. Rather, the project brought together a disparate group of researchers who were motivated by to obtain a major ESRC grant. Beyond that, clearly some members of the team were pursuing personal goals (micropolitics), which at times were complementary to the project and at other times conflicted with the overall objectives.

I believe that revealing some of the problems associated with working in academic teams is important because of pressure from the funding bodies (Spiller et al., 2015) and single-authored papers are rare in top journals. While many of those teams may comprise members of equal status, there will certainly be others which are based on more hierarchical relationships. As discussed already, it is likely that there will be a clear division of labour in such teams with junior members having responsibility for the more mundane and time-consuming tasks (Mauthner & Doucet, 2008; Mauthner & Edwards, 2010). Furthermore, readers are rarely given any insight into the dynamics of 'doing' research and writing papers as a team. I know from my own experience of preparing joint papers that team dynamics are not discussed in explaining how the research was carried out nor how the papers were written. Even the paper by Oswick et al. (2000), which initially 'inspired' the EBK members to reflect on their own experiences had little to say about tensions and conflicts between participants. The survey carried out by Bennett and Kidwell (2001) reveals some of the underlying tensions associated with team-written papers. Hopefully, accounts such as this may help those who find themselves operating in dysfunctional teams to make sense of the underlying tensions associated with 'academic knowledge creation'. Given the current REF-based obsession with research outputs (Butler & Spoelstra, 2014) and the importance of publications for future promotion prospects (Beattie & Goodacre, 2012), it is unlikely that working in teams will be conflict free in the future.

NOTES

1. *Academy of Management Journal* (*AMJ*), the *Academy of Management Review* (*AMR*), the *Strategic Management Journal* (*SMJ*), the *Journal of Management* (*JOM*), *Organization Science* (*OS*), *Management Science* (*MS*) and *Administrative Science Quarterly* (*ASQ*).
2. *Entrepreneurship & Regional Development, International Small Business Journal, Management Learning, Long Range Planning, R&D Management.*

REFERENCES

Alvesson, M., & Skoldberg, K. (2000). *Reflexive methodology*. London: Sage Publications.
Beattie, V., & Goodacre, A. (2012). Publication records of accounting and finance faculty promoted to professor: Evidence from the UK. *Accounting and Business Research, 42*(2), 197–231.

Bell, D. (1974). *The coming of post-industrial society: A venture in social forecasting.* London: Heinemann Education.

Berger, P., & Luckmann, T. (1966). *The social construction of reality.* London: Penguin.

Bennett, N., & Kidwell, R. (2001). The provision of effort in self-designing groups: The case of collaborative research. *Small Group Research, 32,* 727–744.

Bird, M., & Zellweger, T. (2018). Relational embeddedness and firm growth: Comparing spousal and sibling entrepreneurs. *Organization Science, 29*(2), 264–283.

Blackburn, R., & Kovalainen, A. (2009). Researching small firms. *International Journal of Management Reviews, 11*(2), 127–148.

Blackler, F. (1995). Knowledge, knowledge work and organizations. *Organization Studies, 16*(6), 1021–1046.

Blau, P. M. (1954). Co-operation and competition in a bureaucracy. *American Journal of Sociology, 59*(6), 530–535.

Burns, T. (1961). Micropolitics: Mechanisms of institutional change. *Administrative Science Quarterly, 6,* 257–228.

Busenitz, L. W., Plummer, L. A., Klotz, A. C., Shahzad, A., & Rhoads, K. (2014). Entrepreneurship research (1985–2009) and the emergence of opportunities. *Entrepreneurship: Theory and Practice, 38*(5), 981–1000.

Butler, N., & Spoelstra, S. (2014). The regime of excellence and the erosion of ethos in **critical** management studies. *British Journal of Management, 25*(3), 538–555.

Callaway, H. (1992). Ethnography and experience. In J. Okely & H. Callaway (Eds.), *Anthropology and autobiography* (pp. 29–48). London: Routledge.

Chang, A., Bordia, P., & Duck, J. (2003). Punctuated equilibrium and linear progression: Toward a new understanding of group development. *Academy of Management Journal, 46,* 107–117.

Clarke, J. (2011). Revitalizing entrepreneurship: How visual symbols are used in entrepreneurial performances. *Journal of Management Studies, 48*(6), 1365–1391.

Cope, J., & Watts, G. (2000). Learning by doing: An exploration of experience, critical incidents and reflection in entrepreneurial learning. *International Journal of Entrepreneurial Behaviour & Research, 6*(3), 104–125.

Curran, J., & Blackburn, R. (2001). *Researching the small enterprise.* London: Sage.

Czarniawska-Joerges, B. (1995). Narration or science? Collapsing the division in organisation studies. *Organization, 2*(1), 11–34.

Davidsson, P. (2004). *Researching entrepreneurship.* New York, NY: Springer.

Davidsson, P. (2016). *Researching entrepreneurship: Conceptualisation and design* (2nd ed.). New York, NY: Springer.

DeChurch, L. A., Mesmer-Magnus, J. R., & Doty, D. (2013). Moving beyond relationship and task conflict: Toward a process state perspective. *Journal of Applied Psychology, 98*(4), 559–578.

De Dreu, C., & Weingart, L. (2003). Task versus relationship conflict, team performance and team member satisfaction: A meta-analysis. *Journal of Applied Psychology, 88,* 741–749.

Denzin, N. K. (1989). *Interpretive biography.* London: Sage.

Edmondson, A. C., & Smith, D. M. (2006). Too hot to handle? How to manage relationship conflict. *California Management Review, 49*(1), 6–31.

Erickson, K., & Stull, D. (1998). *Doing team ethnography: Warnings and advice.* Thousand Oaks, CA: Sage.

Engeström, Y. (1987). *Learning by expanding: An activity-theoretical approach to developmental research.* Helsinki: Orienta-Konsultit.

Engeström, Y. (1991). Developmental work research: Reconstructing expertise through expansive learning. In M. I. Nurminen, & G. R. S. Weireds (Eds.), *Human jobs and computer interfaces.* (pp. 265–290). Amsterdam: Elsevier.

Engeström, Y. (2001). Expansive learning at work: Toward an activity theoretical reconceptualization. *Journal of Education and Work, 14*(1), 133–156.

Engeström, Y., & Blackler, F. (2005). On the life of the object. *Organization, 12*(3), 307–330.

Gabriel, Y. (1991). Turning facts into stories and stories into facts: A hermeneutic exploration of organisational folklore. *Human Relations, 44*(8), 857–876.

Gibbons, M., Limoges, C., Nowotny, H., Schwartzman, S., Scott, P., & Trow, M. (1994). *The new production of knowledge.* London: Sage.

Griffin-EL, E. W., & Olabisi, J. (2018). Breaking boundaries: Exploring the process of intersective market activity of immigrant entrepreneurship in the context of high economic inequality. *Journal of Management Studies, 55*(3), 457–485.

Hammersley, M. (1992). *What's wrong with ethnography? Methodological explanations.* London: Routledge.

Hood, A. C., Cruz, K. S., & Bachrach, D. G. (2017). Conflicts with friends: A multiplex view of friendship and conflict and its association with performance in teams. *Journal of Business Psychology, 32*, 73–86.

Jakimow, T., & Yumasdaleni, (2016). Affective registers in qualitative team research: Interpreting the self in encounters with the state. *Qualitative Research Journal, 16*(2), 169–180,

Jarzabkowski, P., Bednarek, R., & Cabantous, L. (2015). Conducting global team-based ethnography: Methodological challenges and practical methods. *Human Relations, 68*(1), 3–33.

Jayawarna, D., Jones, O., & Macpherson, A. (2018). Managing social enterprises: The role of socially oriented bootstrapping practices. *British Journal of Management*, DOI: 10.1111/1467-8551.12334. Retrieved from http://livrepository.liverpool.ac.uk/id/eprint/3029060.

Jayawarna, D., Rouse, J., & Macpherson, A. (2014). Modelling pathways to entrepreneurship: A life course perspective. *Entrepreneurship & Regional Development, 26*(3–4), 282–312.

Jehn, K. A. (1995). A multi-method examination of the benefits and detriments of intragroup conflict. *Administrative Science Quarterly, 40*(2), 256–282.

Jones, O. (1995). No guru, no method, no teacher: A critical view of (my) managerial research. *Management Learning, 26*(1), 109–127.

Jones, O., Ghobadian, A., Antcliffe, V., & O'Regan, N. (2013). Dynamic capabilities in a sixth generation family firm: Entrepreneurship and the Bibby Line. *Business History, 55*(6), 910–941.

Jones, O., & Macpherson, A. (2014). Research perspectives on learning in small firms. In E. Chell & M. Karatas-Ozkan (Eds.), *Handbook of research on small business and entrepreneurship.* (pp. 289–314). Cheltenham: Edward Elgar.

Jones, O., Macpherson, A., & Thorpe, R. (2010). Learning in owner-managed small firms: Mediating artefacts and strategic space. *Entrepreneurship and Regional Development, 22*(7/8), 649–673.

Jones, O., Macpherson, A., & Woollard, D. (2008). Entrepreneurial ventures in higher education: Analyzing organizational growth. *International Small Business Journal, 26*(6), 683–708.

Jones, O., & Stevens, G. (1999). Evaluating failure in the innovation process: The micropolitics of new product development. *R&D Management, 29*(2), 167–179.

Kacperczyk, A., & Younkin, P. (2017). The paradox of breadth: The tension between experience and legitimacy in the transition to entrepreneurship. *Administrative Science Quarterly, 62*(4), 731–764.

Kanze, D., Huang, L., Conley, M. A., & Higgins, E. T. (2018). We ask men to win and women not to lose: Closing the gender gap in startup funding. *Academy of Management Journal, 61*(2), 586–614.

Knights, D., & Murray, F. (1994). *Managers divided: Organizational politics and information technology management.* Chichester: Wiley.

Lee, R. (2017). *The social capital of entrepreneurial newcomers: Bridging, status-power and cognition.* London: Palgrave Macmillan.

Lee, R., & Jones, O. (2008). Networks, communication and learning during business start-up. *International Small Business Journal, 26*(5), 559–594.

Lindgren, M., & Packendorff, J. (2009). Social constructionism and entrepreneurship: Basic assumptions and consequences for theory and research. *International Journal of Entrepreneurial Behaviour and Research, 15*(1), 25–47.

Linstead, S., Maréchal, G., & Griffin, R. (2014). Theorizing and researching the dark side of organization. *Organization Studies, 35*(2), 165–188.

Lira, E. M., Ripolli, P., Peiro, J. M., & Orengo, V. (2008). How do different types of intragroup conflict affect group potency in virtual compared to face-to-face teams? A longitudinal study. *Behavior and Information Technology, 27*(2), 107–114.

Maltarich, M. A., Kukenberger, M., Reilly, G., & Mathieu, J. (2018). Conflict in teams: Modeling early and late conflict states and the interactive effects of conflict processes. *Group & Organization Management, 43*(1), 6–37.

Marlow, S., Greene, F. J., & Coad, A. (2018). Advancing gendered analyses of entrepreneurship: A critical exploration of entrepreneurial activity among gay men and lesbian women. *British Journal of Management, 29*(1), 118–135.

Mauthner, N. S. (2015) The past was never simply there to begin with & the future is not simply what will unfold: A posthumanist performative approach to qualitative longitudinal research. *International Journal of Social Research Methodology*, *18*(3), 321–336.

Mauthner, N. S., & Doucet, A. (2008). Knowledge once divided can be hard to put together again: An epistemological critique of collaborative and team-based research practices. *Sociology*, *42*(5), 971–985.

Mauthner, N. S., & Edwards, R. (2010). Feminist research management in higher education in Britain: Possibilities and practices. *Gender, Work & Organization*, *17*(5), 481–502.

McKeever, E., Anderson, A., & Jack, S. (2014). Social embeddedness in entrepreneurship research: The importance of context and community. In E. Chell & M. Karatas-Ozkan (Eds.), *Handbook of research on small business and entrepreneurship*. (pp. 222–236). Cheltenham: Edward Elgar.

McKenna, K. (1991). Subjects of discourse: Learning the language that counts. In H. Bannerji, L. Carty, K. Dehli, S. Heald, & K. McKenna (Eds.), *Unsettling relations: The university as a site of feminist struggles* (pp. 109–28). Toronto, Canada: Women's Press.

Munro, R. (2018). Creativity, organisation and entrepreneurship: Power and play in the ecological press of money. *Organization Studies*, *39*(2–3), 209–227.

Narayanan, V. K., & Fahey, L. (1982). The micropolitics of strategy formulation. *Academy of Management Review*, *7*(1), 25–34.

Newth, J. (2018). "Hands-on" vs "arm's length" entrepreneurship research: Using ethnography to contextualize social innovation. *International Journal of Entrepreneurial Behavior & Research*, *24*(3), 683–696.

Oswick, C., Anthony, P., Keenoy, T., & Mangham, I. (2000). A dialogic analysis of organizational learning. *Journal of Management Studies*, *37*(6), 887–901.

Park, M., & Zafran, H. (2018). View from the penthouse: Epistemological bumps and emergent metaphors as method for team reflexivity. *Qualitative Health Research*, *28*(3), 408–417.

Peterson, R. S., & Behfar, K. J. (2003). The dynamic relationship between performance, feedback, trust and conflict in groups: A longitudinal study. *Organizational Behavior & Human Decision Processes*, *92*, 102–112.

Prewett, M. S., Brown, M. I., Goswami, A., & Christiansen, N. D. (2018). Effects of team personality composition on member performance: A multilevel perspective. *Group & Organization Management*, *43*(2), 316–348.

Ramoglou, S. (2013). On the misuse of realism in the study of entrepreneurship. *Academy of Management Review*, *38*(3), 463–465.

Ramoglou, S., & Tsang, E. W. (2016). A realist perspective of entrepreneurship: Opportunities as propensities. *Academy of Management Review*, *41*(3), 410–434.

Reay, D. (2000). "Dim Dross": Marginalised women both inside and outside the academy. *Women's Studies International Forum*, *23*(1), 13–21.

Ritzer, G. (1998). *The McDonaldization thesis*. London: Sage.

Robins, C. S., & Eisen, K. (2017). Strategies for the effective use of NVivo in a large-scale study: Qualitative analysis and the repeal of *Don't Ask, Don't Tell*. *Qualitative Inquiry*, *23*(10), 768–778.

Rubin, H., & Rubin, I. (2005). *Qualitative interviewing: The art of hearing data* (2nd ed.). London: Sage.

Sanders, C. B., & Cuneo, C. J. (2010). Social reliability in qualitative team research. *Sociology*, *44*(2), 325–343.

Scarbrough, H. (Ed.). (2008). *The evolution of business knowledge*. Oxford: Oxford University Press.

Shane, S. (2009). Why encouraging more people to become entrepreneurs in bad public policy. *Small Business Economics*, *33*, 141–149.

Sharifi, S., & Zhang, M. (2009). Sense-making and recipes: Examples from selected small firms. *International Journal of Entrepreneurial Behaviour & Research*, *15*(6), 555–571.

Spender, J. (1989). *Industry recipes: The nature and sources of managerial judgement*. Oxford: Basil Blackwell.

Spiller, K., Ball, K., Daniel, E., Dibb, S., Meadows, M., & Canhoto, A. (2015). Carnivalesque collaborations: Reflections on 'doing' multi-disciplinary research. *Qualitative Research*, *15*, 551–567.

Stanley, L. (1990). Feminist praxis and the academic mode of production. In L. Stanley (Ed.), *Feminist praxis* (pp. 3–19). London: Routledge.

Stewart, S. A., & Hoell, R. C. (2016). Hire someone like me, or hire someone I need: Entrepreneur identity and early-stage hiring in small firms. *Journal of Small Business & Entrepreneurship*, *28*(3), 187–201.

Storey, D. (2011). Optimism and chance: The elephants in the entrepreneurship room. *International Small Business Journal*, *29*(4), 303–321.

Symon, G., Buehring, A., Johnson, P., & Cassell, C. (2008). Positioning qualitative research as resistance to the institutionalization of the academic labour process. *Organization Studies*, *29*(10), 1315–1336.

Tekleab, A. G., Karaca, A., Quigley, N. R., & Tsang, E. (2016). Re-examining the functional diversity performance relationship: The roles of behavioral integration, team cohesion, and team learning. *Journal of Business Research*, *69*(3), 3500–3507.

Tekleab, A. G., Quigley, N. R., & Tesluk, P. E. (2009). A longitudinal study of team conflict, conflict management, cohesion and team effectiveness. *Group and Organization Management*, *34*(2), 170–205.

Trehan, K., Higgins, D., & Jones, O. (2018). Engaged scholarship: Questioning relevance and impact in contemporary entrepreneurship/small and medium-sized enterprise research. *International Small Business Journal*, *36*(4), 363–367.

Tuckman, B. W. (1965). Development sequences in small groups. *Psychological Bulletin*, *63*, 384–399.

Tuckman, B. W., & Jensen, M. A. (1977). Stages of small group development revisited. *Group & Organizational Studies*, *2*(4), 419–427.

Van Maanen, J. (1988). *Tales of the field: On writing ethnography*. Chicago, IL: Chicago University Press.

Van Maanen, J. (2011). Ethnography as work: Some rules of engagement. *Journal of Management Studies*, *48*(1), 218–234.

Van Woerkom, M., & van Engen, M. (2009). Learning from conflicts? The relations between task and relationship conflicts, team learning and team performance. *European Journal of Work & Organizational Psychology*, *18*(4), 381–404.

Whitehurst, F., & Richter, P. (2018). Engaged scholarship in small firm and entrepreneurship research: Grappling with Van de Ven's diamond model in retrospect to inform future practice. *International Small Business Journal*, *36*(4), 380–399.

Witt, L. A., Hilton, T. F., & Hochwarter, W. A. (2001). Addressing politics in matrix teams. *Group & Organization Management*, *26*(2), 230–247.

Wright, B. M., Barker, J. P., Cordery, J. L., & Malt, B. E. (2003). The ideal participative state: A prelude to work group effectiveness. *Journal of Business & Management*, *9*, 171–188.

Wry, T., & York, J. G. (2017). An identity-based approach to social enterprise. *Academy of Management Review*, *42*(3), 437–460.

Wu, Y., Loch, C., & Ahmad, G. (2011). Status and relationships in social dilemmas of teams. *Journal of Operations Management*, *29*, 650–662.

Appendix: Small Firms in the EBK Sample

	Culture and leisure	Retail	Bespoke advice	Formulaic advice	Low-tech manuf	High- tech manuf
Startup	5	5	5	5	5	5
Stable	5	5	5	5	5	5
Inno-vative	5	5	5	5	5	5
Total	15	15	15	15	15	15

ABOUT THE EDITORS

David Higgins is Lecturer with the University of Liverpool in the area of Management and Entrepreneurship, with over 10 years' experience in the field of entrepreneurial learning/education in the university sector. David is an active researcher and scholar in the field of entrepreneurship with a host of over 30 journals, book chapters and book/conference-related publications. Over this time, David has published his work in journals, such as *International Small Business Journal* and *International Journal of Entrepreneurship and Small Business'*. David is currently serving as the Trustee to the Institute for Small Business and Entrepreneurship (ISBE) Board, for the past three years. He is actively involved in the ISBE community as Vice President for Communities; he also provides services as track chair for the 'Entrepreneurial Practitioner Learning Track', and is serving as the Guest Editor for *International Journal of Entrepreneurial Behavior & Research* (*IJBER*) and *Industry and Higher Education*. In addition, he holds a position on the the British Academy of Management Research Methods Special Interest Group steering community, where he has developed and hosted many professional development workshops for students and practitioners at Entrepreneurial DBA and PhD levels of study. As a scholar in Management and Entrepreneurship, David has developed a deep knowledge and appreciative understanding of the subject matter, which is currently being advanced by his research within the field of Entrepreneurial Learning and Education. His research activity is aimed to contribute to exploring the learning process in the fields of Entrepreneurship/Small Medium Sized Enterprise (SME), which provides a unique and interesting context in terms of extending the current conceptualisations of learning in the Entrepreneurship/SME by paying more attention to a social-process perspective, which understands knowledge as socially constructed, in particular that of a practice-based perspective as a promising way to address the issues of knowing and learning in such a way that the richness and depth of the phenomenon can be considered.

Paul Jones is the Deputy Director of the International Centre for Transformational Entrepreneurship and the Professor in Entrepreneurship at Coventry University with over 24 years' experience in the university sector. Professor Jones is an active researcher in the entrepreneurship discipline with in excess of 200 research outputs, including edited books, academic journals, book chapters and conference papers. He has published his research in journals such as the *International Small Business Journal, Omega* and *Journal of Business Research*. Professor Jones has published research in information communication technology usage, entrepreneurship and small business management and entrepreneurship education. Professor Jones is Editor-in-Chief of the *International Journal of*

Entrepreneurial Behaviour and Research and Associate Editor of the *International Journal of Management Education.* He has guest edited special issues with *Education + Training, International Journal of Management Education, Journal of Small Business and Enterprise Development, Strategic Change* and the *Journal of Systems and Information Technology.* Professor Jones is also the Vice President (Research) of the Institute of Small Business and Entrepreneurship. Professor Jones is a Visiting Professor at Anglia Ruskin and Manchester Metropolitan Universities.

Pauric McGowan holds the Chair for Entrepreneurship and Business Development in the Ulster Business School. Between 2002 and 2009, he was the Director of the Northern Ireland Centre for Entrepreneurship (NICENT), based at the University of Ulster. As the Director of NICENT, he was responsible for providing leadership in the challenge to embed entrepreneurship in the curriculum across all faculties within the partner institutions of the centre, with particular responsibility for the University of Ulster, and for encouraging a greater practical engagement with entrepreneurial new venturing among staff and students. Post NICENT, he lectures in new venturing and business development and continues his research interests in the fields of technology entrepreneurship and entrepreneurship pedagogy. Prior to NICENT, he was involved in enterprise education at the University of Ulster and the development of small to medium-sized businesses through his work with the Northern Ireland Small Business Institute. He is a Fellow of the Marketing Institute of Ireland and a Distinguished Business Fellow of the University of Ulster.

ABOUT THE AUTHORS

Ahmed Abdullah is a Doctoral Researcher and hourly paid Tutor at the University of South Wales. His research interests included e-business and Information and Communications Technology (ICT) adoption in developing countries. He has a BSc in Computer Science from University of Technology and Science, Yemen, and MSc in Information Technology Management from University of Wales, Newport. Ahmed has also worked with IT companies in Yemen.

Gareth Huw Davies is an Associate Professor in Swansea University's School of Management, with research interests in innovation management and regional economic development. He has supported the Welsh Government in policy development as well as working on projects around the world to develop science park and technology-transfer models. He has also worked on a broad range of industry and government-funded projects, across sectors from construction to creative industries. Alongside his academic role, he has practitioner interests, including recently with the Swansea Bay City Region Internet Coast City Deal and other regional initiatives.

David Deakins is Honorary Researcher, Department of Entrepreneurship and Strategy, Lancaster University Management School, Lancaster University. He also is Adjunct Professor, School of Management, Massey University. He retired from a full-time academic role in January 2014 after over 35 years of publishing and leading research in entrepreneurship and small firms in the UK and New Zealand. He is currently working on research in innovation and rural entrepreneurship and on a new textbook on entrepreneurship to be published by SAGE.

Marian Evans is a Lecturer in Enterprise and Entrepreneurship in the Department of Strategic Management and Marketing, De Montfort University. Her research work is focussed on entrepreneurial cognitions, particularly exploring small business decision-making in real-world situations. Marian is an experienced practitioner, previously an owner-manager of several small entrepreneurial businesses. She also works as a consultant in industry for business improvement training and the delivery of Chartered Management Institute (CMI) qualifications. She is interested in developing from her research educational and training applications for other trainers and mentors.

Hanne Haave is an Assistant Professor at Inland School of Business and Social Sciences, Department of Organization, Leadership and Management. She teaches courses in research methodologies, organisation studies and leadership and works with guidance of student assignments. Her research interests are leadership and gender, organisational learning and adult learning, evaluation of students learning outcome and practice-oriented research.

Julie Haddock-Millar is Associate Professor of Human Resource Management and Development at Middlesex University Business School. She is a Senior Fellow of the Higher Education Academy and Chartered Member of the Chartered Institute of Personnel and Development. She is the International Work Group Leader for the International Standards in Mentoring and Coaching Programmes for the European Mentoring and Coaching Council. She has designed, delivered and evaluated a number of mentoring and coaching programmes for organisations such as the UK Cabinet Office, First Division Association, Financial and Legal Skills Partnership and Médecins Sans Frontières.

Lucy Hatt is a Senior Lecturer in Entrepreneurship at Northumbria University. Prior to moving into academia, she was a practitioner for 17 years starting her career at Procter & Gamble. She has also established a management development consultancy and been Head of HR at a multinational recruitment consultancy. As a Doctoral Researcher at Durham University, Lucy is researching the application of the Threshold Concept Framework to entrepreneurship education. She has published in *Education + Training*, *Industry and Higher Education* and *Local Economy*. She was highly commended as an Enterprise Catalyst in 2016 on behalf of National Centre for Entrepreneurship in Education and Enterprise Educators UK (NCEE and EEUK).

Inge Hermanrud, Ph.D., is an Associate Professor at Inland Norway University of Applied Sciences. His PhD addressed organisational learning, knowledge sharing and knowledge creation in distributed organisations. He teaches change management, technology and HR management courses. Currently, he studies digitalisation processes within the Norwegian Labour and Welfare Administration. He has published his research in journals like the *Nordic Journal of Social Science*, *Cases in Information Technology*, *Issues in Informing Science* and *Electronic Journal of Knowledge Management*.

Åse Storhaug Hole is Associate Professor at Inland School of Business and Social Sciences, Department of Organization, Leadership and Management. She has a Master of Science from the Norwegian School of Sport Sciences, and a Master of Public Administration from the University of Karlstad. She teaches several courses in organisational studies and HRM, along with supervising at both graduate and undergraduate levels. Her research interests are within teaching methods and learning outcomes in leadership programs, leadership roles and HRM. She has 15 years of practice as Dean and Director in Higher Education, and as a Headmaster in primary school.

Oswald Jones is Emeritus Professor of Entrepreneurship at the University of Liverpool. He was responsible for the Centre for Enterprise and Entrepreneurial Leadership (CEEL), which provides support for entrepreneurs and owner-managers in Greater Merseyside. CEEL staff delivered the LEAD (Leadership Enterprise and Development) and Growth Catalyst programmes to over 300 small firms since 2010. His early publications were focussed on the management of innovation in the pharmaceutical industry – the subject of his PhD – with publications in Human Relations and the *British Journal of Management*. Subsequently, he has focussed on entrepreneurship and the management of smaller firms Much of his output has examined the nature of learning in smaller organisations and this material has appeared in a wide-range of journals including *Business History, Entrepreneurship & Regional Development, International Small Business Journal, Long Range Planning, Management Learning, R&D Management and Technovation*. His more recent publications have focussed on the resourcing of entrepreneurial firms particularly via bootstrapping. Co-authors for much of this work are his University of Liverpool Management School (ULMS) colleagues Dilani Jayawarna and Allan Macpherson with whom he recently published a textbook: *Resourcing the Start-up Business: Creating Dynamic Entrepreneurial Learning Capabilities* (Routledge).

Neil Kaye is a Research Consultant in the Middlesex University Business School, working on a number of international mixed method longitudinal evaluation projects. In addition, Neil is enrolled on a PhD in social policy and his doctoral studies looks at the role of teachers in promoting resilience among students at risk of leaving school early. His other research interests include educational sociology, youth development, social exclusion and multiple discrimination. He has also had experience in undertaking quantitative and qualitative research for public, private and third-sector organisations, including the Irish Government, the National Health Service, local authorities and community representation organisations.

Daniela Lundesgaard is an Assistant Professor at the Inland School of Business and Social Sciences at Inland Norway University of Applied Sciences, where she teaches and supervises courses in marketing and service management. She is the Leader of the Bachelor's Programme in Service Management and Marketing.

Oliver Mallett has worked in Stirling Management School since 2018, having previously worked at Durham University Business School and Newcastle University Business School. His research focusses on understanding work and employment, principally in terms of the experience of self-employment and employment relationships in small firms. He has researched and written extensively on employment relationships in small and medium-sized enterprises, for example, producing a book published by Routledge, *Managing Human Resources in Small and Medium Sized Enterprises: Entrepreneurship and the Employment Relationship*. His research has also explored identity challenges at work, for example, in relation to the potential difficulties faced by older entrepreneurs marginalised and excluded by dominant conceptions of entrepreneurial legitimacy.

Xiang Ying Mei graduated with Bachelor of International Hotel and Tourism Management with honours at The University of Queensland (UQ), Australia, in

2005. After working a few years within the hotel industry in Norway, she returned to UQ to pursue her PhD focussing on tourism innovation, which was completed in 2012. Dr Mei's research interest includes government policies, international students, consumer behaviour, innovation, sustainability, destination management, regional development, brand management, marketing and co-creation. She is an Associate Professor in Marketing at Inland Norway University of Applied Sciences.

Kamran Namdar, Ph.D., has worked internationally over four decades with adult education, leadership education, organisational development and social entrepreneurship. He is familiar with the workings of civil society organisations, the public sector and the academia alike, having carried out research and innovative development work in all these fields. In all his work, Dr Namdar is especially interested in the role of humans as socially transformative agents and the realisation of transformative potential within the context of globalisation. Currently, Dr Namdar works as a Senior Lecturer in Education at Mälardalen University, Sweden, as well as an International Educational Consultant.

Martin N. Ndlela, Ph.D., is an Associate Professor at the Inland School of Business and Social Sciences, Inland Norway University of Applied Sciences. His research interests include crisis communication, organisational communication, knowledge management and social media innovations. He is the former head of the department of social sciences at Hedmark University College (now part of Inland Norway). Ndlela is also a Research Associate at the Department of Strategic Communication, Faculty of Humanities, University of Johannesburg, South Africa.

Robyn Owen is an Associate Professor of Entrepreneurial Finance at the Centre for Enterprise and Economic Development Research, Middlesex University Business School. She is also a Research Fellow at the Centre for Understanding Sustainable Prosperity and Co-chair of the Institute for Small Business and Entrepreneurship, Entrepreneurial Finance special interest group. Her research focusses on early stage small and medium-sized enterprises (SME) finance and she has undertaken numerous government evaluations and published widely on this subject.

David Rae is a Professor of Enterprise at the De Montfort University, Leicester, UK. He is a leading innovator, researcher and expert in entrepreneurship and small business leadership, learning and management. He has a significant track record in the leadership of business and enterprise in Higher Education as a key member of the Senior Leadership and Executive Management groups in four universities, where he has developed new opportunities and income streams based on enhancing innovation, research, enterprise and learning. He has achieved professional and academic recognition at international level for his contributions to entrepreneurship research, education, policy and regional development, and as an inspirational keynote speaker at international and professional conferences.

Sian Roderick is the Deputy Director of Postgraduate Research and a lecturer in the School of Management, Swansea University. Her background in psychology and industry supports a broad portfolio of applied research in conjunction with multinationals and SMEs. Sian has teaching and research interests in 'Innovation Management' and 'Research Methods'. Her activity in social and work psychology has underpinned a number of significant projects for Local Government, third sector and private organisations and resulted in the adoption and rollout of major initiatives to support the transformation of social care in the region and beyond.

Chandana Sanyal is a Senior Lecturer in Human Resource Management and Development at Middlesex University Business School, a Fellow Member of the Chartered Institute of Personnel and Development and Higher Education Academy. She is an accredited Member of European Mentoring and Coaching Council, an EMCC ISMCP Assessor and the International WorkGroup Leader for EMCC European Individual Accreditations. She has over 20 years' experience as a human resource practitioner and a Senior Manager in the Public Sector. She holds an Advanced Certificate in Coaching and Mentoring from Chartered Institute of Personnel and Development (CIPD), has developed and implemented a number of coaching and mentoring programmes in her practitioner role.

Leandro Sepulveda is an Associate Professor at Centre for Enterprise and Economic Development Research, Middlesex University. Leandro has more than 20 years' experience on research specialising in issues concerning enterprise and socioeconomic development. His current research interests include social enterprise, public services and the social economy; social inequalities; and entrepreneurship and economic development. His work has been commissioned or funded by the different UK government departments, the Economic and Social Research Council (ESRC), the European Commission, Youth Business International and School for Social Entrepreneurs. Leandro worked in Latin America as an External Consultant for the United Nations Economic Commission for Latin America and the Caribbean.

Victoria Konovalenko Slettli, Ph.D., works in the position of an Associate Professor in Organization and Management at the School of Business and Social Sciences, Inland Norway University of Applied Sciences. She holds a Doctoral degree in Business Economics from the University of Nord, Bodø, Norway, and a Master degree in Business Administration from the Baltic State Technical University 'VOENMEH', St-Petersburg, Russia. Victoria is teaching and doing research in the areas of communications, organisational change and knowledge management. In the research, she is especially interested in such topics as organisational and individual learning, knowledge sharing and intellectual capital.

Kjell Staffas is a Senior Lecturer in Electronics and Automation control at Uppsala University with a Ph.D. in Engineering didactics at Aalborg University. His research interest is in pragmatic solutions for studying in higher education in Motivation and Active learning techniques.

Stephen Syrett is a Professor of Local Economic Development and Director of Research at Middlesex University Business School. He specialises in issues of urban and regional economic development, governance and policy and the study of ethnic minority, home-based and social enterprises, microbusinesses and the role of enterprise in regenerating deprived areas. He has published widely on these topics including a number of books and many journal articles and reports. He has worked extensively with national, regional and local government bodies in the UK and internationally, as well as with a wide range of voluntary and community sector and private sector organisations.

Brychan Thomas is a Visiting Professor in Innovation Policy at the University of South Wales, and a Doctoral Supervisor in Entrepreneurship and Innovation at the University of Gloucestershire. He has a Science degree, an MSc in the Social Aspects of Science and Technology from Aston University and a Ph.D. in Science and Technology Policy, Council for National Academic Awards (CNAA), London. Before retiring in October 2012, he was Reader in Innovation Policy at the University of Glamorgan Business School. He has over 400 publications in the areas of science communication, entrepreneurship, innovation and small business – including 137 refereed journal articles and 130 refereed conference papers.

Roderick Thomas, an Academic based at the School of Management at Swansea University, is a Chartered Engineer and Fellow of the Institution of Engineering & Technology. He is author of a number of books, including the *Thermography Handbook,* and has written over 40 industrial papers in new technology including 'Condition Monitoring and Intelligent Asset Management' and is Technical Industrial Editor, *Thermology International Journal,* and an International Expert Witness in Infrared Thermography.

Gareth R. T. White is Reader in Operations and Information Management at the University of South Wales. His interests revolve around transdisciplinary investigation, the synthesis and sharing of knowledge across subject and practitioner boundaries. Research subjects encompass a broad range of operational subjects and disciplines, including information systems and development, and lean production.

Michael D. Williams is Professor and Deputy Dean, and Director of the Swansea Innovation Lab (i-Lab) in the School of Management at Swansea University. Prior to entering academia, he worked in both public and private sectors and since entering academia, has acted as Consultant in the UK and overseas. With research interests surrounding technology and innovation adoption, he is the author of numerous fully refereed and invited papers and has editorial board membership of a number of academic journals. He has obtained external research funding from sources including research councils, government and private sector.

INDEX

Note: Page numbers followed by "*n*" with numbers indicate notes.